THE GLOBAL ENVIRONMENT OF BUSINESS

To the memory of Saint Josemaria Escrivá, whose life and writings have inspired the creation of business schools throughout the world and have led managers to recognize personal responsibilities in business leadership.

THE GLOBAL ENVIRONMENT OF BUSINESS

NEW PARADIGMS FOR INTERNATIONAL MANAGEMENT

DAVID W. CONKLIN
The Richard Ivey School of Business,
The University of Western Ontario

Los Angeles | London | New Delhi
Singapore | Washington DC

For information:

SAGE Publications, Inc.
2455 Teller Road
Thousand Oaks, California 91320
E-mail: order@sagepub.com

SAGE Publications India Pvt. Ltd.
B 1/I 1 Mohan Cooperative Industrial Area
Mathura Road, New Delhi 110 044
India

SAGE Publications Ltd.
1 Oliver's Yard
55 City Road,
London EC1Y 1SP
United Kingdom

SAGE Publications Asia-Pacific Pte. Ltd.
33 Pekin Street #02-01
Far East Square
Singapore 048763

Printed in the United States of America

Library of Congress Cataloging-in-Publication Data

The global environment of business: new paradigms for international management/editor, David W. Conklin.
    p. cm.
Includes bibliographical references and index.
ISBN 978-1-4129-5028-2 (pbk.)
  1. International economic integration. 2. Industrial management. I. Conklin, David W.

HF1418.5.G57146 2011
658′.049—dc22   2009050810

This book is printed on acid-free paper.

10   11   12   13   14   10   9   8   7   6   5   4   3   2   1

Acquisitions Editor:	Lisa Shaw
Associate Editor:	Deya Saoud
Editorial Assistant:	MaryAnn Vail
Production Editor:	Brittany Bauhaus
Copy Editor:	Megan Speer
Typesetter:	C&M Digitals (P) Ltd.
Proofreader:	Eleni-Maria Georgiou
Indexer:	Michael Ferreira
Cover Designer:	Gail Buschman
Marketing Manager:	Carmel Schrire

Brief Contents

Detailed Contents

Introduction

TEXT LEARNING OBJECTIVES

On completion of this text, students should be able to

- understand the impacts of outside (environmental) forces on the firm's profitability and prioritize these risks and opportunities in regard to their relative importance and urgency,

- recognize the differences in these environmental forces among nations,

- assess the changes in these environmental forces over time,

- analyze the relationships among these forces and explain how their impacts differ among business sectors,

- recommend strategies, structures, and practices for a firm to best manage the different and changing environmental forces in each nation where it does business,

- discuss the impact of environmental forces on the relative attractiveness of different nations as alternative sites for doing business and investing,

- recognize the reasons for and the pervasive impacts of government intervention and the importance of managing the firm's business/government relations.

Forces outside the firm's traditional boundaries are often decisive in determining the firm's success. These forces in "the environment of business" differ among nations. Consequently, the multinational enterprise (MNE) must adopt new strategies and management practices as it expands its activities geographically. This text analyzes environmental forces under four broad themes—social, technological, economic, and political—while frequently examining interrelationships among these environmental forces. The introduction to each chapter provides a discussion of the strategies and management practices that are required in order to respond to the environmental forces that are the focus of that chapter.

SOCIAL FORCES

In Part I of the text, managers confront social attitudes that differ among nations—social attitudes concerning appropriate firm policies, corporate responsibility, and ethics. Cultural differences require adjustments in strategies and management decisions throughout the entire array of business activities and relationships. In the economically advanced nations, contractual arrangements can form a basis for interfirm business activities, but in many other cultures, management cannot rely on contracts and must strive to develop close personal relationships with the firm's customers and suppliers. Consumer preferences vary among nations, requiring country-specific modifications to marketing practices. Social forces not only differ among countries, but they are also changing rapidly. A host of global communication technologies are reducing the barriers that have separated cultures in the past, while changes in demographic profiles, often related to and supplemented by substantial migration, are also modifying social forces.

Each of these realities means that as the firm extends its activities globally, the firm finds itself operating within changing business environments. In the context of these social differences, management confronts serious ethical dilemmas. Social norms concerning corruption vary, requiring that management delineate corporate positions in regard to bribery and that they adapt to changing legal provisions that increasingly seek to prevent corruption. Laws differ among nations in regard to fraud, and especially relating to the nature and degree of transparency and accountability toward shareholders. Concepts of corporate social responsibility (CSR) are becoming increasingly important, and the firm may be able to use CSR strategies to create a competitive advantage. In this context, boards of directors have new and expanded responsibilities in some nations. The MNE has to determine its internal division of responsibilities for CSR activities based on the degree to which it decides to create unique strategies and management practices for its operations in different nations. Meanwhile, governments, both individually and through international agreements, are instituting new policies designed to direct management's decisions toward certain social goals.

TECHNOLOGICAL FORCES

Social capital impacts the environment for entrepreneurship and innovation, as does the role of government in regulating business activities and in supporting research and the growth of human capital. Entrepreneurship has increased in importance, both in terms of the creation of new firms that focus on a particular innovation and in terms of established firms that need to create an ongoing innovation process. The extent and nature of social capital differ among nations, creating a significant determinant of each nation's relative attractiveness as an investment site. The phrase "the knowledge economy" rests on the reality that innovation has become central to productivity improvements and international competitiveness, especially in the economically advanced nations where businesses cannot rely on low wages to achieve success. For an increasing number of firms, the adoption of technological advances within a learning organization has become the basis for ongoing profitability. Differences in technologies among nations are a determinant of international trade patterns, and these differences may play a key role in international investment decisions. Each nation has a distinctive innovation system with an increasing emphasis throughout the world on the "triple helix" of research partnerships among universities, governments, and businesses. Within the innovation system, new forms of finance geared to nonphysical assets are major determinants of a firm's success and the nation's growth.

This section of the text analyzes several sectors where the knowledge economy is transforming the nature and the structure of firms. First, the combination of information technologies, microelectronics, and e-business is now permeating all business activities. For each firm, a continual search for innovations seeks to apply or adapt these advances in new ways. For the MNE, "the digital divide" between economically advanced and less developed nations has implications for the degree to which these advances can be applied in different nations, and e-market segmentation has introduced a new dimension to marketing. New ethical and social issues accompany the e-business revolution. Second, within the pharmaceutical sector, biotechnology is altering the research and development process, creating opportunities for entrepreneurial biotech firms and leading to the need for new strategic alliances. Industry structures are changing with the birth of new firms specializing in specific components within the value chain. Compulsory licensing and parallel trade based on price differentials add new complexities to the global nature of the new biotech sector. Third, environmental concerns and the pursuit of clean energy have created new investment opportunities with each firm's adoption of internal systems to encourage the ongoing implementation of new technologies. Opportunities vary among nations due to differences in government policies and programs and differences in social attitudes toward renewable technologies such as wind in comparison with other types of electricity generation. These three sectors illustrate the pervasive and continual impacts of technological changes on management decisions.

ECONOMIC FORCES

Microeconomic forces form the industry structures within each nation. Porter's "five forces" model provides a framework for analyzing the strategies and bargaining strength of the customers, suppliers, and competitors within each industry, as well as substitutes and potential new entrants. The industry structure—from competition through oligopoly and monopoly—determines the ability of management to enhance profitability by raising prices above competitive levels. This ability to influence prices differs among nations and may form a key element in management's decision to invest in one nation rather than another.

For many firms, there is now an ability to locate each business activity anywhere in the world. Many factors enter the decision of whether the firm should maintain each activity within the firm or outsource it to a separate vendor. Related to the "offshoring" or internationalization of production and the ability to outsource is the need to establish a "creative web" of interfirm relationships that can support and facilitate ongoing innovation among the participants. This need for a creative web is leading to the adoption of new forms of interfirm governance.

At each point in time, each nation experiences a unique combination of macroeconomic variables, including rates of inflation, interest, unemployment, and growth, as well as exchange rates. These variables can form an important determinant of the firm's profitability and so can be significant elements in international investment decisions. Changes in exchange rates alter the prices that the firm faces and may require that the firm change its investment and supply chain strategies. Governments regularly impact these variables through their fiscal, monetary, and exchange rate policies, as well as through a wide range of microeconomic policies that seek to enhance the nation's productivity and growth. Taken together, these economic forces play a key role in determining the international competitiveness of each nation and the businesses located in that nation. Porter's "diamond framework" facilitates the analysis of each nation's competitiveness as a business location.

Macroeconomic variables can be volatile, creating repeated business cycles. In many less developed nations, inflation/devaluation cycles are also common. In an attempt to foster economic stability, governments implement fiscal, monetary, and exchange rate policies. Macroeconomic variables form an important component of each nation's environment of business, and managers must devote attention to them in their investment location decisions.

POLITICAL AND GOVERNMENTAL FORCES

Governments play a key role in shaping and responding to social, technological, and economic forces—so the analyses of these forces repeatedly involve the discussion of public policies. In many nations, the public policy paradigm and political risks have been changing in recent years in significant ways. Various published indexes indicate the degree of systemic political risk in each nation, and some nations may simply be too risky for the firm to locate there. Meanwhile, each nation has certain specific political risks that the firm must attempt to manage. Competition policy, or antitrust policy, illustrates specific political risks related to growth, particularly those related to international mergers and acquisitions. Privatization programs, deregulation, taxation, subsidies, and the proliferation of special economic zones are continually altering managers' comparisons among nations as alternative investment sites.

Tariff and nontariff import barriers are still substantial in many countries, while trade agreements seek to reduce these and create a level playing field for international businesses. Several important political forces have been shifting from the national to the international level. Protection of intellectual property has become a global concern, as has environmental protection. Competition policy remains largely in the hands of national governments, but many analysts and business leaders see the need for clearer international collaboration in government decisions. The 2007 to 2009 financial crisis has attracted attention to the possible need for new global financial regulations. Meanwhile, trade disputes arise continually as MNEs find that a wide array of government policies and programs interfere with the free trade objective. Whether to obey certain nations' sanctions often requires difficult management decisions. The rapid growth of sovereign wealth funds can lead to international investments that some nations feel place their national sovereignty and security at risk. In this complex mosaic of political forces and government decisions, management confronts ongoing challenges.

In reviewing the many risks and opportunities resulting from environmental forces, it is necessary to prioritize these issues in terms of importance and urgency. The time profile in the development of each issue becomes a guiding element in this prioritization. Delegation of responsibility for issue management within the firm involves the question of whether the issue should be managed at the local, regional, national, or head office level. Students can put themselves in the positions of prioritization and delegation of responsibility, as well as issue management.

At the end of each chapter are brief excerpts from cases related to the issues analyzed in that chapter. Each case presents "real-world" situations in which management must make decisions in the context of these issues. Questions are included to encourage consideration of how best to manage the issues involved in each set of environmental forces.

Acknowledgments

I would like to thank Danielle Cadieux for extensive research and administrative assistance in preparing this text.

The following editors at Sage have contributed suggestions and support: Al Bruckner, Lisa Shaw, Deya Saoud, MaryAnn Vail, Brittany Bauhaus, and Megan Speer.

I have appreciated the insights of anonymous referees who commented on various versions of the manuscript, as well as the recommendations of colleagues at the Richard Ivey School of Business, particularly Guy Holburn and Rod White.

Above all, I would like to thank my wonderful wife, Marilyn, for her ongoing love and encouragement.

The authors and SAGE gratefully acknowledge the contributions of the following reviewers:

Craig Duckworth, *London Metropolitan University*

Irwin Gray, *The New York Institute Of Technology*

Alan Hamlin, *Southern Utah University*

Stephen W. Hartman, *The New York Institute of Technology*

Thomas D. Jeitschko, *Michigan State University*

John D. Keiser, *SUNY College at Brockport*

Jeanne M. Logsdon, *University of New Mexico*

Steven Maser, *Willamette University*

Catherine Matraves, *Michigan State University*

Abdul Momen, *Framingham State College*

Vitaly K. Nishanov, *University of Washington*

Daniel Ponder, *University of Colorado at Colorado Springs*

David Primo, *University of Rochester*

Jorge E. Rivera, *The George Washington University*

Mark H. Schwiesow, *Marquette University*

Betsey Stevenson, *University of Pennsylvania*

Craig Volden, *Ohio State University*

Sam E. White, *University of Colorado at Colorado Springs*

Part I

Social Forces

Differentiating Strategies in Accordance With Cultural Differences

1

CHAPTER LEARNING OBJECTIVES

On completion of this chapter, students should be able to

- recognize how multinational enterprises (MNEs) may have to tailor their policies and strategies to the unique cultural realities of each nation,

- evaluate differences in consumer preferences among cultural groups and appreciate the need for market segmentation along these cultural lines,

- discuss the need to develop personal relationships in order to do business in certain nations,

- describe how specific social forces may be changing over time, requiring ongoing modifications in corporate strategies,

- understand how the cultural differences among nations can cause differences in other environmental forces.

Cross-cultural management scholars have long noted that managerial values, beliefs, norms, and attitudes are impacted by national culture, causing managers to conceptualize human nature, relationship to nature, work, time, relationships, space, and language very differently (Adler, 1986; Hofstede, 1991). These differences are significant, held at an unconscious level, and impact our perceptions of "right and wrong" and "how things ought to be" (Gopalan & Thomson, 2003, p. 313).

An extensive literature examines the ways in which culture can impact business issues ranging from managerial and employee behavior to customer preferences and marketing. Culture can impact a manager's education and life experiences, and culture can influence individual perceptions of ethical problems, including the consequences of ethical decisions. In some societies, people apply the same rules and treatment consistently to those from all social groups, while in others they make distinctions between insiders and outsiders. Some support universalism where rules are considered to be paramount. However, the cultures in many less developed nations support particularism and personal relationships, with a sharp distinction between loyalty to in-groups and nonloyalty to out-groups. These cultural distinctions lead to different definitions of truth and reality, with particularist cultures tending to reject the notion of universal truths and principles.

In some cultures, people separate business from pleasure. In business discussions, they use communication styles that are direct, concise, and focused on specific issues. However, diffuse cultures view all types of activities as interrelated, so business dealings must rest on long-term personal relationships. Personal and professional lives become mixed. In place of direct comments, these cultures practice ambiguity in communication with comments that avoid negative connotations.

In some cultures, people believe that they have mastery over the circumstances that they face, relying on science and technology and personal effort to maintain control of their own destinies. However, cultures in Asia and the Middle East place a heavier emphasis on the power of outside events, with outcomes being preordained by divine power or the result of fate or luck or destiny. Cultural differences can impact the types of information that individuals consider in their decision making and can also impact individual evaluations of certain actions as ethical or unethical. From these perspectives, management must carefully analyze cultural differences in order to operate effectively internationally and in order to develop global strategies that combine global objectives with local differentiation.

For MNEs, continual changes in social forces have created a set of moving targets. It is no longer adequate for the MNE to develop a standard set of reaction patterns within each nation's static culture. Rather, the MNE must undertake ongoing analyses of changes in social forces that are relevant for its operations, together with ongoing studies of related changes in other environmental forces as well. Consequently, social forces enter our analyses of technological, economic, and political forces throughout this text. Frequently, academic publications utilize Hofstede's typology as a framework for research and commentary.

Hofstede's Typology

In analyzing cultural differences, many academics base their research on the typology created by Hofstede (1991, 2001) who developed his conclusions from a survey of 117,000 IBM employees in 66 countries. Originally presented as four sets of issues, he later added a fifth on the basis of a survey undertaken in China. Hofstede ranked countries in accordance with these five dimensions, and other authors have related these dimensions to a wide range of issues that confront management. For example, many authors have pointed to differences between the United States and China that require U.S. multinationals to alter their behavior and practices in order to be successful if they invest in China. Some authors have applied Hofstede's typologies to differences among countries in regard to general issues such as ethical behavior, including systemic corruption and corporate social responsibility (CSR) activities. Some authors have applied his typologies to specific managerial decisions, such as marketing strategies, that must be modified in accordance with differences in consumer preferences.

First, "individualism/collectivism" refers to the cultural attitude concerning individual achievement or well-being, as opposed to collective achievement or well-being. Cultures where individualism is pervasive lead to the common practice of people caring only for their personal or immediate family success. They see individuals as responsible for their own advancement or failures. However, within collectivist cultures, people rely on group decisions rather than their own individual decisions. People look to groups to protect them, and they make decisions based on their loyalty to these groups.

Second, "uncertainty avoidance" refers to a general desire to avoid ambiguous or uncertain situations. In cultures where they feel threatened by ambiguous situations, people seek relationships that create certainty and predictability. They strive to avoid conflict, and they look to experts and authorities for decision making. They do not tolerate people or ideas that are out of the mainstream. Consequently, for both government and business, systems are centralized within a hierarchical power structure. Individual initiative is discouraged. In cultures with lower levels of uncertainty avoidance, these tendencies are replaced with decentralized decision making where managers are prepared to take greater risks and are encouraged to do so.

Third, "power distance" refers to the degree to which people are willing to accept an unequal distribution of power and wealth. Cultures that have a high degree of power distance also tend to be hierarchical, with decision making concentrated in the managerial/political elite. Compensation is based on static structures that relate to differences in job status rather than being geared to individual achievement. In contrast, low power distance cultures convey less respect for titles and formal status, and employees are more comfortable questioning the decisions of senior management.

Fourth, Hofstede's "masculinity/femininity" dimension relates to a distinction between aggressive objectives, such as the pursuit of money and power, and nurturing objectives. Masculine cultures support values such as personal assertiveness and materialism. They tend to distinguish gender roles in which men are automatically given the superior job descriptions. Work has priority over other duties. On the other hand, feminine cultures place a stronger emphasis on personal relationships that are multidimensional. They value the quality of life and nonmaterial success. Employment security is important, together with group decision making.

Hofstede's fifth cultural dimension, long-term orientation, relates to the difference between a focus on short-term outcomes and long-term outcomes, and it relates to the value placed on characteristics such as perseverance, reliability, respect for tradition, and established relationships. Hofstede developed this fifth dimension on the basis of surveys in China, so many authors link this dimension to the values of Confucianism. With Confucianism, a stable and lasting social order is achieved through generally accepted principles of human wisdom rather than through the imposition of laws and regulations. All human relationships should be motivated by sincerity, benevolence, and goodness, with respect and courtesy and ongoing consideration for the needs of others. In this context, business organizations have a hierarchical structure within which there is a generally accepted respect for seniors and for authority. Employees exhibit unquestioned obedience. The pursuit of personal success is not admired, and humility is regarded as a virtue.

Hofstede's fifth cultural dimension underlies many significant differences between Western and Asian business practices. In contrast with Confucian values, Western businesses tend to encourage individualistic and self-interested behavior. Western businesses regard transactions as separate from personal relationships. Western businesses rely on their legal rights, and they engage in litigation to resolve disputes. Miles (2006) raises the question, "How does a corporate governance model embodying all these traits fit in with Confucian beliefs? The truth is that to a large extent, it does not" (p. 307). As a result, Anglo-American corporate governance practices cannot be implemented easily in Asian countries. An example is the concept of appointing independent directors to corporate boards. Governments in China, Japan, and Korea have required this practice within each of their listed companies. However, independent directors in this culture may not be able to play the role that is expected of them in asking questions that might be embarrassing to management and in pursuing issues that could disrupt existing corporate practices. Other examples of differences in corporate governance include the increasing support for minority shareholder rights and shareholder activism practices. These rights and practices may be limited in many nations due to cultural characteristics and beliefs. From this perspective, the adoption of modern corporate governance practices may be very difficult in such cultures.

The Role of Personal Relationships

Managers in China have frequently noted the entrenched cultural norm of *guanxi*, and such a cultural norm is also commonplace in many other nations. Business negotiations often require that participants first develop a personal relationship with one another. These relationships are based on a gradual creation of trust and friendship through the process of an ongoing exchange of favors. Relationships require significant time and effort as individuals interact to build credibility between them. Some argue that the lack of strong institutions requires this informal network. Without a long-standing legal system, business law, or judicial precedents, it is not possible to rely solely on the enforcement of contracts. Furthermore, circumstances in the environment of business continually change, and this may require frequent modifications in written agreements due to developments beyond the control of either party. Other commentators point to the need to deal with inefficiencies that permeate the bureaucracy. A manager needing government approval for any particular activity, such as sale of a new product or construction of a plant, can bypass the complex system of government approvals and reduce time delays. Guanxi is generally seen as a personal asset. Nevertheless, a firm can establish practices that strengthen relationships between their employees and those with whom they must negotiate or gain approval. Systematic invitations to participate in expense-paid entertainment or travel, personal gifts, and the development of intermediaries to strengthen network contacts may all serve as ways of strengthening the firm's guanxi.

Meanwhile, the environment of business is changing in ways that are placing a greater emphasis on the Western practice of rule of law. Corporate governance is becoming stronger in many nations, and the freedom of individual managers to engage in guanxi may be restrained by corporate codes of conduct. Greater reliance on free markets and the extension of privatization are reducing the interventionist role of government and its agencies, thereby reducing the need for guanxi. MNEs have greatly expanded their international activities, and this has brought Western practices into a wider array of negotiations.

Culture and MNE Operations

These cultural differences have important implications for the decision-making structure within the MNE and in particular for the ability of the head office to manage a foreign subsidiary's marketing operations. On the one hand, the MNE requires a globally consistent set of policies and behaviors for a number of reasons, including the development of a global brand. Yet the need for creating trust and dependence in negotiations that extend beyond formal contracts adds complications to the firm's internal balance of power. In collectivist cultures, trust is more important relative to economic rewards as a motivation in cooperative behaviors. This conclusion has implications for the relationships between a firm and its employees in each country, as well as the division of decision-making responsibility between the parent and its subsidiaries.

Significant differences among nations in regard to cultural differences can impact the ethical sensitivities of employees, creating challenges for the MNE. Meanwhile, MNEs do influence their employees' perceptions in regard to ethical issues in ways that are changing employee perceptions in these countries. If cultural values are collectivist and passive with submission to authority, employees may not feel that they have a clear ethical framework to guide their decisions and may feel helpless in exerting their personal opinions against the common practices within the firm. As a result, there may be a lack of uniformity and consistency in regard to ethical practices. Management within the MNE must become more culturally sensitive and aware of its host country's ethical environment, hiring local managers and staff, as well as designing cultural and sensitivity training for expatriates.

Many commentators have studied the implications of cultural differences for daily business activities within international business operations. Oertig and Buergi (2006) discuss the difficulties of leading cross-cultural project teams when members of the teams live and work in different countries and must rely on long-distance communications. Their interviews led them to conclude that "virtual" communication lacks the ability to develop trust in a broad sense compared with face-to-face discussions, so physical rather than virtual meetings should be organized as often as possible. Apart from this issue, they note that trust has an important time component, with confidence in each other being built with long-term consistency in mutual experiences and decisions. Language differences enter as another important element in the challenges of cross-cultural communication, particularly when it is virtual rather than face-to-face. These realities add a complexity to management procedures.

Cultural differences form an important subject in the creation of international alliances and joint ventures. Arino, de la Torre, and Ring (2001) relate cultural differences to the degree of trust that is initially part of the international alliance, and they emphasize the importance for management to understand both the trust that the participants share and the ways in which this trust may be strengthened over time. They point to Russia in the 1990s as a particularly dramatic example.

> Western European managers negotiating alliances in Russia were unanimous in their view that legal contracts were of little consequence in that environment. Furthermore, language difficulties and differences in the worth attributed to verbal agreements rendered initial assessments of trustworthiness suspect at best. (p. 115)

Negotiations may have to be an ongoing process rather than being firmly established in a contract. Initial trust is fragile, so negotiation must involve a considerable effort in regard to understanding the other party.

Furthermore, management must recognize that its own behavior is being closely monitored by the other party and must engage in practices and personal behavior that may be different from those it would practice in its own country. Management should expect that cultural conflicts will arise, and management must devote considerable effort to ensuring that these conflicts are resolved. Overall, in managing its international operations, the MNE must emphasize the creation and strengthening of trust.

Many authors have focused on the need for trust in joint ventures that involve different cultures. For many cultures, trust depends on social relations among the decision makers, and this is particularly difficult when the decision makers live and work in different countries. Madhok (1995) emphasizes that "Relationship management is increasingly important in today's business environment where the forces of global competition and technological dynamism compel even the strongest firms to enter collaborative relationships in order to remain competitive" (p. 133).

Kauser and Shaw (2004) point to a substantial literature that concludes that the success of international strategic alliances is impacted significantly by the degree of commitment, trust, coordination, interdependence, and communication between the strategic alliance partners. They have developed a database for the period 1988 to 1995 for strategic alliances between British MNEs and their U.S., European, and Japanese partners. Of these alliances, 287 participated in the study, which examines the relationships between the degree of success in strategic alliances and the behavioral characteristics within these alliances, as well as the key structural or organizational characteristics. The authors conclude that the behavioral characteristics were more significant in predicting the degree of success of international strategic alliances than any structural or organizational features. Hence, they conclude that firms entering strategic alliances should emphasize ways of coordinating activities that will lead to ongoing interdependence and commitment. Trust may be strengthened through a number of practices, such as improving the quality of information that is shared, as well as participating together in planning procedures and setting goals and in creating procedures for resolving conflicts.

Rodriguez (2005) presents an analysis of the opportunities for managers from different cultures to create a new shared culture, or "a third culture," that can facilitate the success of a joint venture. Rodriguez uses data from U.S.-Mexican strategic alliances to test hypotheses in regard to this concept. He concludes that the different management styles converge into a more participative and consultative style that combines U.S. managers' focus on task innovation with Mexican managers' focus on personal relationships (p. 67).

Recognizing that managers have a set of personal attitudes that have been shaped by the culture in which they live, it is helpful in international alliances if managers focus on ways of aligning cultural backgrounds. An important mechanism for this is the creation of procedures through which managers from both countries regularly share in joint decision making. A shared working culture can create new cultural norms and attitudes that are different than the traditional norms and attitudes from the participants' countries. In this process of shared decision making, it is essential to focus on the resolution of conflicts, and personalities play an important role. In general, the development of a third culture within international joint ventures depends on the personal determination and adaptability of management.

Consumer Preferences and Market Segmentation

> Values help direct a consumer's behavior in that an individual develops their value system and beliefs based on the culture in which they are raised. . . . Obviously, cultural values influence how people think and behave. Consequently, ethical characteristics such as Machiavellianism, opportunism, trust, consumer ethical perceptions, and moral philosophies may be useful to segment and understand markets. (Al Khatib, D'Auria Stanton, & Rawwas, 2005, p. 228)

Al Khatib et al. (2005) have used surveys in order to segment consumers in the countries of Saudi Arabia, Oman, and Kuwait. In their surveys, consumers were asked to indicate their position on a wide variety of scales measuring cultural attributes, demographics, and ethical beliefs. In spite of the fact that respondents came from the same geographical area, the analysis has resulted in the delineation of three distinct segments. "Principled purchasers" emphasize ethical behavior in their day-to-day activities, including their purchasing patterns. They trust others and do not search for ulterior motives. Their personal standards are high. They tend to be older than the average. For MNEs to succeed with such customers, it is necessary to develop marketing strategies and practices that will present themselves as ethically and socially responsible. This approach impacts the products and services offered, as well as the procedures for marketing. Principled purchasers want the firms where they deal to exhibit the idealism, trust, and high moral standards to which they adhere. Since this group has a culture that is collectivist, opinion leadership plays an important role. Consequently, advertising should include the identification and recognition of a "moral champion" as a supporter of the MNE's products and services.

A second distinct segment consists of the "suspicious shopper," who is mistrustful of other people. These consumers are cautious in their purchases for fear that they will be dealt with unfairly. While they are not likely to engage in unethical actions themselves, they may not be completely transparent for fear of being exploited. In order for the MNE to market successfully to suspicious shoppers, the firm must be honest and forthright with a conscious determination to develop trust. The firm must ensure that customers perceive that both the firm and the customer will benefit from the transaction. Specific practices include great care that pricing is accurate and that sufficient stock is available.

A third segment, the "corrupt consumers," may engage in clearly unethical practices within a store, such as changing price tags on merchandise or telling lies in order to negotiate a better deal. They view morality as situationally specific. With such customers, the MNE must be culturally sensitive but impose a strict code of ethics. Managers must be aware of situations in which members of this group might try to exploit or deceive the firm and must invest in practices that can apprehend inappropriate behavior such as product theft, altered returns, or consumption on the premises.

Malhotra, Ulgado, Agarwal, Shainesh, and Wu (2005) emphasize the significance of culture in determining consumer perceptions of quality in the provision of services. The authors present 10 dimensions of service quality: reliability, access, understanding of the customer, responsiveness, competence, courtesy, communication, credibility, security, and tangible considerations. The authors note that some dimensions of service quality are related to the stage of economic development. For example, reliability and access depend on the country's infrastructure, technology, and even educational levels. They conclude that cultural factors do play a decisive role and that these must be understood by the firm if it is to be successful in its marketing. From this perspective, marketing will have to differ among nations and perhaps even within nations. The authors refer to Hofstede's typology of cultural dimensions, and they focus on power distance and individualism/collectivism as particularly important aspects of culture in international marketing. International marketing programs should be geared to these realities, with the firm's reliance on alternative marketing techniques differing among countries as discussed in these comparisons.

Straughan and Albers-Miller (2001) conclude that retail MNEs must create international expansion strategies on a country-by-country basis because culture is a crucial factor in determining loyalty to existing domestic retailers. They compare survey data from the United States, Australia, France, and South Korea. They use Hofstede's dimensions of culture, focusing on the importance of individualism and uncertainty avoidance. These cultural variables indicate that the higher the level of uncertainty avoidance, the greater the loyalty to existing domestic retailers. The more individualistic a culture is, the less loyal the customers are to existing domestic retailers. The authors have found substantial differences in loyalty patterns between men and women, with men being more loyal to existing domestic retailers. This suggests that women may be a more responsive target market for MNE retailers. The authors have found that age is not an indicator of loyalty.

Cultural differences impact the degree to which consumers are likely to adopt new products readily and to find new characteristics or features of products desirable. Therefore, marketing strategies should differ among cultures, being designed in accordance with the predominant cultural characteristics. In cultures where power distances are significant, where uncertainty avoidance is strong, and where so-called feminine character- istics are common, marketing strategies should use normative influences with interpersonal communication as a framework for introducing new products and new product characteristics. Hierarchical forms of commu- nication lead to the recommendation that role models or authority figures should be used in marketing programs. Advertisements should enable consumers to observe the product in use, with sales people and opinion leaders extolling the virtues of a product. Distribution of free samples may also be an effective marketing technique. In order to reduce perceived risk and skepticism, marketing programs should offer guarantees, after sales services, and lenient refund policies.

Alam (2006) has investigated the ways in which new developments in the service sector are influenced by cultural forces, focusing on financial service firms in Australia and the United States. His results from 300 ques- tionnaires indicate that U.S. firms more often use a well-defined team leader, relying on cross-functional teams to a greater extent. The degree of customer uncertainty in the context of the heterogeneity of a service requires that the provision of training for personnel differ significantly between the countries. U.S. firms devote more effort to personnel train- ing and take more care in the selection of staff delivering new services. U.S. firms see a need to undertake more extensive internal marketing in order to strengthen the understanding and support of employees for the introduction of new services. Alam extends his study to businesses operat- ing internationally, noting that this international perspective has become of greater importance to an increasing number of firms. He concludes that "overall the results support the central argument of the article that signifi- cant cross-national differences do exist with regard to a firm's new service strategy and new service development (NSD) process" (p. 247).

Modifications in Cultural Differences Over Time

In their news coverage, the global media convey cultural attitudes from throughout the world in ways that enable people everywhere to see a wider variety of social norms and individual objectives as increasingly acceptable globally. Entertainment, especially through television, pre- sents disparate behavior patterns in a vast array of circumstances. Movies with world-famous actors convey a set of images that people throughout the world may emulate. Literature can now appeal to a global market. In this process of cultural interaction, the English language has become commonly used, and this reality has facilitated more extensive communication linkages. Travel has become commonplace for people from all nations, so the exposure to other cultures has become increasingly frequent. Student exchanges create opportunities to live in another culture for an extended period of time. A vast expansion of international trade has created globally branded products that are now available anywhere. Worldwide advertisements and retail chains have created global fashions and fads that now permeate cultures everywhere. The Internet has become a means through which people in any nation in the world can communicate with people in any other nation, thereby enhancing their understanding of other cultures. In this process, many aspects of the cultures of Western Europe and North America have penetrated traditional cultures in developing countries, while aspects of these traditional cultures have also penetrated the economically advanced nations.

For many decades, the schisms between capitalism and communism created solid barriers to cultural exchange in much of the world. The philosophies underlying capitalism and communism encouraged very different personal goals and behavior patterns. Since 1990, with the overthrow of communism in Eastern Europe and Russia, these barriers have largely disappeared. With China's gradual movement toward free markets, openness to foreign cultural influences has expanded. Throughout the world, responsibilities for one's employment and income have shifted from the government to the individual—with the result that attitudes toward the employment relationship, success criteria, and appropriate norms have all been changing.

MNEs have increasingly responded positively to global nongovernmental organization pressures in implementing CSR activities and in adopting reporting procedures uniformly through all of their operations. Many MNEs have come to recognize that common technologies and CSR practices throughout the world may be the most cost-efficient approach to CSR, and in this way MNEs have become a vehicle for local adaptation to global norms. Meanwhile, governments are signing international agreements in which they pledge to create local laws and regulations that are consistent with the objectives of these international agreements. As indicated in Chapter 2, for example, Organisation for Economic Co-operation and Development (OECD) agreements and World Bank pressures are leading governments everywhere to impose penalties for corruption.

Urbanization has become a powerful reality throughout the world as rural inhabitants flood to the cities in pursuit of jobs and a more exciting lifestyle. In each nation, this urbanization is facilitating the absorption of the forces for change described above, relegating traditional rural cultural traits to an ever-decreasing proportion of the populations. The cities themselves create a culture of adaptation as individuals from a myriad of villages suddenly confront a wider range of cultural alternatives.

Migration

For many nations, immigration is a process that is continually changing local social forces. While some nations such as Japan have experienced limited immigration and so have not been subject to this cause of change, Western Europe and North America have experienced annual immigration numbered in the millions. Immigrants bring their traditional cultural practices and may alter the nation's cultural characteristics. In the extreme, a country such as Canada has become multicultural, where the national culture to a large degree consists of dozens of separate ethnic cultures. In recent years, many millions of Hispanics have entered the United States, making the Spanish language a significant presence, especially in certain cities such as Miami. European countries are also experiencing a substantial immigration.

Many immigrants maintain linkages and ongoing dialogue with relatives in their home countries, and this communication can convey cultural attributes of their new homes in ways that may modify the norms and values of their original homelands. Immigration can lead to social fluidity and to modifications in the culture of the new home country. Immigrants strengthen their impact through their ethnic networks. Immigration can enhance the understanding and acceptance of cultural differences, as well as serving as a force of change. The presence of immigrants heightens the sensitivity of traditional residents to cultural traits of other nations. Yet these interactions can reveal widespread social biases and can result in divisive conflicts. For the MNE, immigration provides an opportunity to hire individuals who have been raised in other nations, speak other languages, and understand other nations' cultures. The MNE from a multicultural home base has an automatic advantage in regard to hiring employees who can enable it to be competitive in other cultures. Andrea Mandel-Campbell (2007) uses Canada as an illustration of the advantages for MNEs of the new social capital that immigrants bring with them.

> Multiculturalism is arguably the country's most defining feature. With one foot in Canada and the other in their country of origin, these cultural double agents have the ability to act as trade bridges, whether by filling in knowledge gaps and lowering the fear factor involved in foreign ventures or infiltrating ostensibly closed societies and forging relationships, while reporting back home in a language Canadian companies can understand. (p. 219)

The Malleability of Youth

Increasingly, young people are part of the adaptation to global norms at a pace and with an intensity that appears to be quite different from older residents. It is the youth who seem to be most involved in watching global entertainment and adopting global fashions. It is the youth who use the Internet to a greater degree than older people, developing the skills necessary for using information technology to communicate internationally. It is the youth who can participate in student exchanges. It is the youth who most readily leave rural areas to create a new life in the cities. It is the youth who are involved in formal education that increasingly exposes them to what is happening in other nations and to the cultural traits that exist elsewhere. As a result, it is possible that Hofstede's cultural dimensions may differ not only geographically but also across age groups, with youth being more aggressive and individualistic and less inclined to accept hierarchical decision making.

It is the youth who form the bulk of the immigrants to advanced economies, forming a process for intensive cultural adaptation. It is the youth who may marry someone from another cultural background, creating an additional vehicle for cultural fusion. It is the youth who will be hired by MNEs and will have to adapt to new cultural norms in their employment. As young people age, their malleability in regard to cultural norms will become a more common component of each nation's culture and will lead to a shift in dominance from "traditional" to "modern." Enhanced availability of formal education may alter the attitudes of young people and—with the aging process—eventually alter general social attitudes. One might expect that the impacts of formal education might change the relative significance in any society of each of Hofstede's five cultural dimensions.

As a result of the above forces, cultural attributes and preferences have become age-dependent to some degree. For the MNE, this reality forms an important element of market segmentation. For example, the potential for e-business activities on the Internet will generally be much higher among the youth than among older population groups. As employees, young people may adopt a pattern of changing jobs several times in their careers as opposed to their parents' pattern of lifetime employment with loyalty to a specific firm. Meanwhile, the changes in the age structure in a country will automatically lead to changes in the social forces in that nation.

Changes in Demographic Profiles

Some economic demographers have concluded that each age cohort has unique preferences and consumption patterns. Consequently, it is necessary to gear the firm's production and marketing to specific age cohorts. A firm's success will depend on the number of people in the age cohorts that it chooses as a target. By examining the different numbers in each age group in each nation, a manager can project the future numbers in each age group in, say, 5 or 10 years. In this way, a manager can understand how much the target market will grow or decline over time.

Social forces are impacted by changes in the dependency ratio. As birth rates fall and life expectancy increases and as women enter the workforce, the percentage of the population that is employed is changing. When the Treaty of Rome created the European Union in 1957, all the signatories had fertility rates above 2.1. Today none does, and for many the fertility rate has fallen below 1.5, guaranteeing an eventual decline in the population unless enormous immigration occurs. The decrease in child labor in many nations, often accompanied by more years of formal education, also impacts the dependency ratio. In many countries, the aging population will change demographic profiles dramatically. The number of older people continuing to work may increase. These phenomena differ from country to country, presenting each country with unique changes in social forces.

For the MNE, these demographic changes have implications for many business issues. For example, a growing percentage of the MNE's employees may be women, so the MNE may need to create systems that can facilitate the occupational promotion of women. With an increase in the dependency ratio, taxation rates for both employees and the firm may have to rise to cover higher costs of pensions and healthcare for the growing percentage of the population that is elderly. At the same time, the change in composition of the population alters the demand for various types of goods and services, creating new business opportunities and requiring new types of market segmentation. Growing numbers of the elderly may alter the general attitude of a population toward social forces, leading, for example, to pressures on governments to alter their public policies. An International Monetary Fund report by Batini, Callen, and McKibbin (2006) points to several trends:

- Population aging in industrial countries will reduce growth, beginning in Japan in the next decade and then the rest of other industrial countries by the middle of the century.

- In contrast, as the relative size of their working-age populations increases, developing countries will enjoy a "demographic dividend" that should result in stronger growth over the next 20 to 30 years, before aging sets in.

- Demographic change will also affect saving, investment, and capital flows. Japan and to a much lesser extent the other industrial countries—the fastest aging countries—could see large declines in saving and a deterioration in their current account positions as the elderly run down their assets in retirement.

Interactions Between Social Forces and Other Forces in the Environment of Business

Many government policies seek to change social forces, creating incentives and punishments for behaving in certain ways. In some circumstances, political leaders take the initiative in order to achieve their vision of a better society. In recent decades, for example, many governments have sought to reduce discrimination through the imposition of affirmative action programs. Bills of rights and charters of rights have created a legal foundation for individual actions that may violate traditional social norms. On the other hand, certain public policies such as environmental or labor legislation aim to prevent individual actions that might violate new social norms.

New technologies will also likely change social forces. The Internet and e-business together with the recent expansion of satellite technologies will alter the ways that people view their daily lives. Biotechnology is raising a host of new ethical issues with which societies must wrestle. For Europeans, genetically modified foods may be socially unacceptable, while for Americans the prospects of productivity improvements may lead to a general acceptance of such products. New possibilities of cloning farm animals may raise new social challenges. Throughout the implementation of new technologies, the need for new skills is impacting educational systems—and hence social norms and values. For each nation, increases in per capita incomes alter consumer choices and lifestyles—and so may also alter the relative significance of Hofstede's five cultural dimensions. For the MNE, changes in social forces are adding greater complexity to the creation of strategies and management practices.

De Beers used advertising programs to alter cultural values so as to expand its potential market. Within the United States and Europe, De Beers sought to increase the occasions when a diamond ring should be the gift of choice, and it also sought to make diamond jewelry culturally desirable in Asia. The case of De Beers illustrates the opportunities for a firm to change social forces in ways that can increase the firm's profitability.

In Practice 1.1   **Changes in Cultural Preferences for Diamonds**

De Beers convinced the world that a diamond symbolized love. The "diamond is forever" slogan was a brilliant marketing ploy that was invented in the 1930s when diamond demand was at an all-time low. Hollywood actresses cooperated by sporting the glamorous rocks and the public ate it up. Although a luxury item, this penetrating marketing transformed the stone into a necessity in the public eye. As a token of love and devotion and the symbol of marriage, this diamond marketing created a tradition. Some ads advised men that they should spend two months' salary on an engagement ring. The phrase "a diamond is forever" was an ongoing theme in De Beers' retail advertising. De Beers also succeeded in portraying the idea that diamonds were rare. Although sales had been largely in Western Europe and North America, De Beers' advertising was an important element in convincing the rest of the world that diamonds were a key element of the Western lifestyle and romance. Japan was quickly becoming a major market for diamond jewelry.

(Continued)

(Continued)

Both China and India were experiencing rapid increases in diamond jewelry sales, and they could become huge markets in the future. Nevertheless, the United States still purchased 51% of the world's diamond jewelry, the Euro region 14%, Japan 14%, and the rest of the world 21% (Rapaport Research, 2004).

For the retail consumer of diamond jewelry, the market structure created an opportunity for long-term investment. De Beers' control of the value chain, together with De Beers' market intervention to ensure stability and gradual escalation of prices, meant that a retail customer was assured that his or her investment would not decline in value.

The Diamond Trading Company (DTC) hired J. Walter Thompson to develop advertising campaigns based on themes other than just the wedding. Some campaigns were targeted at men looking for a way to rekindle a sense of excitement and passion in their relationships. A "Celebrate Her" campaign was designed to motivate men to purchase solitaire, three-stone and right-hand diamond rings. Men were urged to show their significant other how valued their relationship was. The diamond gift would prove his love for her. The three-stone ring campaign included a memorable ad of a forty-something man on bended knee offering the three-stone and asking, "Will you marry me again?" The "Women of the World Raise Your Right Hand" print campaign targeted the affluent, fashion-savvy woman who had probably been married at some point, previously received diamond jewelry, and needed no one's permission to indulge herself. The ad copy encouraged women to think of rings for their right hands as expressions of personal style for the independent, worldly, assertive sides of their personalities, and to make their left hands jealous.

By using De Beers as the brand name, identified by the "forevermark" logo, De Beers wanted consumers to associate their diamonds with good ethics, corporate social responsibility, and enduring genuine quality.

De Beers invested heavily in the creation of an Internet site for the promotion of diamonds and diamond jewelry. This was basically an information site enabling the user to gain knowledge and appreciation for De Beers' expertise and guarantee. This site allowed the user to examine a very wide variety of jewelry designs. The question remained whether the actual sale of luxury jewelry through the Internet might devalue the brand equity.

In Africa, civil wars had become numerous and extensive and various groups used diamonds as a way of raising funds and obtaining military equipment. Concerns had developed throughout the world that the retail customer might turn against diamonds on the basis that a purchase might indirectly support civil conflict. Many in the industry feared a consumer boycott similar to that experienced by the fur industry. De Beers took a leadership role in demanding a guarantee from its suppliers that they were not selling "conflict diamonds" smuggled out of Africa.

The government of South Africa had put in place new legislation to shift a certain percentage of equity ownership in all South African companies to black shareholders and to raise the proportion of employee and management positions held by black South Africans. Instead of fighting against these government policies, Mr. Oppenheimer publicly discussed how the objective of black empowerment might be implemented with least disruption to the economy. In particular, Mr. Oppenheimer argued for a public discussion in regard to precise steps to achieve black empowerment and urged that firms taking part in this transformation should be rewarded with tax concessions. With this, Oppenheimer and De Beers once again cultivated an image of public leadership.

SOURCE: Conklin and Cadieux (2005).

Critical Thinking Questions

1. For the United States and Western Europe, discuss the relationships between changes in social forces and changes in De Beers' strategies.

2. Will consumers in all nations come to accept the diamond ring as a necessary element in a loving relationship? Will such a shift in global norms and values be the result of De Beers' advertising or the result of the adoption of the norms and values of the United States and Western Europe—or both?

3. New global cultural norms and values have included concerns about conflict diamonds. In South Africa, the "black empowerment" movement has also raised new challenges. Evaluate De Beers' responses to these changes in social forces.

References and Suggested Readings

Adler, N. (1986). *International dimensions of organizational behavior.* Boston: Kent.

Al Khatib, J., D'Auria Stanton, A., & Rawwas, M. (2005). Ethical segmentation of consumers in developing countries: A comparative analysis. *International Marketing Review, 22*(2), 225–246.

Alam, I. (2006). Service innovation strategy and process: A cross-national comparative analysis. *International Marketing Review, 23*(3), 234–254.

Arino, A., de la Torre, J., & Ring, P. S. (2001). Relational quality: Managing trust in corporate alliances. *California Management Review, 44,* 109–131.

Batini, N., Callen, T., & McKibbin, W. (2006, January). *The global impact of demographic change* (IMF Working Paper No. 06/9). Washington, DC: International Monetary Fund.

Conklin, D. W., & Cadieux, D. (2005). *De Beers and the global diamond industry.* London: Ivey. (Ivey Case No. 9B05M040)

Gopalan, S., & Thomson, N. (2003). National cultures, information search behaviors and the attribution process of cross-national managers: A conceptual framework. *Teaching Business Ethics, 7*(3), 313.

Hofstede, G. (1991). *Cultures and organizations: Software of the mind*. New York: McGraw-Hill.

Hofstede, G. (1993). Cultural constraints in management theories. *Academy of Management Executive, 7*, 81–94.

Hofstede, G. (2001). *Culture's consequences: Comparing values, behaviors, institutions, and organizations across nations* (2nd ed.). Thousand Oaks, CA: Sage.

Hofstede, G., & Bond, M. (1988). The Confucius connection: From cultural roots to economic growth. *Organizational Dynamics, 16*(4), 4–21.

Kauser, S., & Shaw, V. (2004). The influence of behavioural and organizational characteristics on the success of international strategic alliances. *International Marketing Review, 21*(1), 17–52.

Madhok, A. (1995). Revisiting multinational firms' tolerance for joint ventures: A trust-based approach. *Journal of International Business Studies, 26*(1), 117–137.

Malhotra, N., Ulgado, F., Agarwal, J., Shainesh, G., & Wu, L. (2005). Dimensions of service quality in developed and developing economies: Multi-country cross-cultural comparisons. *International Marketing Review, 22*(3), 256–278.

Mandel-Campbell, A. (2007). *Why Mexicans don't drink Molson*. Vancouver: Douglas & McIntyre.

Miles, L. (2006). The application of Anglo-American corporate practices in societies influenced by Confucian values. *Business and Society Review, 111*(3), 305–321.

Oertig, M., & Buergi, B. (2006). The challenges of managing cross-cultural virtual project teams. *Team Performance Management, 12*(1/2), 23–30.

Rapaport Research. (2004, February). *Rapaport Research Report*, Part 1, 7. Retrieved from www.rapaport-research.com

Rodriguez, C. (2005). Emergence of a third culture: Shared leadership in international strategic alliances. *International Marketing Review, 22*(1), 67–95.

Straughan, R., & Albers-Miller, N. (2001). An international investigation of cultural and demographic effects on domestic retail loyalty. *International Marketing Review, 18*(5), 521–541.

Coping With New Concerns About Corruption and Fraud

2

CHAPTER LEARNING OBJECTIVES

On completion of this chapter, students should be able to

- analyze differences in the extent and nature of corruption and fraud among nations,

- recognize the ambiguities in defining corruption and fraud,

- see the challenges in developing strategies for business/government relations in the context of corruption and fraud,

- appreciate the significance of recent changes in laws and their enforcement,

- understand the need for corporate guidelines and ethical codes.

Many nations have become increasingly concerned with the subjects of corruption and fraud, and managers today must cope with changes in laws and ethical norms. New laws and international agreements seek to create a worldwide shift toward the reduction of corruption and fraud; so management responsibilities are continually evolving. The subjects of corruption and fraud both emphasize the importance of ethics within each multinational enterprise's (MNE's) corporate culture.

Corruption constitutes a major obstacle to democracy and the rule of law. It is often responsible for the funnelling of scarce public resources to uneconomic high-profile projects. . . . It hinders the development of fair market structures and distorts competition, thereby deterring investment. . . . It undermines people's trust in the political system, in its institutions and its leadership. . . . Environmental degradation is yet another consequence of corrupt systems. (Transparency International, n.d.)

Transparency International and the World Bank provide estimates of the relative pervasiveness of corruption in different countries. Yet this subject is ambiguous and complex, creating significant challenges for managers. Both Volkswagen and Siemens have recently experienced public criticism and legal prosecution over corruption issues, some relating to internal and inter-corporate relations. Some cultures appear to accept corrupt practices as part of normal business-government relations. In China, guanxi is widely seen as a requirement for business success with the establishment of personal rela-tionships that include an ongoing exchange of gifts and personal favors. Some managers may argue that the giving of gifts is acceptable, that bribes to expedite decisions may be necessary, and that only certain types of bribes should be seen as inappropriate corruption. This perspective draws atten-tion to the difficulty of drawing a line to guide decisions of corporate employees, yet for many managers it is now necessary to implement clear corporate guidelines in regard to what they consider to be corruption. In this context, some managers may decide to avoid investing in certain nations until the culture of corruption in these nations has changed.

Traditionally, the firm experienced considerable freedom in choosing how much information to provide to the public. Investors had to base their decisions on whatever information the firm provided. To a major degree, management could determine their own remuneration, including bonuses, stock options, and severance packages. Management could manipulate pub-lished financial results to create a more positive image than was accurate. Maximizing short-term results on which personal financial gain depended could lead management to risk long-term crises or even bankruptcy. Faced with a series of fraudulent actions, some governments have prosecuted senior management on the basis of traditional criminal law. In addition, led by the U.S. Sarbanes-Oxley Act, a global attempt has been made to create new corporate guidelines for transparency, reporting, and accountability with specific rules to direct management decisions. Government prosecution has extended to the huge brokerage houses whose "tainted research" may have led their clients to invest in questionable firms that were paying substantial fees to these brokerages. Nevertheless, management is still left with ethical decisions regarding how to implement the new guidelines. The fact that laws now differ among nations in this regard may even tempt some firms to shift their head offices to nations with less stringent practices.

The Ethical Responsibilities of the MNE

Luo (2006) views the ethical responsibilities of the MNE through three lenses at the same time—political strategies, corporate social responsibility

(CSR), and corruption. A wide variety of academic disciplines examine various components of these three lenses, including economics, law, political science, sociology, ethics, management, and international business. Within the MNE, the three lenses influence one another in an integrated manner.

With the lens of political strategies, each MNE must choose to either be assertive in its relations with government, relying on its bargaining power, or be cooperative, working interdependently with the government. For any MNE, the decision must be made whether to bargain at arm's length in formal procedures or whether to rely on social networks with their ongoing gifts as the basis for resolving issues with government officials.

With the CSR lens, Luo divides MNE ethical activities into philanthropic contributions, ethical codes, organizational credibility, and resource accommodation. While philanthropic contribution and ethical codes are rather straightforward, organizational credibility lies in the attitudes of local stakeholders to various MNE activities such as transparency, accountability, integrity, and quality of products and services. Resource accommodation relates to the degree to which an MNE contributes to the host country's economic and social development needs. These various components are the building blocks for an MNE's achievement in the area of CSR, and they rest on the ethical foundation of the MNE's corporate culture.

The third lens, corruption, is ubiquitous and raises transaction costs. The MNE's role in politics and in CSR is intimately linked with the MNE's position in regard to corruption. An MNE's assertiveness with a host government is positively related with its CSR focus on ethical codes. When confronted with corruption, MNEs that focus more on ethics tend to use arm's-length bargaining, while those focusing less on ethics rely on social connections. Luo's study emphasizes the central role of ethics in each of the three lenses—political strategies, CSR, and corruption.

Adjusting to Changes in Ethical Norms and Values: Volkswagen and Siemens

Prior to the 1990s, German companies could engage in payments to foreign government officials without facing the threat of prosecution within Germany. Furthermore, bribery payments in order to win procurement contracts could be legally deducted from income for taxation purposes. However, new legislation in the 1990s made such payments illegal, and the German government also began to prosecute inappropriate domestic payments. Both Volkswagen and Siemens suddenly faced a series of charges in regard to these practices. German companies traditionally had two boards. A management board was responsible for day-to-day operations and was led by the chief executive. A separate supervisory board was responsible for overseeing the company's strategies and had equal representation from each of the employees and the shareholders. In order to win approval for its strategies, management was tempted to offer various forms of bribes to employee representatives on the advisory board.

In the 2005 to 2007 period, a series of charges were laid against Volkswagen and some of its management in regard to inappropriate payments to union leaders who served on the company's advisory board. It was alleged that these payments were intended to gain the support of union leaders in approving management decisions. "This relationship between VW managers and labor leaders underpinned what is often called 'the Volkswagen system,' a decision-making network more geared to protecting jobs in VW's money-losing German factories than to running a profitable business" (Meiners, 2007, p. 96). BBC News has reported that in 2007, VW's former head of personnel, Peter Hartz, was given a 2-year suspended prison sentence for sanctioning illegal payments to employee representatives. In 2008, the former head of VW's supervisory board received a jail term of 2 years and 9 months for his role in giving illegal privileges to employee representatives.

Meanwhile, some purchasing managers within Volkswagen were accused of accepting kickbacks from parts suppliers. These kickbacks included cash payments, furniture, free holidays, and jobs for friends. It was alleged that fake companies had been created to hide bribes. As a result of these various scandals, several of Volkswagen's executives resigned and a number faced ongoing prosecution.

For Volkswagen, a series of issues also arose related to Porsche's purchase of substantial shareholdings in Volkswagen. Porsche asserted that its investment entitled it to two seats on the Volkswagen board. However, some directors and commentators objected on the basis that Porsche was attempting to gain too much control over Volkswagen.

> The dispute laid bare the web of interlocking ties among German companies, at times made all the closer by family holdings. It also raised troubling questions about corporate governance at Volkswagen, a far-flung automotive empire with public and private shareholders that has been rocked by a bribery and corruption scandal. (Landler, 2006, p. C3)

For Siemens as well, a series of corruption allegations threatened the reputation of the firm. Beginning in 2004, European prosecutors initiated an extensive investigation of Siemens' corporate records. Allegations covered a wide range of issues, including money laundering, fraud, and income-tax evasion. As with Volkswagen, there were allegations of funds being transferred to a labor union considered friendly to the company. Most of Siemens' inappropriate payments appeared to have been bribes paid to foreign officials. Critics saw this situation as the result of an endemic system of bribery put in place to win contracts. "This individual case is of significance because it shows clearly that a system of bribery was installed," said Manuel Theisen, a professor of business and tax law at Ludwig-Maximilians-Universität in Munich. "The rest is now just a question of numbers and dimension" (Sims, 2007, p. 4).

By 2007, an internal probe at Siemens had identified about €1.6 billion (about $2.3 billion) in suspicious transactions. By April 2007, Siemens' chief executive office and supervisory board chairman had both resigned. On October 5, 2007, the *Financial Times* reported,

> Siemens was last night fined €201m ($285m) by the German authorities over a bribery scandal in its telecommunications unit in the first of several rulings that could end up costing Europe's largest engineering group billions.
>
> The fine by the Munich district court represents the first step by the German conglomerate to address what senior directors have called a "systematic" approach to bribery that has spawned investigations by several regulators including the US Securities and Exchange Commission. (Milne, 2007, p. 17)

In December 2008, Siemens agreed to pay fines of more than $1.3 billion to settle corruption probes in the United States and Germany. The scandal also resulted in the loss of jobs for Klaus Kleinfeld, former chief executive, and Heinrich von Pierer, former CEO and former supervisory board chairman. Neither von Pierer nor Kleinfeld was accused of crimes, and both denied any wrongdoing. Nevertheless, Siemens agreed to appoint an independent monitor for up to 4 years to cooperate with the U.S. government's continuing investigation in the case.

Transparency International's Corruption Perceptions Index

Transparency International conducts annual surveys in nations throughout the world to elicit opinions concerning the extent and nature of corruption in each country.

> A country or territory's Corruption Perception Index (CPI) score indicates the degree of public sector corruption as perceived by business peoples and country analysts, and ranges between 10 (highly clean) and 0 (highly corrupt). (Transparency International, 2008)

Exhibit 2.1 presents CPI scores for 180 nations. In 2008, only 6 nations had a CPI score of 9.0 or higher. More than half the nations had a CPI score of less than 5.0, and 70 countries had a CPI score of less than 3.0.

A global survey by Transparency International of 73,000 people took place between October 2008 and February 2009. Respondents were asked

Exhibit 2.1 Corruption Perceptions Index

Rank	Country	2008 CPI Score	Rank	Country	2008 CPI Score	Rank	Country	2008 CPI Score	Rank	Country	2008 CPI Score
1	Denmark	9.3	45	Czech Republic	5.2	85	Serbia	3.4	134	Pakistan	2.5
1	New Zealand	9.3	47	Cape Verde	5.1	92	Algeria	3.2	134	Ukraine	2.5
1	Sweden	9.3	47	Costa Rica	5.1	92	Bosnia and Herzegovina	3.2	138	Liberia	2.4
4	Singapore	9.2	47	Hungary	5.1	92	Lesotho	3.2	138	Paraguay	2.4
5	Finland	9.0	47	Jordan	5.1	92	Sri Lanka	3.2	138	Tonga	2.4
5	Switzerland	9.0	47	Malaysia	5.1	96	Benin	3.1	141	Cameroon	2.3
7	Iceland	8.9	52	Latvia	5.0	96	Gabon	3.1	141	Iran	2.3
7	Netherlands	8.9	52	Slovakia	5.0	96	Guatemala	3.1	141	Philippines	2.3
9	Australia	8.7	54	South Africa	4.9	96	Jamaica	3.1	141	Yemen	2.3
9	Canada	8.7	55	Italy	4.8	96	Kiribati	3.1	145	Kazakhstan	2.2
11	Luxembourg	8.3	55	Seychelles	4.8	96	Mali	3.1	145	Timor-Leste	2.2
12	Austria	8.1	57	Greece	4.7	102	Bolivia	3.0	147	Bangladesh	2.1
12	Hong Kong	8.1	58	Lithuania	4.6	102	Djibouti	3.0	147	Kenya	2.1
14	Germany	7.9	58	Poland	4.6	102	Dominican Republic	3.0	147	Russia	2.1
14	Norway	7.9	58	Turkey	4.6	102	Lebanon	3.0	147	Syria	2.1

Rank	Country	2008 CPI Score	Rank	Country	2008 CPI Score	Rank	Country	2008 CPI Score	Rank	Country	2008 CPI Score
16	Ireland	7.7	61	Namibia	4.5	102	Mongolia	3.0	151	Belarus	2.0
16	United Kingdom	7.7	62	Croatia	4.4	102	Rwanda	3.0	151	Central African Republic	2.0
18	Belgium	7.3	62	Samoa	4.4	102	Tanzania	3.0	151	Côte d'Ivoire	2.0
18	Japan	7.3	62	Tunisia	4.4	109	Argentina	2.9	151	Ecuador	2.0
18	United States of America	7.3	65	Cuba	4.3	109	Armenia	2.9	151	Laos	2.0
21	Saint Lucia	7.1	65	Kuwait	4.3	109	Belize	2.9	151	Papua New Guinea	2.0
22	Barbados	7.0	67	El Salvador	3.9	109	Moldova	2.9	151	Tajikistan	2.0
23	Chile	6.9	67	Georgia	3.9	109	Solomon Islands	2.9	158	Angola	1.9
23	France	6.9	67	Ghana	3.9	109	Vanuatu	2.9	158	Azerbaijan	1.9
23	Uruguay	6.9	70	Colombia	3.8	115	Egypt	2.8	158	Burundi	1.9
26	Slovenia	6.7	70	Romania	3.8	115	Malawi	2.8	158	Republic of the Congo	1.9
27	Estonia	6.6	72	Bulgaria	3.6	115	Maldives	2.8	158	Gambia	1.9
28	Qatar	6.5	72	China	3.6	115	Mauritania	2.8	158	Guinea-Bissau	1.9
28	St. Vincent and Grenadines	6.5	72	Macedonia	3.6	115	Niger	2.8	158	Sierra Leone	1.9
28	Spain	6.5	72	Mexico	3.6	115	Zambia	2.8	158	Venezuela	1.9

(Continued)

Exhibit 2.1 (Continued)

Rank	Country	2008 CPI Score	Rank	Country	2008 CPI Score	Rank	Country	2008 CPI Score	Rank	Country	2008 CPI Score
31	Cyprus	6.4	72	Peru	3.6	121	Nepal	2.7	166	Cambodia	1.8
32	Portugal	6.1	72	Suriname	3.6	121	Nigeria	2.7	166	Kyrgyzstan	1.8
33	Dominica	6.0	72	Swaziland	3.6	121	Sao Tome and Principe	2.7	166	Turkmenistan	1.8
33	Israel	6.0	72	Trinidad and Tobago	3.6	121	Togo	2.7	166	Uzbekistan	1.8
35	United Arab Emirates	5.9	80	Brazil	3.5	121	Vietnam	2.7	166	Zimbabwe	1.8
36	Botswana	5.8	80	Burkina Faso	3.5	126	Eritrea	2.6	171	Democratic Republic of the Congo	1.7
36	Malta	5.8	80	Morocco	3.5	126	Ethiopia	2.6	171	Equatorial Guinea	1.7
36	Puerto Rico	5.8	80	Saudi Arabia	3.5	126	Guyana	2.6	173	Chad	1.6
39	Taiwan	5.7	80	Thailand	3.5	126	Honduras	2.6	173	Guinea	1.6
40	South Korea	5.6	85	Albania	3.4	126	Indonesia	2.6	173	Sudan	1.6
41	Mauritius	5.5	85	India	3.4	126	Libya	2.6	176	Afghanistan	1.5
41	Oman	5.5	85	Madagascar	3.4	126	Mozambique	2.6	177	Haiti	1.4
43	Bahrain	5.4	85	Montenegro	3.4	126	Uganda	2.6	178	Iraq	1.3
43	Macau	5.4	85	Panama	3.4	134	Comoros	2.5	178	Myanmar	1.3
45	Bhutan	5.2	85	Senegal	3.4	134	Nicaragua	2.5	180	Somalia	1.0

about their experiences in regard to petty bribery, perceptions of corruption in national institutions and the private sector, and government effectiveness in fighting corruption. Of the respondents, 53% considered the private sector to be corrupt, and this was an 8% increase over the previous 5 years. Respondents were of the opinion that bribery can shape government policies and regulations in a company's favor. In Europe, only 44% believed that their governments' efforts to fight corruption were effective. Globally, only 3 in 10 said their governments' efforts to fight corruption were effective. Of the respondents, 10% worldwide admitted to having paid a bribe in the previous year. The latter statistic differed significantly among countries, ranging from 5% in Europe as a whole to 30% in Lithuania and 18% in Greece. The chair of Transparency International has concluded that in order to reduce corruption, "governments must think very carefully about how to make it safe and simple to report corruption" (*Business Corruption*, 2009).

World Bank Estimates

In recent years, the World Bank has adopted a new role in the investigation of corruption within projects and programs it finances. In its publications, it now emphasizes,

> The Bank also has global partnerships to fight corruption and help countries recover stolen assets, and provides extensive analytical work and diagnostics on governance and anticorruption.
>
> The Bank's Integrity Vice Presidency (INT) investigates allegations of fraud and corruption in Bank-financed projects—inside and outside the bank—and refers its findings to the Bank's sanctions system. Since 1999, INT has handled nearly 3,000 cases of alleged fraud, corruption, or other wrongdoing, resulting in the public debarment of 351 companies and individuals whose names have been listed on the Bank's website. (World Bank, 2008, p. 21)

The World Bank currently undertakes surveys to determine the extent and nature of corruption in nations throughout the world. Exhibit 2.2 presents some recent (2003–2009) data in regard to three measures: percentage of firms that expected to pay informal payments to public officials to get things done, percentage of firms that expected to give gifts to secure a government contract, and percentage of firms that identified corruption as a major constraint. For managers, these estimates provide another guide to the challenges their MNEs will face. In many countries, these percentages are astonishing. For the three measures, estimates in Bangladesh were 85%, 34%, and 55%; in Sub-Saharan Africa, 41%, 44%, and 33%; in India, 47%, 24%, and 26%; and in Russia, 29%, 46%, and 50%.

| Exhibit 2.2 | Corruption Measures |

Country	Percentage of Firms Expected to Pay Informal Payments to Public Officials (to Get Things Done)	Percentage of Firms Expected to Give Gifts to Secure a Government Contract	Percentage of Firms Identifying Corruption as a Major Constraint
All countries	30.61	31	36.52
East and Pacific Asia	59.8	43.59	29.84
Eastern Europe and Central Asia	16.79	26.15	34.06
Latin America and Caribbean	22.58	15.02	53.37
Middle East and North Africa	28.74	30.91	49.27
Organisation for Economic Co-operation and Development	12.56	15.62	8.12
South Asia	42.9	22.16	32.91
Sub-Saharan Africa	41.12	44.26	33.32
Afghanistan (2009)	41.49	44.04	53.64
Albania (2009)	36.76	53.78	38.54
Algeria (2007)	64.72	40.56	64.33
Angola (2006)	46.8	38.45	36.06
Argentina (2006)	18.72	25.08	59.92
Armenia (2009)	11.62	1.73	39.61
Azerbaijan (2009)	32.01	37.58	25.07
Bangladesh (2007)	85.07	33.81	54.9
Belarus (2008)	13.53	28.98	30.66
Benin (2004)	57.65	75.43	83.85
Bhutan (2009)	10.05	6.96	6.04
Bolivia (2006)	32.41	35.69	65.8
Bosnia and Herzegovina (2009)	8.08	5.63	35.14

Country	Percentage of Firms Expected to Pay Informal Payments to Public Officials (to Get Things Done)	Percentage of Firms Expected to Give Gifts to Secure a Government Contract	Percentage of Firms Identifying Corruption as a Major Constraint
Botswana (2006)	27.62	22.92	22.58
Brazil (2009)	6.99	1.65	64.87
Bulgaria (2009)	8.51	20.27	33.52
Burkina Faso (2006)	86.96	80.77	53.96
Burundi (2006)	56.46	44.36	19.72
Cambodia (2007)	61.23	76.25	53.73
Cameroon (2006)	77.6	85.23	52.05
Cape Verde (2006)	5.63	14.08	16.33
Chile (2006)	8.22	11.38	35.9
China (2003)	72.57	27.04	27.33
Colombia (2006)	8.23	5.11	48.93
Congo, Democratic Republic of the (2006)	83.79	80.54	20.02
Congo, Republic of the (2009)	49.21	75.18	65.02
Costa Rica (2005)	33.8	18.71	39.94
Côte d'Ivoire (2009)	30.64	32.34	74.99
Croatia (2009)	14.71	20.3	31.49
Czech Republic (2009)	8.73	30.31	25.12
Dominican Republic (2005)	26.34	15.1	72.89
Ecuador (2006)	21.45	25.14	72.07
Egypt (2007)	7.34	92.22	59.29
El Salvador (2006)	34.28	21.02	62.52
Estonia (2009)	1.6	0.28	5.43
Ethiopia (2006)	12.42	11.8	23.08

(Continued)

Exhibit 2.2   (Continued)

Country	Percentage of Firms Expected to Pay Informal Payments to Public Officials (to Get Things Done)	Percentage of Firms Expected to Give Gifts to Secure a Government Contract	Percentage of Firms Identifying Corruption as a Major Constraint
Gabon (2009)	26.09	26.61	41.35
Gambia (2006)	52.42	50.3	9.78
Georgia (2008)	4.08	0	20.42
Germany (2005)	. .	. .	3.87
Ghana (2007)	38.77	61.23	9.86
Greece (2005)	21.61	14.51	10.02
Guatemala (2006)	15.67	16.76	62.93
Guinea (2006)	84.75	74.58	47.66
Guinea-Bissau (2006)	62.72	48.41	44.01
Guyana (2004)	20	8.28	17.79
Honduras (2006)	16.67	18.4	59.79
Hungary (2009)	3.95	30.51	20.38
India (2006)	47.49	23.79	25.65
Indonesia (2003)	44.18	3.27	41.51
Ireland (2005)	8.32	7.69	3.02
Jamaica (2005)	17.65	0	46.07
Jordan (2006)	18.08	5.8	40.69
Kazakhstan (2009)	23.25	54.84	43.85
Kenya (2007)	79.22	71.2	38.35
Korea (2005)	14.05	25.84	8.54
Kosovo, Republic of (2009)	2.16	18.47	73.42
Kyrgyz Republic (2009)	37.48	56.38	58.93
Lao People's Democratic Republic (2006)	98.26	100	8.94
Latvia (2009)	11.32	48.06	33.91

Country	Percentage of Firms Expected to Pay Informal Payments to Public Officials (to Get Things Done)	Percentage of Firms Expected to Give Gifts to Secure a Government Contract	Percentage of Firms Identifying Corruption as a Major Constraint
Lebanon (2006)	51.19	33.33	66.57
Lesotho (2009)	13.96	26.37	46.71
Liberia (2009)	55.22	51.59	31.19
Lithuania (2009)	8.48	12.24	38.61
Macedonia, Former Yugoslav Republic (2009)	11.52	0.47	27.11
Madagascar (2009)	19.2	14.13	42.71
Malawi (2006)	35.65	12.26	46.84
Malaysia (2002)	. .	. .	14.49
Mali (2007)	28.88	80.35	15.7
Mauritania (2006)	82.12	76.16	17.1
Mauritius (2009)	1.59	8.81	50.72
Mexico (2006)	22.57	10.49	48.1
Moldova (2009)	25.41	24.2	40.92
Mongolia (2009)	30.41	40.63	31.14
Montenegro (2009)	7.39	23.41	3.02
Morocco (2007)	13.39	6.38	27.34
Mozambique (2007)	14.84	31.65	25.36
Namibia (2006)	11.36	8.08	19.14
Nicaragua (2006)	17.22	11.52	70.57
Niger (2006)	69.7	80	58.54
Nigeria (2007)	40.9	44.57	24.7
Oman (2003)	33.21	. .	11.9
Pakistan (2002)	57.01	. .	40.35
Panama (2006)	25.42	6.99	32.86
Paraguay (2006)	84.76	37.62	67.99

(Continued)

Exhibit 2.2   (Continued)

Country	Percentage of Firms Expected to Pay Informal Payments to Public Officials (to Get Things Done)	Percentage of Firms Expected to Give Gifts to Secure a Government Contract	Percentage of Firms Identifying Corruption as a Major Constraint
Peru (2006)	11.3	9.3	55.54
Philippines (2003)	44.74	17.54	35.17
Poland (2009)	4.95	16.71	24.07
Portugal (2005)	14.46	27.63	15.42
Romania (2009)	9.75	37.67	52.34
Russian Federation (2009)	29.44	46.32	50
Rwanda (2006)	19.96	14.37	4.35
Senegal (2007)	18.12	36.32	23.84
Serbia (2009)	17.98	15.93	35.62
Sierra Leone (2009)	18.8	33.85	36.87
Slovakia (2009)	11.63	23.06	33.11
Slovenia (2009)	5.41	1.2	9.76
South Africa (2007)	15.09	33.2	16.87
Spain (2005)	4.36	2.41	7.84
Sri Lanka (2004)	16.28	2.21	16.89
Swaziland (2006)	40.6	31.85	24.89
Syria (2003)	. .	. .	57.55
Tajikistan (2008)	40.51	31.09	37.82
Tanzania (2006)	49.47	42.69	19.73
Thailand (2006)	. .	. .	41.04
Turkey (2008)	17.7	23.12	42.3
Uganda (2006)	51.7	46.43	23.57
Ukraine (2008)	22.9	44.87	50.21
Uruguay (2006)	7.26	7.23	43.05

Country	Percentage of Firms Expected to Pay Informal Payments to Public Officials (to Get Things Done)	Percentage of Firms Expected to Give Gifts to Secure a Government Contract	Percentage of Firms Identifying Corruption as a Major Constraint
Uzbekistan (2008)	56.19	50.81	27.2
Venezuela (2006)	. .	. .	39.97
Vietnam (2005)	67.2	40.38	15.18
West Bank and Gaza (2006)	13.25	7.19	66.5
Zambia (2007)	14.33	27.39	12.08

SOURCE: World Bank Enterprise Surveys (www.enterprisesurveys.org).

Other World Bank surveys provide the percentage of firms that expected to give gifts to get an operating license, percentage of firms that expected to give gifts in meetings with tax officials, and percentage of revenue given as gifts.

In 2007, the World Bank published *The Many Faces of Corruption: Tracking Vulnerabilities at the Sector Level* (Campos & Pradhan, 2007). This manuscript examines the myriad forms of corruption in a series of specific sectors, including pharmaceuticals, education, forestry, electricity, transportation, petroleum, and water and sanitation. In each sector, this World Bank manuscript provides a detailed analysis of how corruption can enter the business process.

The pharmaceutical sector is particularly susceptible to fraud and corruption because it is subject to a significant degree of government regulation. Government officials have discretion in making regulatory decisions at many points in the pharmaceutical supply chain: manufacturing, registration, selection, procurement, distribution, and prescribing and dispensing. The educational system in many countries is vulnerable to a variety of forms of corruption, including bribes for admission and examinations and illegal procurement practices. In the forestry sector, firms are given access to specific timber stands, and this access may depend on bribery, while payments to government officials may result in the evasion of royalties and taxes. In the transport and export stage of forestry, a firm may be allowed to deal in illegal logs that have not been taken under official permits and programs. In the electricity sector, corruption can range from petty theft at the level of meter readers and linemen to grand larceny by the politicians who award lucrative concessions with power purchase agreements.

> The infrastructure sectors are seen as being particularly vulnerable to corrupt practices given inter alia the large and lumpy expenditures involved (therefore easier to hide bribes), the reality that there are often relatively few qualified contractors (which can, in turn, lead to collusion), the presence of natural monopolies and the limits to competition (even with reform), the prevalence of "regulatory capture," and the numerous opportunities for discretionary decisions and "rent taking" by public and private officials. (Campos & Pradhan, 2007, p. 115)

China's Guanxi: Corruption or Not?

While they may seem of relatively minor importance in many instances, decisions based on personal relationships may have an overall negative impact on efficiency and growth by distorting free market outcomes. Such decisions benefit a relatively small number of those in authority, and one might expect that this is often at the expense of those who do not receive personal favors. This decision-making process may violate the participants' sense of fiduciary duties and may lead some of them to more significant corruption. Firms that reject traditional practices may experience ongoing difficulties in conducting business. While this informal system of personal commitments may be most clearly observable in China, the culture of many nations involves phenomena similar to guanxi. Meanwhile, successful MNE operations in some other nations depend much less on developing personal relationships that include an exchange of gifts.

A tough question for managers has to do with the line where acceptable gifts become unacceptable corruption. In May 2009, *The Economist* discussed an extensive list of expensive gifts from local contractors to Mr. Ndebele following his appointment as the new transport minister in South Africa. Among these gifts was a Mercedes worth $130,000.

> The temptation apparently proved too great. He gleefully accepted, hotly denying that he was doing anything wrong. . . .
>
>   Under the government's code of ethics, ministers may accept business gifts provided they are properly declared and anything worth over 1,000 rand gets presidential approval. Many people were nevertheless quick to express outrage at this first apparent instance of sleaze in the new government of President Jacob Zuma. ("Not a Whiff," 2009, p. 49)

Faced with a negative public outcry, Mr. Ndebele "voluntarily" decided to sell some of the gifts and donate the funds to poor communities.

Linkages Between Culture and Corruption

Many comparative studies assume that the major reason underlying variations in ethical practices across nations has to do with cultural differences. In their detailed analysis of cross-country differences in corruption, Davis and Ruhe (2003) examine the relationship between corruption in a nation and that nation's cultural characteristics. They use Hofstede's classifications in regard to culture to test a variety of hypotheses in regard to this belief. They find support for three of Hofstede's cultural dimensions as being antecedents of a country's corruption. Their multiple regression analysis concludes that countries low in power distance have cultures where people question the leaders' actions, so there is less corruption. In contrast, cultures with high power distance involve a hierarchical system that may encourage corruption. A culture that is high in individualism emphasizes performance outcomes, with rewards geared to outcomes rather than rewards geared to personal connections that involve corruption. In countries with a universalistic culture, people believe that laws should apply to everyone equally. In contrast, in particularist societies corruption may be commonplace as part of favoritism and special privileges for the elite. Davis and Ruhe do find that other institutional, organizational, and personal factors are additional elements beyond Hofstede's classifications of cultures in determining the degree of corruption in a country. In particular, they conclude that there is a clear relationship between disillusionment with democracy and the degree of corruption.

Sanyal (2005) also relates bribery to Hofstede's basic cultural divisions, and his statistical analyses support the linkage between cultural traits and levels of bribery. This finding is important in considering the time that will be required to reduce corruption.

> Since cultural values and practices are deeply embedded in a society, they are difficult to change, and in fact, are more likely to persist. To that extent, efforts to curb bribery are going to be a long-drawn and frustrating process. (p. 144)

Government weaknesses or shortcomings may provide opportunities for corruption with relatively low expectation of being apprehended. Extensive government intervention in the economy encourages corruption. If government officials have the authority to impact economic transactions in general, then the opportunity for bribery is widespread. The nation's judicial system and rule of law form a major determinant of the degree of corruption. Here, the functioning of various agencies that are required for customs procedures and police work, as well as the judiciary, all interact to create a social attitude toward corruption. In very poor nations, public officials are paid such low wages that it is generally understood they must accept illegal payments in order to survive. Government officials who have low educational levels may fail to appreciate the implications of corruption for their nation's economic development. Nations with widespread corruption have generally had governments that have been independent of foreign dominance for only a short period of time with a relatively recent political constitution and a weak financial base. These nations tend to be relatively poor with problems of inflation and unemployment, and they tend to be illiterate with little formal education. They have large rural populations, extended families, and shorter life expectancies. This "demand side" perspective suggests that corruption may be reduced through the strengthening of political rights and civil liberties, job creation, and improved education.

Corruption can be divided into two quite separate types of illegal activities. With petty bribery, government officials are paid in order to expedite their normal duties. In many cases, government decisions are not changed by the bribery, but bribery may have to be used in order to get the officials to provide appropriate approvals within a reasonable period of time. A quite different type of corruption involves the diversion of substantial revenue from the government or the public into the hands of specific businesses. Here, senior officials may work with MNEs to determine the terms and conditions under which the MNE may operate in their country, including the creation of barriers to the entry of potential competitors. Such corruption may involve the payment of huge sums of money to government officials. Widespread poverty can be an explanation for petty corruption, while the possession of major reserves of natural resources can be a cause of the second kind of corruption. A substantial literature describes the history of linkages between oil rights and corruption, and Nigeria and Venezuela illustrate these linkages. Both petty bribery and major corruption may reduce economic development and misallocate resources. Major corruption creates a form of regressive taxation, and in the extreme, corruption can threaten the legitimacy of the government itself.

By themselves, payments or petty bribery may not involve clear injustice, and they may be seen as unavoidable. One might distinguish between gifts on the one hand and bribes or facilitating payments on the other. With a gift, there is a purpose of creating an atmosphere of friendship with a long-term relationship, whereas a facilitating payment is directed at a particular issue and is given in return for a favorable decision. A series of problems arise in a culture that permits gifts and facilitating payments. Government officials may have an interest in not resolving issues as swiftly or efficiently as they could, since this might reduce the payments. The firm may be given a permit or license to which it is not really entitled. The firm experiences a loss of money and time. Government officials in such a culture may develop the habit of automatically demanding payments. Since such payments generally violate domestic laws, government officials fall into a pattern of illegality, creating a culture of corruption. Although these payments are small, they may impede the multinational political efforts to fight against corruption. A network of extortion can readily develop. Politicians and public officials have an incentive to create regulations that give them the power to demand payments. Meanwhile, facilitating payments can lead to a deterioration in corporate morale as a culture of corruption becomes commonplace within the MNE.

Each MNE must make a clear decision concerning the use of gifts and facilitating payments. The MNE should clarify the precise circumstances or specific cases in which they may be permitted. Whatever the policy, all employees and managers must adhere to it. Employees require training that focuses on how to respond to the solicitation of payments. The MNEs should create problem-solving procedures so employees can obtain advice in specific situations. The firm should ensure that any employee has the right to be a whistle-blower with a guarantee of confidentiality. The firm should put in place control systems that can detect noncompliance with its code, and it should actively gather information in regard to expectations in the local culture. If certain payments are to be permitted, such payments should be recorded clearly rather than being taken from a general slush fund. Argandona (2005) concludes,

> Companies tend to have a permissive attitude towards facilitating payments. Yet they should adopt the opposite attitude, at least as a general rule, given the internal and external consequences of facilitating payments for the company, its stakeholders and society at large. (p. 261)

A Global View of Corruption

> Corruption is everywhere, to be sure, but it is not the same everywhere. Indeed, corruption varies across countries as much as labor costs or corporate tax rates. The challenges firms face on entering foreign countries largely reflect their efforts to understand and adapt to local corruption. (Rodriguez, Uhlenbruck, & Eden, 2005, p. 383)

Corruption significantly reduces direct investment flows for manufacturing, and corruption can even deter MNE entry for the purpose of purchasing for export. Attitudes toward corruption determine the generally accepted rules of business, and corruption is embedded to varying degrees and in different ways in the norms and behaviors of each culture. The greater the degree of government regulation, the higher the levels of corruption, as public servants hold greater power over corporate success. There seems to have been a change in levels of corruption over time, with current corruption levels being significantly lower in countries that have had high foreign direct investment (FDI) flows. "The harmful effects of culture on corruption are lower and the beneficial effects of education on corruption are higher in countries with higher FDI in the past" (Rodriguez, Siegel, Hillman, & Eden, 2006, p. 742).

It is useful to divide corruption into two very different dimensions. The term "pervasiveness" describes the likelihood that a firm will encounter corruption in its normal interactions with government officials. Pervasiveness of corruption refers to an expectation of the frequency and degree to which the firm will be obliged to deal with the subject of corruption—that is, the degree to which corruption is a regular and meaningful part of business activity. This concept underlies the indices developed by organizations such as Transparency International. However, corruption has an additional dimension related to the degree to which it is arbitrary due to uncertainty concerning the size, the target, and the number of payments necessary in any situation requiring government approval.

In analyzing corruption in each nation where it is considering doing business, the MNE must understand both the pervasiveness and arbitrariness of corruption. Arbitrary corruption encourages the development of social networks that are able to serve as coping mechanisms. Consequently, an MNE will likely choose a joint venture partner if a country has highly arbitrary corruption. On the other hand, corruption that is pervasive but not arbitrary can be understood by the MNE, and a wholly-owned subsidiary may be able to conduct business successfully once it understands the conditions of corruption. An MNE may even be able to develop a competitive advantage based on its experiences with pervasive corruption. However, where corruption is highly arbitrary, an MNE's experience with corruption may not lead to a competitive advantage.

Cuervo-Cazurra (2006) has examined the impact of corruption on trends in FDI. In particular, he has analyzed FDI from countries that have signed the Organisation for Economic Co-operation and Development (OECD) convention on combating bribery of foreign public officials in international business transactions. He contrasts MNEs from this group of countries with MNEs from countries that themselves have high levels of corruption and have not signed the OECD convention. He concludes that investors from the latter countries have been exposed to bribery in their home countries and may actually seek foreign countries where bribery is more prevalent as the sites for their investments. He concludes that not all foreign investors are concerned about corruption in the host country. Not all investors view corruption in the same way. Further, a foreign investor may use a joint venture structure in order to avoid paying bribes directly itself. Managers at the MNE head office may hire local managers with experience in bribery and give them responsibility for organizing bribes in countries with which they have had business experiences.

A historical analysis of developed countries might reveal that most have experienced corruption in the past. From this perspective, one might see the degree of corruption as related to the level of per capita income, with the expectation that economic growth may automatically reduce the level of corruption. Related to this is the gradual strengthening of the legal system as part of the growth process. Developing nations today are at a major disadvantage in dealing with corruption because they need foreign investment and they have a weak bargaining position in the international competition for capital. While corruption may appear to lead to some forms of national value maximization in the short run, it will not in the long run.

Business corruption also exists in the economically advanced nations. Western businesses have developed sophisticated techniques with payments to political parties and to individual election campaigns. In western nations, this type of corruption has become almost invisible as it has taken a permanent place in the election process. Chief Justice David Souter, a former member of the U.S. Supreme Court, has been quoted as saying,

> I think most people assume—I do, certainly—that someone making an extraordinarily large (political) contribution is going to get some kind of an extraordinary return for it. . . . I think there is . . . an appearance of . . . an attenuated corruption. . . . Large contributors are simply going to get better service . . . from a politician than an average contributor, let alone no contributor. (Khera, 2007, p. 31)

In the economically advanced nations, political donations are accompanied by an extensive network of lobbyists who maintain ongoing interactions with elected officials and also with the public service bureaucracy, including various government agencies. Lobbyists work intently to advance the financial interests of the firms who hire them. Generally, firms in less developed nations do not have this array of go-betweens to handle their business/government relations. To some degree, the firm must fulfill this role itself, and petty bribery with personal relationships may be seen as an alternative to formal lobbyists. Over time, it is possible that the creation of a network of lobbyists may serve to reduce petty bribery as currently practiced.

While many surveys of corruption omit the economically advanced nations, even the United States is often the focus of corruption scandals. In July 2009, *The Wall Street Journal* reported,

> Federal agents swept across New Jersey and New York on Thursday, charging 44 people—including mayors, rabbis and even one alleged trafficker in human kidneys—in a decade-long investigation into public corruption and international money laundering. (Efrati, Sataline, & Searcey, 2009, p. A1)

The Corruption Path Ahead: Ethical Challenges Facing Managers

The subject of corruption has received increasing public attention in recent years. Managers now have to make decisions concerning their corporation's international position in regard to giving or accepting bribes. Some managers may institute corporation-wide policies with the threat of dismissal if violated, while other managers may promulgate policies that differ among countries. Some managers may conclude that they wish not to invest in certain countries where corruption is too extensive and unpredictable to permit regular business practices.

GE's corporate position is among the most well-known. In the early 1990s, GE adopted uniformly high ethical standards throughout the firm. GE management has concluded that the firm's clear and decisive line in regard to corruption has actually helped it win contracts in many countries. IKEA was a major shopping center developer and retailer in Russia. In June 2009, IKEA received global attention as a result of its decision to suspend further investment in Russia because of pervasive corruption. IKEA's Russian management cited "the unpredictability of administrative processes" in Russia. At this time, Russia's president, Dmitry Medvedev, signed a law prohibiting surprise inspections of corporate property that had often been used to extort bribes. He also required civil servants to disclose the income and assets of their spouses, as well as themselves, so the receipt of bribes could be monitored. A Moscow correspondent emphasized the importance of IKEA's decision and stated, "The Swedish retailer's public stance could mark an economic turning point if it leads to more Western businesses speaking out against corruption here" (Kramer, 2009, p. B11).

A July 2009 *Financial Times* article pointed to an increase in the international coordination of corruption investigations based on the global harmonization of anticorruption regulation and prosecution. As a result, managers now face far more severe prosecution than in the past. Prosecutions are now directed at individual managers and board members rather than just the corporation. This has raised corruption to a "top corporate governance issue." Routine tasks such as securing government permits now carry "risk that could ultimately impact company executives." A PricewaterhouseCoopers (PWC) report has calculated an increase in global settlements and penalties from $3.1 million in 2002 to more than $1.7 billion in 2008. PWC has created a division specializing in advice concerning corruption regulation, and it has warned that

> Business leaders and board members must be aware that the level at which their companies prepare for geopolitical risk and anti-corruption compliance could make or break the viability of doing business in a desired region. (Chung, 2009, p. 2)

In 2009, a study commissioned by Klynveld Peat Marwick Goerdeler (KPMG) found that 40% of the British companies surveyed had begun internal investigations of alleged corruption within the previous 3 years. Many companies had established whistle-blower hot lines to encourage reporting. Nevertheless, 67% of respondents said there were places where it was impossible to do business without bribery. The U.K. Parliament was set to debate a new bribery bill that would make executives personally responsible for corrupt activities whether or not they were aware of them. For managers, corruption continues to create new and difficult ethical challenges. The international evolution of new management challenges in regard to corruption has become increasingly important. Specific challenges differ among nations, and they may involve internal relationships and intercorporate relationships, as well as business/government relationships. For managers, personal ethics may be a central element in delineating corporate policies. Solutions will not be easy, yet the penalties for failure will become increasingly severe.

New Concerns About Fraud and Ethics

No doubt fraud has existed throughout human history as some individuals have tried to take advantage of others in their economic exchanges. By not revealing the truth, one may convince others to purchase things they might not purchase if told the truth. Many nations have long had laws that make certain fraudulent exchanges illegal and that subject the perpetrators of fraud to prosecution. Purchasers deceived by false advertising and purchasers of defective merchandise have long been able to obtain legal redress.

In recent decades, a new type of fraud has attracted widespread public attention. Some senior managers have been tempted to issue false and misleading information to their investors and potential investors. Their bonuses have been geared to the firm's current profits, and the value of their stock options has been dependent on the escalation in the firm's share prices. Issuing false and misleading information has been a way to maintain public perceptions of the firm's success and so support the firm's ongoing growth. Brokerage firms have been tempted to offer overly optimistic advice in hopes of selling more shares to investors, especially when they have been hired by the firm to raise capital for it. Management may be offered falsely dated stock options whose value has already risen substantially when the management receives them. A series of major corporate and accounting scandals has shocked investors, the general public, and governments. With some firms—such as Enron, Tyco International, and World Com—existing legislation has been used to prosecute senior management. However, a widespread public feeling has developed that many such managers may have avoided the prosecution that they deserve. In response, new laws and regulations have been proposed that hopefully might prevent these types of investor-related fraud before they occur.

New internal controls may be required to ensure that management and the board of directors are fully aware of the issues that may impact the firm's profitability and can be honest in revealing these issues to the public. More precise methodologies for estimating and describing risk may have to be used. The function of audit and consulting may have to be performed by separate firms so the financial statements will be compiled objectively by "independent" auditors. Senior management may have to bear personal responsibility for the accuracy of the firm's financial statements, with the threat of personal prosecution if errors are later found. However, subjective judgment based on corporate ethics is still involved in providing information to the public. Management must still make decisions that involve ethics. So the implementation of new laws and regulations still leaves the subject of ethics at the core of the firm's management.

A series of enormous investment frauds by Bernie Madoff, Allen Stanford, and others has emphasized the importance of personal ethics when investors trust advisers with their savings. The general suspicion has developed that with each fraud a large number of other employees must have known and been complicit. The strengthening of personal ethics may encourage whistle-blowers to reveal fraudulent practices early in the process. Since laws and regulations differ among nations, some managers may be tempted to shift the firm's head office to a jurisdiction that has not imposed such stringent requirements. For all these reasons, the subject of ethics and an ethics code has become a new and important element in the environment of business.

New Laws to Prevent Corruption and Fraud

The U.S. Foreign Corrupt Practices Act (FCPA) came into effect in 1977. The FCPA has two sets of provisions. The accounting provisions require strict accounting and record keeping that can assure management's control over international activities and prevent the concealment of foreign bribery. The foreign payments provisions prohibit all U.S. businesses and persons from paying bribes to foreign government officials. However, the U.S. government has not enforced the FCPA aggressively for most of its history. The number of prosecutions has been relatively small. Over the first 20 years, only 17 companies were charged with fines ranging from $10,000 to $3.5 million. Nevertheless, U.S. business executives have often expressed the view that the FCPA places them at a competitive disadvantage. This argument emphasizes the need for a concerted international prohibition of corruption.

> Ever since the enactment of the FCPA in 1977, U.S. business executives have complained that enforced honesty was leaving them at a competitive disadvantage. Their European and Asian counterparts were not only beating them out of lucrative deals all over the world, but they were also deducting the bribes as business expenses. (Kaikati, Sullivan, Virgo, Carr, & Virgo, 2000, p. 216)

In 1997, the OECD adopted an anti-bribery convention (The OECD Convention in Combating Bribery of Foreign Public Officials in International Business Transactions). Under this convention, an OECD Working Group on Bribery has established procedures for monitoring and evaluating bribery in its signatory countries, which consist of the 30 OECD nations plus 6 additional countries. The OECD convention requires that its signatories impose severe penalties, including fines and imprisonment, for the bribery of foreign public officials. These punishments must apply to both individuals and firms. Member governments must confiscate the bribes and any profits obtained through the bribery. As part of this process, the OECD undertakes regular examinations of each country's national laws to determine whether they achieve these objectives. In addition, the working group studies linkages between corruption, money laundering, and the finance of terrorism. Since the 36 signatory countries account for most of the international trade in the world today, this OECD convention has a role of increasing importance in reducing corruption.

The most powerful new legislation to prevent fraud has been the U.S. Sarbanes-Oxley Act of 2002. This act requires the U.S. Securities and Exchange Commission (SEC) to create and enforce new regulations that will compel conformance with specific sections of the act. The officers of the corporation must certify their responsibility for establishing and evaluating the effectiveness of internal control procedures and for disclosing this information to the auditor and the board of directors. Information in this regard must also be included in the corporation's quarterly and annual reports.

Other sections of Sarbanes-Oxley require certain standards of quality and transparency in financial reporting so that investors will better understand the financial position of the corporation and material changes in that position over time. Boards of directors are to be given new and additional responsibilities in regard to matters of internal controls and financial disclosure. Senior corporate executives must take individual responsibility for the accuracy and completeness of corporate financial reports. Criminal penalties are included in the legislation for "white-collar crimes" and "conspiracies" to commit fraud.

Nevertheless, Sarbanes-Oxley inevitably leaves considerable discretion to management and the board of directors in regard to the analyses of risks and material changes. Individuals must still refer to ethical standards for guidance in individual decisions. Furthermore, many critics of Sarbanes-Oxley argue that compliance costs are too severe. Managers and boards may be tempted to withdraw their shares from the public stock exchanges in order to avoid the need to comply with the new SEC regulations. Some may be tempted to shift head offices to other jurisdictions with less onerous restrictions. In a sense, these decisions also involve ethical judgments.

Many would argue that new laws and regulations by themselves can have only a limited impact, since decisions are ultimately driven in many situations by a manager's personal ethics. From this perspective, progress may require a heightened universal appreciation for the role of ethics. Furthermore, progress may require a more active involvement by each firm's board of directors, involving changes in corporate governance practices. It is to these subjects that we turn in Chapter 3. Meanwhile, the Citigroup case illustrates the challenges of creating a new corporate culture that emphasizes ethics, and it highlights the difficulties of ensuring ethical behavior within an MNE that operates in many nations.

In Practice 2.1 | **Evaluating and Improving the Corporate Ethical Culture**

Citigroup's vision of the ultimate financial company, manufacturing and selling every financial product, is lost. A series of scandals betrayed the fact that the structure Sanford Weill built had reached the limits of manageability. (Lee, 2005, p. 1)

Over the period 2000–2005, many divisions within Citigroup were charged with illegal or unethical behavior. It seemed that Citigroup had simply become too large and complex for central management to prevent inappropriate decisions on the part of various groups scattered throughout the world. Business crises included

- lawsuits by shareholders and creditors of WorldCom, Enron, Global Crossing, and Parmalat SpA concerning inappropriate loan arrangements;

Citigroup took a $1.3 billion charge in 2002 relating to settlements concerning tainted research and IPO analyses. In 2004, it made a payment of $2.65 billion related to WorldCom. In 2005, it paid $75 million to investors in Global Crossing and $208 million to settle alleged wrongdoing in regard to mutual funds. In 2005, Citigroup also agreed to pay $2 billion to settle a class action lawsuit by Enron investors.

- the Japanese government's retraction of Citigroup's private-banking license in Japan after a series of financial scandals;
- imposition of the largest fine on a U.K.-regulated bank after the sale of a large quantity of bonds in Europe over a short time period that abruptly decreased bond prices, enabling Citigroup to then purchase bonds at a lower price.

Analysts criticized the corporate culture:

Employees indicated that cost cutting had gone too far, eating away core capabilities without offering adequate support. In addition, there was a sense that there was inadequate support for developing talent within the company and little consideration was given to work-life balance. Local corporate franchises were undermined by an organization that was driven by products and results without the necessary investment in people and culture. (Harker, 2005, p. 16)

In response to these scandals,

> The Federal Reserve barred Citigroup Inc. from major acquisitions until the company fixes regulatory problems that have gotten the financial-services giant in trouble around the world. (Pacelle, 2005, p. C1)

It appeared that Citigroup needed a new corporate culture to guide globally decentralized decision making. In response, CEO Charles Prince appointed Lewis Kaden, a recognized expert in business ethics, as vice-chairman and chief administrative officer. On March 1, 2005, Prince launched his Five Point Plan:

> A comprehensive, forward-looking program of training, development and cultural change that was to cascade down throughout the organization, from New York, to Johannesburg, to Hong Kong. The Five Point Plan consists of five key areas: 1. expanded training, 2. enhanced focus on talent and development, 3. balanced performance appraisals, 4. improved communications, and 5. strengthened controls. (Harker, 2005, p. 16)

SOURCE: Conklin and Cadieux (2006).

Critical Thinking Questions

1. How can an MNE create a global culture of ethics that provides guidance concerning corruption and fraud throughout the firm?

2. Evaluate Charles Prince's attempts to create a new and better corporate ethical culture. What recommendations would you make?

3. Was Citigroup just too big and too diverse and complex to cope effectively with ethical issues?

References and Suggested Readings

Argandona, A. (2005). Corruption and companies: The use of facilitating payments. *Journal of Business Ethics, 60,* 251–264.

Business corruption on the rise, says report. (2009, July 4). Retrieved July 13, 2009, from http://www.euractiv.com/en/pa/business-corruption-rise-report/article-182858

Campos, J. E., & Pradhan, S. (Eds.). (2007). *The many faces of corruption: Tracking vulnerabilities at the sector level.* Washington, DC: World Bank.

Chung, J. (2009, July 27). Regulators in drive to curb bribery. *Financial Times,* p. 2.

Conklin, D. W., & Cadieux, D. (2006). *Citigroup in post-WTO China (B).* London: Ivey. (Ivey Case No. 9B06M043)

Cuervo-Cazurra, A. (2006). Who cares about corruption? *Journal of International Business Studies, 37,* 807–822.

Davis, J., & Ruhe, J. (2003). Perceptions of country corruption: Antecedents and outcomes. *Journal of Business Ethics, 43*(4), 275–288.

Efrati, A., Sataline, S., & Searcey, D. (2009, July 24). Jersey mayors stung in graft probe. *Wall Street Journal* (Eastern ed.), p. A1.

Harker, J. (2005, September/October). Ethics and strategy innovation at Citigroup. *Strategic HR Review*, 16.

Kaikati, J., Sullivan, G., Virgo, J., Carr, T., & Virgo, K. (2000). The price of international business morality: Twenty years under the Foreign Corrupt Practices Act. *Journal of Business Ethics, 26*(3), 213–222.

Khera, I. P. (2007). Business ethics, East vs. West, myths and realities. *Journal of Business Ethics, 30*(1), 31.

Kramer, A. (2009, June 25). Citing corruption, IKEA suspends investment in Russia. *Globe and Mail*, p. B11.

Landler, M. (2006, January 20). Volkswagen chairman will step down. *New York Times*, p. C3.

Lee, P. (2005, July). What Citigroup needs to do next. *Euromoney*, 1.

Luo, Y. (2006). Political behavior, social responsibility, and perceived corruption: A structuration perspective. *Journal of International Business Studies, 37*, 747–766.

Meiners, J. (2007). VW corruption figure admits payoffs. *Automotive News, 81*(6240), 96.

Miles, L. (2006). The application of Anglo-American corporate practices in societies influenced by Confucian values. *Business and Society Review, 111*(3), 305–321.

Milne, R. (2007, October 5). Siemens hit with € 201m fine. *Financial Times* (U.S. 1st ed.), p. 17.

Not a whiff of corruption is allowed. (2009). *The Economist, 391*(8632), 49.

Organisation for Economic Co-operation and Development. (2006). *Working group on bribery annual report 2006*. Paris: Author.

Pacelle, M. (2005, March 18). Fed ties the hands of Citigroup. *Wall Street Journal* (Eastern ed.), p. C1.

Rodriguez, P., Siegel, D. S., Hillman, A., & Eden, L. (2006). Three lenses on the multinational enterprise: Politics, corruption, and corporate social responsibility. *Journal of International Business Studies, 37*, 733–746.

Rodriguez, P., Uhlenbruck, K., & Eden, L. (2005). Government corruption and the entry strategies of multinationals. *Academy of Management Review, 30*(2), 383–396.

Sanyal, R. (2005). Determinants of bribery in international business: The cultural and economic factors. *Journal of Business Ethics, 59*, 139–145.

Sims, T. (2007, May 15). Two convicted of bribery; Siemens is fined millions. *New York Times*, p. 4.

Transparency International. (2008, September 22). *Corruption perceptions index.* Retrieved December 3, 2009, from http://www.transparency.org/news_room/in_focus/2008/cpi2008

Transparency International. (n.d.). *Frequently asked questions about corruption.* Retrieved July 3, 2009, from http://www.transparency.org/news_room/faq/corruption_faq

World Bank. (2008). *The World Bank annual report: An inclusive and sustainable globalization* (p. 21). Washington, DC: Author.

Adopting an Ethics Code and Corporate Social Responsibility 3

Why, What, and How?

CHAPTER LEARNING OBJECTIVES

On completion of this chapter, students should be able to

- list and discuss the elements they would include in corporate codes of ethics and social responsibility and indicate whether they would implement different codes in different nations,

- suggest how they would relate with various stakeholder groups in responding to their interests and concerns,

- describe how they would structure corporate social responsibilities (CSR) within a multinational enterprise (MNE),

- explain the changing nature and responsibilities of the board of directors as they relate to ethics and CSR.

The issues concerning corruption and fraud discussed in Chapter 2 are leading to new and clearer government guidelines for corporate decisions. Throughout the world, laws are being changed to compel the firm to adhere to higher standards of transparency and honesty. Both firms and business schools are adopting formal codes in regard to ethics and CSR in hopes of improving management decisions. Corporate employees, as well as students, are being urged to pursue values beyond the maximization of their individual income and short-term profits. How best to implement these values underlies a recent shift to new expanded responsibilities for boards of directors. However, throughout the world these new paradigms for strategies and management are being created to varying degrees and in different ways.

Countless authors have commented on Milton Friedman's (1970/2001) article "The Social Responsibility of Business is to Increase its Profits," in which Friedman argues that business activities should be limited to those that increase profits. Many regard Friedman's famous dictum as a rationale for ignoring ethical perspectives, social forces, corporate philanthropy, and obligations to stakeholders. In recent years, however, authors have analyzed the linkages between specific CSR policies and programs on the one hand and shareholder value on the other hand, emphasizing that a CSR strategy can be an important mechanism for increasing profits and shareholder value. A firm can use CSR to differentiate its reputation and brand from those of its competitors. Employees may contribute more effectively in their work if they have pride in their firm's CSR. Furthermore, various stakeholder groups have significantly increased their ability to disrupt corporate activities—through boycotts, for example—so the maximization of shareholder value requires a new involvement in CSR activities in order to minimize negative impacts of activist groups. Opportunities to create a new competitive advantage based on CSR, together with this ongoing threat of negative public responses greatly expands the activities that are consistent with Friedman's dictum.

Some authors disagree strongly with Friedman's (1970/2001) interpretation of the principal/agent argument, which states that "in his capacity as a corporate executive, the manager is the agent of the individuals who own the firm . . . and his primary responsibility is to them" (p. 51). Many authors emphasize that management today must acknowledge the firm's obligations as a member of the society in which it operates. From this perspective, management may feel that it has a responsibility to use corporate resources in some ways that might not increase shareholder value. An important element of this debate concerns the time horizon of management. If management considers only the short-term maximization of shareholder value, then it may feel justified in limiting CSR activities. However, if management is concerned with long-term shareholder value maximization, then management may see a much larger array of CSR activities as being appropriate.

As indicated in Chapter 2, significant differences exist among countries in regard to what is considered ethical or appropriate business behavior. MNEs must confront the conflict between adapting to cultural relativism in each country and adhering to global ethical positions. Many believe that MNEs should adhere to more stringent standards than may be required by some of the countries in which they do business and that each MNE must create global moral foundations. Fundamental human rights give rise to fundamental MNE duties and obligations. These obligations may include actions to advance the long-term welfare of employees and customers and obedience to minimum standards of justice. Further, most managers do have some personal sense of public responsibility, and their preferences and choices can underlie a firm's "corporate culture" in regard to ethics and CSR. In regard to responsiveness, the firm must be involved in managing issues whenever it confronts them and must respond to these issues in the context of an ongoing analysis of the environment in which the firm operates. Stakeholders cannot be ignored, and the firm should develop procedures for relating with them and responding to them. Finally, each firm should focus on the outcomes of its CSR activities, including analyses and measurement of the social impacts of the programs and policies that have been put in place.

The New Emphasis on Ethics

A recent advertisement by the Chartered Financial Analyst Institute (CFA) consists of the word "ethics" prominently displayed, followed by the assurance that the CFA designation brings with it a thorough awareness of ethical responsibilities.

> When someone has achieved the CFA designation—make no mistake he or she is well aware of ethical responsibilities. He upholds the Code of Ethics and Standards of Professional Conduct. She knows why GIPS [global investment performance standards] were created and to whom they apply. He has acknowledged his obligation to act in an ethical manner and to encourage others to do the same, with integrity, competence, diligence and respect. (CFA Institute Advertisement, 2009, p. 12)

Cacioppe, Forster, and Fox (2008) published their results from "A Survey of Managers' Perceptions of Corporate Ethics and Social Responsibility and Actions that may Affect Companies' Success." The authors emphasize the positive impacts of a corporate culture that rests on clear guidelines for ethical decision making.

> As research is beginning to document, companies that bring ethical discipline to bear on their activities and tap into the moral capabilities of their people start to reap a variety of economic benefits from doing so. . . . Given a choice, most people prefer to work for and do business with companies that are honest, fair, reliable and considerate. (p. 681)

The media in many countries have adopted a new investigative role in uncovering decisions that reflect questionable ethics. Corporations and their employees are not the only focus for such news stories. In Britain, reports of bloated and inappropriate expense claims by members of

Parliament raised a public outcry, and throughout the world, British strictures against corruption and fraud were mocked as hypocrisy. In Brazil, three senate presidents were suspended or resigned because of scandals over the period 2001 to 2009, and a fourth was similarly criticized in 2009. Meanwhile, media themselves have been accused of unethical behavior. A *Financial Times* article in 2009 reported that employees of one of Rupert Murdoch's British newspapers had been accused of hacking into the mobile phones of celebrities. "If true, this would represent an unpleasant invasion of privacy that could prove very costly to the present company ("Tapped for the Top," 2009).

Academic journals now place greater emphasis on research concerning ethics, and some journals such as *Corporate Responsibility Management* are devoted to this subject. There are now research centers that specialize in ethics. Simon Webley (2006), research director for the Institute of Business Ethics, has advocated a clear code of ethics to inform and guide all employees, together with the following procedures:

- Make a distinct (senior) person responsible for implementing the ethics part of the function.
- Have a clear reporting route to the CEO/board.
- Make clear the role of internal audit.
- Make sure there is an effective and continuous ethics training program.
- Always base the case for compliance on corporate values. (Webley, 2006)

Using CSR to Create a Competitive Advantage

Porter and Kramer (2002) argue that corporate philanthropy can be designed so as to improve the firm's competitive advantage, which will also improve the firm's profitability over time. From this perspective, the firm should align its long-term business interests in each nation with each nation's social and economic goals. A purpose in the design of charitable activities should be to leverage the firm's capabilities and relationships in order to create social benefits that exceed those that could otherwise be achieved. Porter and Kramer refer to this as "context-focused philanthropy." This perspective can be successful, for example, in financially supporting the education of the local workforce. In addition, efforts to preserve the environment through pollution reduction can also strengthen the firm's productivity and create goods for which consumers have special preferences and for which they will pay higher prices. Here the firm's profitability goals need not conflict with CSR objectives. "It is only where corporate expenditures produce simultaneous social and economic gains that corporate philanthropy and shareholder interests converge" (p. 33). Consequently, management should analyze the elements of its competitive context in order to identify overlaps between these social and economic values.

Porter and Kramer (2006) also emphasize the importance of creating a strong competitive cluster of related CSR activities in which many firms and institutions may collaborate. Education and water and sewage treatment are obvious areas in which firms can collaborate in efforts to strengthen research institutions, the legal system, and physical infrastructure—each of which can improve the international competitiveness of all local firms. Philanthropy can also increase the size and nature of the local market, leading consumers to demand product and service improvements that can be the basis for international competitiveness. A variety of collaborations among firms can create a more productive cluster. Both Transparency International and the International Corporate Governance Network have developed successful collaborations. Strengthening the network of suppliers, exchanging information, and lowering transaction costs can all stimulate the development of clusters that can help each member firm. A central element in this analysis is that a firm can gain a competitive edge for itself even when collaborating with competitors. In this process, the firm's philanthropy can enhance the performance of grant recipients and on a more general scale can advance the social capital in a region. With strategic philanthropy as a foundation for its CSR, MNEs should increasingly take an activist stance on social issues such as hunger, community development, literacy, school reform, AIDS, and environmentalism. CSR should involve different activities for each firm and for each country in which it does business. Furthermore, the expectations of the public and governments for a firm's citizenship role may change over time. This cross-national and intertemporal perspective leads to the conclusion that management must be involved in CSR decisions on an ongoing basis.

> Each company can identify the particular set of social problems that it is best equipped to help resolve and from which it can gain the greatest competitive benefit. When a well-run business applies its vast resources, expertise, and management talent to problems that it understands and in which it has a stake, it can have a greater impact than any other institution or philanthropic organization. (Porter & Kramer, 2006, p. 14)

In the 1980s, only a few firms reported anything publicly in regard to their CSR activities. Today, several organizations, such as Ethical Investment Research Services (EIRS), conduct research in regard to CSR activities, with EIRS providing performance indicators in regard to about 3,000 firms worldwide. To a major degree, EIRS receives its funding from institutional investors, especially pension funds, which make their investment decisions in the context of each firm's CSR. Hence, the firm's access to capital may now be impacted by its CSR activities. CSR has now evolved into a mainstream business responsibility that integrates a firm's CSR activities into its core business strategy. EIRS predicts that investors will increasingly be concerned with social performance indicators since there is a growing belief that CSR does impact long-term financial performance. EIRS also goes beyond specific performance indicators to place an emphasis on corporate governance as a driving force in each firm's CSR activities. They point to the need for independent directors and the importance of governance codes that increase corporate transparency and director responsibilities.

Hillman and Keim (2001) examine the ways in which stakeholder management and participation in social issues can ultimately result in improvements in long-term shareholder value. They suggest that stakeholder management and social issue participation are very different activities and may have opposing impacts on a firm's financial performance. Stakeholder management can have positive impacts while general social issue support may not. Effective stakeholder-management relations may include ongoing structural dialogues with customers, employees, suppliers, community residents, and environmental groups. These relations can constitute intangible, socially complex resources that may enhance a firm's ability to outperform competitors in terms of long-term value creation (Hillman & Keim, 2001). Many other authors have also attempted to analyze the relationship between corporate social performance (CSP) and corporate financial performance (CFP). An objective has been to determine whether or not a CSR strategy can in general enhance shareholder value. Orlitzky, Schmidt, and Rynes (2003) have undertaken a meta-analysis of 52 studies containing a total sample size of nearly 34,000 observations. While many of these studies have suggested a negative relationship, indicating that CSR may be a net expense to the firm, the authors demonstrate flaws in statistical techniques that can explain these results. In general, Orlitzky et al. conclude that a positive relationship does exist between CSP and CFP across a wide variety of industries and studies.

> Portraying managers' choices with respect to CSP and CFP as an either/or trade-off is not justified in light of 30 years of empirical data. This meta-analysis has shown that (1) across studies, CSP is positively correlated with CFP, (2) the relationship tends to be bidirectional and simultaneous, and (3) reputation appears to be an important mediator of the relationship. (p. 427)

Managing the Activists

Each firm today confronts a wide variety of stakeholders whose objectives may often conflict. Pressures now emerge continually from employees, suppliers, customers, various community groups, nongovernmental organizations (NGOs), and institutional shareholders. Somehow, management must develop CSR strategies that can cope effectively with their conflicting goals and objectives. CSR today means going beyond obedience to the law and creating strategies that can differentiate the firm from its competitors. For this to be successful, the firm must have a public relations strategy designed to build its reputation. Cost-benefit analysis can be used for potential CSR activities in the same way that the firm would analyze other investment decisions. The ability of activists to damage the firm—and the avoidance of this damage—becomes a major component of the cost-benefit analysis.

Groups of activists can compel a firm to transfer some of its resources to satisfy the interests of each activist group. Here, activist groups may solicit support from the general public in regard to their wishes concerning the CSR activities of the firm. Each firm today must develop a thorough understanding of the objectives of these various stakeholder groups, as well as their ability to impact its activities—through boycotts, for example. While managers may be motivated by altruistic preferences, this compulsory redistribution of firm resources must now be considered carefully. Furthermore, each firm must strive to mitigate the impacts of incomplete information provided by activists to potential customers and must actively bolster its reputation and market image in regard to CSR. Activists may have strategies that not only impact the firm directly but also impact the political process with the objective of changing laws and regulations that affect the firm.

In recent years, media have developed an increased interest in the interactions of firms with society and in the ethical performance of firms. To some degree, this may be the result of ethical scandals in firms such as Enron, Tyco, and Parmalat. This increased media attention has become a global phenomenon, as various media organizations have themselves become global. The Internet has also enabled a new level of global communication and unified global action on the part of concerned individuals and NGOs. As a result, CSR decisions throughout the world have become linked in terms of public perceptions. This globalization of media and interest groups has made the CSR activities, or lack thereof, in faraway countries of immediate concern to consumers in the economically advanced nations. Consequently, the decisions that are made in subsidiaries or suppliers in China may impact the firm's success in the United States or Western Europe. International conflict resolution concerning CSR has become a new responsibility of management. For example, corporations such as Nike and Gap have suddenly faced global campaigns and threats of boycotts due to their treatment, or their suppliers' treatment, of employees abroad. By 2009, Wal-Mart had initiated a widespread campaign in China to ensure continual adherence by its suppliers to its global environmental standards.

Teegan, Doh, and Vachani (2004) have emphasized the global reach of NGOs and their impact on the concepts of value creation and governance.

They suggest that increasingly citizens have lost trust in the institutions that they have relied on in the past. Consequently, citizens are turning to NGOs to further their interests. They note that some NGOs focus on advocacy in regard to certain CSR objectives and have become expert in lobbying, conducting research, holding conferences, disseminating information, defining agendas, developing and promoting codes of conduct, and organizing boycotts. Throughout the world today, NGOs are giving voice to citizens who otherwise would lack the ability to impact firm decisions. Some NGOs have developed operational activities where they feel that both private and public markets have failed. Such NGOs have developed skills and expertise in providing certain goods and services to the public. Teegan et al. note the huge increase in the number of NGOs within Organisation for Economic Co-operation and Development (OECD) countries. The result of these developments is that management cannot ignore NGOs without the risk of suffering financially. "In conclusion, we recognize the emerging role of NGOs in advancing broad social issues of major concern around the world and providing critical goods and services" (p. 477).

To some degree, a "governance gap" is caused by the failure of governments at the country or regional level to participate effectively in economic and social development. The need for global public policies is particularly challenging since there is no global government and international institutions lack adequate authority and enforcement capabilities. Furthermore, pressures to create free trade can conflict with government intervention aimed at social issues. Consequently, this subject of global CSR will not be dealt with easily in the near term. As part of this social change process, the firm's employees develop their own vision of the firm and may become activists themselves. These perceptions influence employee commitment to the firm. A particularly important managerial implication is that each firm can play a leadership role in relating universal ethical principles to local cultural norms as part of the social change process.

Creating Unique CSR Strategies for Each Nation

Hillman and Hitt (1999) examine the linkages between the firm's involvement in CSR activities and the firm's political strategy. A political strategy may rest on alternative approaches. First, the firm can deal with specific issues as they arise. Second, beyond a transactional approach, a firm can develop long-term relationships that enable it to deal more effectively in an ongoing manner with an array of potentially significant issues. Third, the firm must also decide whether to participate in this process by itself alone or whether it can be more effective in collaboration with other firms and stakeholder groups. Based on these alternative approaches, each firm must delineate its unique political strategy.

Hillman and Hitt focus on three components of the firm's political strategy. First, the firm provides information to political decision makers in the expectation that this information will influence government decisions in the interests of the firm. Second, the firm provides political decision makers with financial contributions necessary in election campaigns. Third, the firm develops support in the general electorate for the policies and programs that it believes can enhance its profitability. Optimal CSR activities and political strategies depend on relationships between social forces, corporate strategies, and government decisions. For the MNE, the many differences among countries may require that the firm develop multiple political strategies that differ among nations.

Ernst & Young interviewed senior executives at 147 of the largest MNEs in order to determine the impacts of the CSR concept and to understand likely trends in firm activities in response to CSR pressures. While most of these companies did not have a CSR strategy in 2002, those interviewed emphasized the need for their firms to adopt a much greater role for CSR. Ernst & Young concluded that

> CSR has emerged as a significant business issue with the majority of survey respondents. . . . Even though CSR rates highly on the boardroom agenda, few survey respondents feel that they have an adequate understanding of the relevance of CSR to their company, nor do they believe that the business case for the CSR strategy has been systematically developed. (Grant, Buttle, McKenzie, & Veale, 2000, p. 3)

In this Ernst & Young survey, 63% of the MNEs considered stakeholder dialogue to be necessary in developing a CSR strategy, while an additional 33% thought that it would be useful. Nevertheless, only 8% of the firms felt that they had effectively engaged with stakeholders in creating a strategy. Only 19% believed that their CSR agenda was understood throughout the firm. Nearly half of the companies published reports regularly on various aspects of CSR, and three quarters believed such reporting to be critical. However, the survey found that much remained to be done in terms of developing reporting strategies. CSR was generally the responsibility of personnel in corporate affairs and public relations rather than being an element of corporate strategy at the senior management level. The survey suggested that the following factors were believed to be critical in improving the reporting process:

- More effective dialogue with stakeholders
- Greater awareness of the relevance of CSR to the organization
- Better understanding of critical risks

- Improved metrics/measurement
- Data collection on the basis of measurable metrics

Survey respondents pointed to a series of important nonfinancial issues that they thought could be impacted by a CSR strategy: brand value, company reputation, risk mitigation, staff retention and attraction, market position, customer attraction, and customer loyalty. Respondents also pointed to a series of stakeholder groups that saw themselves as having an important role to play in determining these nonfinancial issues, including employees, customers, suppliers, the local community, NGOs, and government, quite apart from shareholders. Throughout the interviews, respondents expressed their conviction that an appropriate CSR strategy could lead to an increase in shareholder value. As the Ernst & Young survey indicates, CSR has been increasing greatly in importance for the MNE.

A central issue is whether the MNE should apply the laws and norms of its home country to the issues it confronts in other nations. MNEs may be motivated to locate facilities in certain nations because of lower costs related to less stringent requirements in regard to environment and labor standards. A further complication is that some analysts feel that firms in less developed nations should use resources to address issues that in developed nations would typically be dealt with by governments. Many authors point to the challenges for a firm in applying CSR concepts to nations where law may not be as extensive in regard to these issues, where social expectations of corporate behavior may be quite different from those in the economically advanced nations, and where cultures may place a different emphasis or priority on various CSR issues. In many countries, corporate ownership is held by powerful elites who play an instrumental role in the determination of government laws and regulations. Consequently, CSR activities face more complex challenges where the MNE has to translate its business citizenship into the culture, economics, and government practices in these countries.

Competition continually exerts pressure on the MNE to minimize costs in ways that may violate its home-country vision of CSR. Certain business sectors, such as textiles, footwear, and the assembly of electronics, may face this risk to a greater degree than others. Different countries have different cultural priorities and so have different stakeholder groups. Consequently, cultural differences must be considered carefully by management as they develop a global CSR strategy. In some cases, MNEs may choose not to do business in a given country because of the gap between their corporate ethics and that country's norms. Nevertheless, globalization is causing an automatic transfer of CSR activities and practices from the advanced nations to less developed nations over time. An important component of this spread of CSR has to do with values of senior management within the MNE. From this perspective, senior management of an MNE has a new responsibility: understanding how to articulate a common global vision within different cultures. This reality emphasizes the importance of international governmental agreements that attempt to create global CSR standards in regard to labor and environmental issues, as well as in regard to general human rights and codes of conduct.

The Division of Responsibilities for CSR Within the MNE

A basic challenging question concerns the appropriate division of responsibilities between the head office and the subsidiaries of MNEs as management struggles to create optimal CSR strategies and respond to issues, some of which may be global and some local. Subsidiaries may have limited functions and may lack the staff to be able to monitor and respond successfully to local CSR issues. This need for local responsiveness may require changes in the governance structure of the MNE. Social causes that are seen as important in one particular geographical area will not be seen as important everywhere, and community projects that the public want to promote will also differ. Consequently, the mechanics of nonmarket strategies have to be geared to the particular host country or city, and a CSR strategy that includes political involvement and stakeholder relationships may have to be tailored to local conditions.

Decentralization of responsibility could lead subsidiaries to pursue lower standards than those of the parent firm in the home country. Hence, an MNE needs global strategies and standards in regard to some issues and practices while permitting the decentralization of responsibility for others. An additional complication is that managers may have nonbusiness-related motives for engaging in CSR since some managers are internally driven to adhere to their personal ethical code. This perspective supports the importance of ongoing evaluation in regard to the optimal location of CSR decision-making responsibility.

Neef (2003) uses the risk of mistakes as a CSR focus in his book *Managing Corporate Reputation and Risk*. With widespread de-layering and downsizing, more employees within a firm have responsibility for decision making. Neef emphasizes that today a series of challenges could lead to financial penalties, consumer boycotts, lawsuits, greater regulation, damage to reputation, a decrease in profits, and a loss of share value. The Internet and international news services have completely changed the environment of business, exposing firms everywhere to public scrutiny and criticism. Furthermore, individual members of senior management and the board of directors are increasingly being held accountable legally for the actions of the firm. From this perspective, business integrity is necessary quite apart from ethical motivations. At the same time, incentive-based remuneration provides continual pressure for management to minimize the costs of corporate actions that could prevent these kinds of mistakes.

Neef (2003) recommends a combination of managing corporate integrity and ethical behavior; managing knowledge and information that is necessary for appropriate decisions, which he refers to as knowledge and risk management (KRM); and creation of reporting techniques that clarify risks prior to accidents happening. MNEs should transform the pursuit of ethics and the knowledge management that is required to enforce ethical behavior into a core competency. Increasingly, new international standards are requiring that firms develop frameworks for monitoring and auditing the firm's social performance. The opportunity to use new information technology systems can enable MNEs to communicate their CSR strategies easily and effectively with employees, customers, suppliers, and other stakeholders throughout the world.

For Neef (2003), the firm's board of directors should be playing a far more active role in this subject area. In the past, board members did not make themselves aware of risks that the firm faced in regard to these issues. They failed to control senior management who were placing too great an emphasis on short-term profitability or who were even involved in personal unethical behavior. International investments have made this subject increasingly important. MNEs are now operating in countries and cultures where senior management may not be aware of what is happening within subsidiaries, joint ventures, suppliers, or strategic alliances. A particularly difficult area concerns labor standards overseas. Many U.S. firms have suddenly faced public outcries and damage to reputation as a result of employment conditions within their own subsidiaries or within supplier organizations. "Here, innovative policies by companies that pay for housing, education, and health care can not only ensure a humane response, but can also help to ensure stability and continuity of a workforce" (p. 59). Senior management and board members must have "an integrated KRM process that helps them to know whether they are being ethically compliant or not" (p. 63). While many MNEs have a series of departments within their organization that consider some of these issues, most firms have not yet integrated or coordinated these multiple areas to develop a consistent global corporate culture.

Today, an appropriate governance structure includes procedures for involving many groups of stakeholders, referred to as multiple stakeholder collaborative processes. As part of this new approach to governance, most firms have to create new kinds of networks with a wide variety of organizations. This perspective has revolutionized traditional views of corporate governance. As part of this process, most governments have adopted new responsibilities for supervising firm decisions that can impact society, so corporate governance now involves new and intensified interactions with a wide range of government agencies.

The Development of Trust

The above perspectives emphasize the need for mutual trust among personnel within the MNE if CSR is to be successful. This mutual trust has to be based on a set of beliefs shared globally with an implicit code of conduct for some issues and an explicit code of conduct for others. This trust has to be based on shared values related to these shared beliefs. Leaders at both the head office and subsidiary level have to set the right example both in terms of specific decisions and also in terms of the objectives that they encourage. In this process, it is necessary to create benchmarks so that success can be measured and failures can be the target of remedial action. With a positive global CSR, the various stakeholders, including NGOs, may develop loyalty and support for the firm that can add significantly to shareholder value.

The above perspectives are also important in risk minimization and in dealing effectively with crises. For the firm, the assessment and management of CSR risks and the appropriate management of human error have become essential. MNEs continually confront risks, and many of these pose difficult challenges in regard to measurement of the risk, judgments about risk taking, and appropriate crisis management. The firm requires an ongoing risk-scanning process that provides analyses in regard to risks and also early alerts of oncoming crises. The firm should develop reporting procedures for creating transparency in regard to how the firm is dealing with these various issues.

This subject of the relationship between culture and trust with its implications for management decisions and strategies is explored more fully in Chapter 4. Here, it is important to note the problems that asymmetry in trust between the MNE and its stakeholders can cause for the creation and implementation of a global CSR strategy. When one sees CSR as an investment strategy, then one can appreciate the challenge of developing an optimal pattern of investment in trust building and monitoring within CSR activities. The structural and social dimensions of trust may differ across cultures. Trust may be more difficult to instill in subsidiaries or partners in certain countries. Legal, political, and social systems monitor and sanction social behavior, and these differ significantly among countries. Institutional differences cause differences in behavior relating to trust. A central concern has to do with expectations on the part of stakeholders in different countries.

Many MNEs have put considerable effort into developing a wide variety of firm-specific CSR codes of conduct. In CSR codes, corporate values or practices are formalized in order to guide the decisions of firm employees operating in different countries. A code is "an aspirational strategy" that encourages employees to behave in certain ways. The need to preserve and convey a reputable public image may require codes that can be readily understood by employees in different countries. The creation of codes can be the result of a series of motivations ranging from the need for internal control systems, the differentiation of the firm in the marketplace, the reduction of insurance premiums, and the prevention of activist criticisms and boycotts.

International CSR Agreements

The OECD (2008) has created *Guidelines for Multinational Enterprises* with the objective of encouraging CSR initiatives. In this international code, the 39 signatory countries have expressed their shared commitment. The OECD guidelines provide recommendations in the major areas of CSR, and the government signatories have pledged to promote the guidelines within their nations. The guidelines include recommendations in regard to managements' decisions and activities that bear on human rights, labor relations, the environment, consumer protection, and corruption. In addition, the OECD has promulgated its "Declaration and Decisions on International Investment and Multinational Enterprises." This declaration relates to government treatment of foreign investors and indicates the OECD's objective of encouraging a more widespread balance of rights and commitments between businesses and governments.

The New Responsibilities of Boards of Directors

Janet Arnold (2008) has written an article titled "It's Not Your Father's Board Seat: The Evolution of Corporate Governance in an Era of Scandal." Arnold describes how the evolution of the concept of "fiduciary duty" has extended the legal responsibilities of board members. She presents eight "critical lessons":

1. Be independent.

2. Be loyal to the organization.

3. Be informed. Really informed.

4. It's all about process. Have one.

5. Have a supportable basis for your decisions and document, document, document.

6. Devote sufficient time and analysis to your decisions.

7. Don't be passive. Ask questions.

8. Trust, but verify.

Increasingly, boards of directors in many nations must act as adjudicators, standing guard between management's day-to-day operations and the long-term interests of shareholders. This means that board members must incorporate a new attention to ethics into their adjudication process. A particular concern relates to the appropriate timeline for the maximization of shareholder value. While management's interests are geared to the short term, many shareholders are focused on the long term. Recent corporate disasters have emphasized the importance of this trade-off, as management in certain corporations has sacrificed the corporate entity itself in order to maintain short-term profitability and share values. Individual shareholders and institutional investors are now playing a far more active role in pressuring boards to consider long-term value. Until recently, individual investors had little means of monitoring a company's performance other than the occasional report in the media or the annual financial reports that public companies were legally bound to provide.

Today, many nations are experiencing the rise of investor education and investor mobilization. Through the Internet, individual investors are now able to access a vast array of information, not only on the financial results of most public companies but also on upcoming annual meetings, on the issues being addressed, and on how institutional investors are planning to vote. Investors are now voting online at annual meetings of companies that allow such practice. The Internet has empowered small investors—who can now make their voices heard—to communicate with other investors, present their points of view, and influence decisions. Contacting other shareholders is inexpensive and rapid. New Web sites are created regularly for investors to exchange information and strategies about publicly traded companies. A number of sites now offer information that can help individual investors decide whether to renew a director's term of service, hire new auditors, or change management's compensation. Individual investors are now forcing public companies to change the way they deal with their shareholders. Companies must now consider even small investors in their communication strategy, as well as in their governance policies.

The Internet has spurred a movement to make corporations more transparent. The rise of this new, better informed class of investors is forcing companies to comply with what is publicly perceived as ethical governance behavior. The increase in class action lawsuits initiated by unsatisfied shareholders is another way to make management and boards more accountable. Companies have been sued for releasing financial statements that were false or misleading or even for questionable management decisions that affect share prices, such as those related to mergers, acquisitions, and takeovers.

Unlike individual investors, institutional investors often take such large positions in companies that they cannot just sell the stock when they are concerned with the way management operates, since this could drive the stock price down considerably, hence affecting their returns. Consequently, their most effective way of affecting the performance of their investment is to take an active role in influencing the management of the company. A key mechanism for such influence consists of more open and transparent governance structures and policies.

Today, American, Canadian, and European institutional investors are pressuring large domestic and foreign companies (and, increasingly, mid-size and small companies) into electing directors who are independent from management and who have a diverse portfolio of experiences and competencies to fulfill the board's new responsibilities. Their actions have played a role in the gradual disappearance of the "old boys' network" approach of selecting directors and helped replace them with independent, value-adding, competent members that constitute a stronger and broader portfolio of skills. As enterprises become more international, boards of directors will also be modified to include qualified individuals who represent both the new, large shareholder blocks and all parts of the MNE's operations. More diverse representation will bring more objectivity to the board table, as well as international experience and a network of contacts that can enrich the board's contribution to company decisions.

The rise of the Internet, the growth of institutional investors and the intensified pressures of international competitiveness are doing a great deal to change the form and function of boards. The impacts of these three influences are far-reaching, affecting the composition of boards, their responsibilities, the way they function, and the compensation and time commitment of directors. In this new corporate governance paradigm, questions remain about how to ensure the right "balancing of power" between mammoth institutional investors, Internet-enabled individual investors, company management, the public, and each stakeholder's agenda, be it the maximization of shareholder value or responses to social or environmental concerns. It is in this "balancing of power"—particularly in the context of an ethical analysis of short-term versus long-term shareholder-value maximization—that boards are playing a new, powerful role in corporate governance.

Apart from the firm's own ethical code and internal organization, a firm's supplier relationships can create difficult CSR challenges. Decisions within supplier organizations can lead the firm indirectly to inappropriate management practices. In the 1980s and 1990s, the Mexico-U.S. border region became severely degraded because a series of realities outside the manufacturing firms limited the MNE's scope of responsible environmental behavior. This case illustrates the complexity of managing change within Mexico's laws and enforcement agencies, within Mexico's cultural norms and values, and within all of the organizations that supply goods or services to the MNE.

In Practice 3.1	**Environmental Degradation: The Result of Corruption and Fraud and Deficiencies in Ethics and CSR**

One example of the difficult nature of multination negotiation over environmental problems is the situation that has been observed along the Mexico-U.S. border. As a result of incentives created through multilateral trade agreements, it is economically advantageous for American companies to assemble products in the border region of Mexico. The result of the increased manufacturing activity in Mexico has been the production of significant volumes of hazardous waste. This waste was supposed to be returned to the United States for safe disposal, however, this has not been what has evolved over time.

Hazardous waste has not been adequately stored and has leaked into the groundwater, affecting both Mexicans and Americans. The reasons for this are numerous. First, although Mexico does have stringent environmental regulation, the implementation and monitoring of the adherence to these regulations is, at best, lax. Fines for noncompliance are often significantly less than the costs of adhering to the regulations. The economic benefit these American factories provide the people of Mexico makes it undesirable for the Mexican government to come down hard on Americans who have violated the regulations. To lose investment in these regions would risk putting a great number of Mexican workers into poverty. Second, the legal system in Mexico does not hold the offending parties responsible for their actions. Individual lawsuits brought against companies for environmental damage are rare, and class-action lawsuits are virtually nonexistent. Mexican companies contract with trucking services to dispose of hazardous waste but are not held liable if those contractors dump the hazardous material inappropriately. Given the costs involved with appropriate disposal, it is only reasonable for these contractors to disregard regulations and use illegal dumping locations.

The problem of American-owned Mexican factories polluting the environment would, at first glance, appear to be solely within Mexican control. However, the United States is also impacted in a number of ways. First, its companies are responsible for much of the pollution problem. So long as it is cheaper to produce in Mexico because it is less costly than adhering to U.S. environmental standards, the U.S. companies will continue to contribute to the problem. Second, and most pressing, is that the health of U.S. residents has been placed in jeopardy as a result of the Mexican pollution seeping into the groundwater that eventually flows into U.S. soil. The incidence of birth defects in Texas has increased drastically in the past few decades, and this increase has been attributed to the pollution produced in the Mexican border regions.

The Chilpancinco settlement in Tijuana sits in the shadow of Otay Mesa, on top of which sprawl dozens of the city's *maquiladora* factories, on the California-Mexico border. Many of them are owned by U.S. corporations, including a now closed battery recycling plant. A white chemical crust rims the clods of dirt in the field outside the plant, and pools of strange, yellow water dot the barren landscape.

(Continued)

(Continued)

Lead and heavy metal deposits have been measured in the soil on the mesa at concentrations 40,000 times over safe levels. In this unincorporated settlement, or *colonia*, 6 babies were reported born without brains in 1993, and 13 in 1994, just one of several clusters of this rare birth defect, called anencephaly, on the border.

Contrary to what was often portrayed in the public press, solutions to the pollution problem in the border region were neither obvious nor easy to implement. Many economists argued that it was misplaced for a developing country like Mexico to implement U.S. and Canadian-level environment standards. In fact, the chief economist for the World Bank, Lawrence Summers, had written an internal memo (subsequently leaked to the press) stating that "the economic logic behind dumping a load of toxic waste in the lowest wage country is impeccable." According to this view, environmental consciousness, along with greater enforcement of environmental laws, should—and surely would—follow Mexico's long march out of poverty toward economic prosperity. To environmental groups, such arguments were misconceived and ignored both the very real costs of the pollution hazards for those living in the region, as well as the long-term costs of a badly degraded natural environment.

Based on U.S. legislation, Mexican environmental laws and regulations were relatively strict. Where Mexico and the United States diverged in terms of environmental legislation was mostly in areas that were only secondarily related to the environment, such as so-called "right to know laws" and provisions for civil liability. For example, companies in Mexico were not required to make public the nature of their manufacturing activities to interest groups or the general public. Even when individuals or groups were able to collect evidence of damages caused to them by a polluting company, the Mexican legal system did not provide an adequate opportunity to seek restitution. Multimillion-dollar class-action settlements were nonexistent in Mexico.

Most of the criticism surrounding Mexico's environmental record was aimed at the country's ability to enforce the legislation already in place. Fears of lax enforcement were, in fact, central to the so-called "pollution haven hypothesis"—the notion that free trade would precipitate a race to the bottom in environmental standards as countries competed for foreign investment.

The controversy over the environmental impact of NAFTA (North American Free Trade Agreement) led the Clinton administration to negotiate a parallel side agreement pertaining to the environment. The agreement established several bodies designed to deal with environmental issues and to investigate "persistent patterns of failure to effectively enforce (a country's) environmental law."

Despite claims that NAFTA was the "greatest trade agreement in history," its environmental provisions had been criticized on several accounts. First, environmentalists complained that the dispute resolution process was secretive, exclusive, and lacked provisions for enforcement. No apparent means existed for public comment on environmental matters presented before NAFTA panels. A second complaint was with the burden of proof provisions, which required the challenging party to establish that the sanitary (health) or phytosanitary (plant health) measure in question is inconsistent with or in violation of NAFTA. In addition, no specific trade sanctions were provided as a means to combat noncompliance with the provisions of either NAFTA or the side agreement on the environment. Moreover, the sanctions specified under NAFTA were considered to be unenforceable and too complex to be of much use.

SOURCE: Frost, Campbell, and Eaton (1997).

Critical Thinking Questions

1. What are the ethical and CSR obligations of an MNE investing in the U.S.-Mexico border region? Do these obligations extend to supervision of companies that transport their hazardous wastes?

2. How can a head office monitor the environmental impacts of its subsidiary and supply chain in Tijuana? How can a head office enforce its environmental standards?

3. Are new international agreements and international enforcement mechanisms necessary in order to deal effectively with such social issues?

References and Suggested Readings

Arnold, J. (2008). It's not your father's board seat: The evolution of corporate governance in an era of scandal. *Management Quarterly, 49*(3), 28–47.

Cacioppe, R., Forster, N., & Fox, M. (2008). A survey of managers' perceptions of corporate ethics and social responsibility and actions that may affect companies' success. *Journal of Business Ethics, 82*(3), 681–700.

CFA Institute advertisement. (2009, July 27). *Financial Times,* p. 12.

Friedman, M. (2001). The social responsibility of business is to increase its profits. In T. Beauchamp & N. Bowie (Eds.), *Ethical theory and business* (6th ed., pp. 51–55). Upper Saddle River, NJ: Prentice Hall. (Reprinted from *New York Times Magazine,* pp. 32–33, 122–126, September 13, 1970)

Frost, T., Campbell, D., & Eaton, D. (1997). *Note on the pollution problem in the Mexico-U.S. border region.* London: Ivey. (Ivey Case No. 9A98H001)

Grant, A., Buttle, J., McKenzie, S., & Veale, G. (2002). *Corporate social responsibility: A survey of global companies.* Sydney: Ernst & Young.

Hillman, A., & Hitt, M. (1999). Corporate political strategy formulation: A model of approach, participation and strategy decisions. *Academy of Management Review, 24,* 825–842.

Hillman, A., & Keim, G. (2001). Shareholder value, stakeholder management and social issues: What's the bottom line? *Strategic Management Journal, 22,* 125–139.

Neef, D. (2003). *Managing corporate reputation and risk.* Burlington, MA: Elsevier Butterworth-Heinemann.

Organisation for Economic Co-operation and Development. (2008). *OECD guidelines for multinational enterprises.* Paris: Author.

Orlitzky, M., Schmidt, F., & Rynes, S. (2003). Corporate social and financial performance: A meta-analysis. *Organization Studies, 24*(3), 403–441.

Porter, M., & Kramer, M. (2002, December 1). The competitive advantage of corporate philanthropy. *Harvard Business Review on Corporate Responsibility*, 1–16. Boston: Harvard Business School Press.

Porter, M., & Kramer, M. (2006, December). Strategy and society: The link between competitive advantage and corporate social responsibility. (Reprint R0612D). *Harvard Business Review*, 1–14.

Tapped for the top; The implications of the hacking scandal are widespread. (2009, July 11). *Financial Times*, p. 10.

Teegan, H., Doh, J., & Vachani, S. (2004). The importance of nongovernmental organizations (NGOs) in global governance and value creation: An international business research agenda. *Journal of International Business Studies, 35*, 463–483.

Webley, S. (2006, October 26). Making business ethics work: The foundations of effective embedding. *Institute of Business Ethics.*

Williamson, O. E. (1996). *The mechanisms of governance.* New York: Oxford University Press.

Part II

Technological Forces

Social Capital 4

Implications for Entrepreneurship and Innovation

CHAPTER LEARNING OBJECTIVES

On completion of this chapter, students should be able to

- discuss the relationships between a nation's environmental forces and the nature and extent of entrepreneurship and innovation in that nation,

- appreciate how the impacts of social capital in shaping entrepreneurship and innovation differ among nations and among firms,

- understand how the culture and role of governments impact a nation's innovative capacity,

- compare and contrast India and China in regard to their social capital and the implications for investment opportunities in each nation,

- relate these issues to the advantages and disadvantages for the firm of alternative investment locations.

Several academic disciplines have studied networks of personal relationships within a culture, and the term *social capital* is now commonly used in regard to these networks. Adler and Kwon (2002) present a series of some 20 definitions of social capital. They summarize the basic concept with their phrase "the goodwill that others have toward us is a valuable resource. By 'goodwill' we refer to the sympathy, trust, and forgiveness offered us by friends and acquaintances" (p. 18). An important aspect of social capital is the nature of the hierarchy within the organization and the interactions between this hierarchy and social relations. From this perspective, social capital plays an important role in daily business activities within the firm. The processes for establishing and maintaining relationships should be seen as expensive investments, and these investments may not be cost-efficient in all circumstances. For each firm, the nature and value of social capital may be unique. This perspective suggests that each firm should create its own types of networks that contribute to social capital in response to its particular objectives.

Many authors have used the social capital perspective to analyze differences among nations in regard to entrepreneurship. Social capital can facilitate transactions that are crucial for start-up entrepreneurs. Social capital can also be the basis for joint problem solving as entrepreneurs seek to deal with a set of new challenges. The significance of social capital can differ among business sectors and geographical locations. These differences may influence the relative desirability of alternative nations and regions within them as business locations that support the innovative activities of the firm.

The social capital literature emphasizes "clusters" as the basis for international competitiveness. To the extent that innovation is an interfirm process with one company's entrepreneurial activity being linked with that of others, it may be essential for some firms to locate near one another. To the extent that innovation depends on university research facilities, firms will locate near the leading universities and, consequently, near one another. To the extent that innovation requires highly sophisticated and specialized scientific skill, it may be necessary for an entrepreneurial firm to locate near similar firms from which it may entice employees. Each of these relationships links social capital with entrepreneurship and innovation.

Social Capital

Weaknesses exist in the concept of social capital. There is a lack of conceptual clarity, particularly since each academic discipline has tended to interpret the subject differently. The nature of causality is uncertain between social capital and the various issues related to it. For example, social capital may stimulate economic growth, while economic growth may also strengthen social capital. Various aspects of social capital cannot be measured easily. Some aspects of social capital may have negative impacts on desired outcomes, in which case social capital may be seen as more complex than the positive interpretations that are generally attributed to it. Nevertheless, the extensive literature on this subject indicates that social capital does matter and that it differs among nations.

In economics, social capital research has focused on the relationships within each society that support a generalized level of trust in that society. A strong level of trust may reduce the costs of economic transactions, the extent of criminality, and the degree of corruption and inefficiency in government. Furthermore, networks can create social norms of cooperation in business dealings. These aspects of social capital are seen by some economists as being an important determinant of economic growth. Many World Bank publications discuss the positive relationships between a nation's social capital and its economic development.

Bolino, Turnley, and Bloodgood (2002) use the phrase organizational citizenship behaviors (OCBs) to discuss social capital. They emphasize the extent to which employees within the firm are interconnected and relate with one another. Employee willingness to respect and comply with the rules and procedures of the firm forms a key element. OCBs in this sense "play a critical role in facilitating the effective functioning of organizations" (p. 517). In this sense, OCBs contribute to the development of social capital, as well as being dependent on social capital.

Definitions of trust focus on relationships and organizational structures. "Just as perceptions about an individual's ability, benevolence, and integrity will have an impact on how much trust the individual can garner, these perceptions also affect the extent to which an organization will be trusted" (Schoorman, Mayer, & Davis, 2007, p. 345). The three factors of ability, benevolence, and integrity are important contributors to trust both within and among organizations. These aspects of trust are particularly important in daily activities and in relationships between supervisor and subordinate in the workplace. An important aspect of trust is that it facilitates risk taking and entrepreneurship.

Generally, academics separate networks of personal relationships into two categories. "Bridging" social capital refers to the degree to which a society has open networks that cross social divisions and create society-wide forces. "Bonding" social capital refers to relationships that are unique within specific groups of people and that tend to support the identity and homogeneity of each particular group. Within the sociology literature, a common focus concerns the degree to which social capital relates to particular groups that are closed and preserve their unique identities. Some researchers have extended this perspective to focus on immigrants as closed groups, and some have linked this reality to the tendency for immigrants to become involved in entrepreneurial activities.

The political science literature has focused on the relationships between various aspects of social capital and the role of government in representing separate groups and in dealing with organized crime. With a high level of general trust in a culture, people work toward the betterment of the system as a whole rather than fighting against the system. Bonding social capital encourages adherence to social norms and may result in mutual help and loyalty. Trust based on social capital may fill in gaps in contracts that cannot cover all aspects of a rapidly changing environment. Trust builds reputations readily and can thereby facilitate collective action. However, to the degree that bonding social capital excludes others, the success of one group may be to the detriment of members who are not part of it. In particular, bonding social capital may play a major role in the perpetuation of business-political elites.

The Social Foundations of Entrepreneurship

Firms may differ in their ability to utilize social capital. In particular, a firm may have a particular set of capabilities for creating and sharing knowledge that gives it a competitive advantage. There is a crucial interaction between trust and cooperation, and this interaction plays a key role in creating and transferring knowledge. Social capital is created through a firm's accumulated history. Social capital plays a key role in the creation of intellectual capital, facilitating the creative actions of individuals within the firm. Social capital impacts the degree of cooperative behavior within each MNE and facilitates the development within the firm of new forms of association and value creation. As a result of these realities,

> Differences between firms, including differences in performance, may represent differences in their ability to create and exploit social capital. Moreover, at least regarding the development of intellectual capital, those firms developing particular configurations of social capital are likely to be more successful. (Nahapiet & Ghoshal, 1998, p. 260)

Many authors emphasize knowledge and skills as types of social capital that are essential for innovation, yet they are not adequately developed if left entirely to private decisions. Knowledge and skills form the framework for today's entrepreneurial activities, and many have termed our age "the era of human capital." Consequently, many see the government's financial participation as crucial. Some emphasize the need for government adjustment assistance to enable those workers displaced by economic change to develop new skills for new jobs. Individual investment in one's education and skills entails a large risk of obsolescence, and this alone could justify public funding as the only means for insuring the otherwise uninsurable risks involved. Third-party effects of educational and research facilities provide a strong additional argument for public funding to strengthen these aspects of social capital.

Social capital can be an important determinant of a community's entrepreneurship. Social capital consists of relationships that facilitate flows of information. A social network, or even a structure for having confidence in communication, can facilitate the exchange of information necessary for entrepreneurship. From this perspective, social capital provides individuals with a type of credential or social identity. "Social capital may well exert its primary impact fairly early in the process, determining which entrepreneurs gain initial access to venture capitalists, customers, and suppliers" (Baron & Markman, 2000, p. 108). Skill in social perception is an important component of the entrepreneur's ability to utilize the community's social capital most effectively. The entrepreneur will be more successful to the degree that he or she is able to gauge the attitudes or emotions, the motives, and the personal characteristics of others with whom he or she is negotiating. For entrepreneurs, a key success determinant is the ability to choose appropriate partners and key employees. Here again, the entrepreneur's ability to relate effectively with others can maximize the value of the community's social capital in the entrepreneurial process. This ability to create positive feelings and goodwill will enable an entrepreneur to expand the social capital available to him or her through expansion of his or her personal networks, thereby facilitating access to capital, information, and markets.

A country's commercial environment impacts the ability of an entrepreneur to profit from success. This "appropriability regime" differs significantly from one country to another. Furthermore, soft infrastructure such as a country's legal, financial, fiscal, and educational systems are important elements of social capital and can create significant differences among countries.

> We have argued that opportunity costs and appropriability are subjective reference points that entrepreneurs rely on when evaluating opportunities. Further, we have described how the institutional and cultural features of a nation influence these reference points by affecting the amounts and type of benefits that an entrepreneur can expect to appropriate from a discovered opportunity, the range of options available to individuals and the costs of abandoning current circumstances to pursue opportunities. (Baker, Gedajlovic, & Lubatkin, 2005, p. 498)

The desire to attain material success and advanced social status has long served as a major incentive for entrepreneurial activities, so entrepreneurship has been linked with social changes. In some nations, entrepreneurship has been able to alter existing social relationships, and many people have seen it as their best means of social advancement. However, in some nations, social rigidities and attempts to maintain the status quo can act as strong barriers to entrepreneurship. Criticisms of mercantilism, arguments for free trade, and insistence on the rights of individuals vis-à-vis the state have all dealt with the relationships between economic change and the rigidity of the social and political structure. Many studies of entrepreneurship have emphasized that in certain nations the fluidity and openness of social structures have permitted the speedy introduction of new techniques, the rapid growth of new corporations, and the swift acquisition of wealth, power, and prestige by successful entrepreneurs. In the 19th century, the United States stood out as a nation whose social structure permitted economic change to a degree not found in other nations. Many writers have commented positively on the lack of government intervention and the general laissez-faire environment in U.S. history.

Some studies of entrepreneurship and growth look at the same subject from a more negative perspective, discussing the obstacles to change that many governments establish in their efforts to protect vested interests. Olson (1982) in particular has investigated this theme, concluding that governmental protection of vested interests almost inevitably ossifies a society. He points to the lobbying by special interest groups that leads a government to create barriers to change. In his opinion, a society that protects existing interests slows down its own progress. Only a dramatic and pervasive shock, such as military loss in a major war, can smash the rigidity of such arrangements and open a society once more to economic change and progress. Olson concentrates on the process of government decision making within democracies, referring to the literature on public choice. This literature examines the impact of vested interests on the governmental process and the ability of established groups to maintain their income, wealth, and social status by preventing change. Several of Olson's central tenets bear on this issue:

- On balance, special-interest organizations and collusions reduce efficiency and aggregate income in the societies in which they operate and make political life more divisive.

- Distributional coalitions slow down a society's capacity to adopt new technologies and to allocate resources in response to changing conditions, and thereby reduce the rate of economic growth.

- The accumulation of distributional coalitions increases the complexity of regulation, the role of government, and the complexity of understandings, and changes the direction of social evolution. (p. 74)

Olson (1982) explains the "economic miracles" of nations defeated in World War II, particularly Japan and West Germany. Military defeat shattered the protective privileges that government had established in response to traditional vested interests and enabled new groups and individuals to advance unhampered by restrictions. "At least in the first two decades after the war," Olson writes, "the Japanese and West Germans had not developed the degree of regulatory complexity and scale of government that characterized more stable societies" (p. 76). At the other extreme, Olson describes the calcification of relationships and practices in Britain, prior to Thatcher's reforms. Britain was the nation with the longest period of time since suffering from any major national disaster such as revolution, invasion, or dictatorship. Olson links this political stability with the fact that the economic growth of other large democracies surpassed Britain's in the period 1945 to 1980. Olson discusses Britain's calcifying special interest groups, particularly the trade unions, professional associations such as lawyers, and producers' organizations such as farmers' groups. "In short, with age, British society has acquired so many strong organizations and collusions that it suffers from an institutional sclerosis that slows its adaptation to changing circumstances and technologies" (pp. 77–78). Thatcher's reforms sought to create a new business environment that would stimulate and reward entrepreneurship and innovation.

India's Segmented Social Capital

In comparing India and China, Martin Wolf (2005) emphasizes that India has tried to minimize social dislocation, and India's politicians have sought to protect special interests. China's leaders, on the other hand, have focused on economic development and have been prepared to accept any social transformation that is necessary.

> China has accepted both growth and social transformation. India welcomes growth but tries to minimise social dislocation. The Chinese state sees development as both its goal and the foundation of legitimacy. Indian politicians see the representation of organised interests as their goal and the foundation of their legitimacy. Chinese politics are developmental, while India's remain predominantly clientelist. (p. 13)

In 2001, McKinsey Global Institute estimated that regulations reduced India's gross domestic product (GDP) growth rates by 2.3 percentage points each year, and merely to remove these regulations would raise India's growth rate substantially. They pointed to India's liberalized automotive industry as an example of the success that India's businesses could achieve if the regulations constraining their decisions and actions were removed. McKinsey pointed to five features that made India's regulations very damaging to the competitiveness and productivity of India's businesses.

• Many regulations were inequitable, as they did not treat all businesses the same. In particular, regulations protected incumbent firms from new entrants. In the telecom sector for example, new entrants had to pay expensive fees for new licenses, while the incumbents did not face these fees. New entrants had to access the networks of incumbents, but their access fees were set at very high levels. McKinsey concluded that regulations were not only inequitable, but they were also ill conceived and they damaged the public good rather than enhancing it.

• India had uneven enforcement of its regulations. Regulations were not applied equally to all businesses, so profitability was impacted by the ability of the firm to avoid regulatory costs. McKinsey pointed to tax avoidance as an example, as well as different prices paid for public utilities.

- At the time of the McKinsey study, some 830 products were reserved for small-scale businesses. These products could be manufactured only by firms that were smaller than a specified size, so they prevented the achievement of economies of scale. These regulations covered a wide variety of products, including clothing and textiles. At the same time, import restrictions enabled these small and inefficient firms to survive.

- India prohibited foreign direct investment in many sectors of the economy. This prohibition damaged the economy as a whole, as it created inefficient sectors that could have benefited greatly from the modern technology, managerial practices, and capital that foreign investors could have provided. India's politicians were motivated by the desire to protect incumbent firms that might be destroyed by more efficient foreign investment.

- In many sectors, to open a new firm required a license from the government. Government officials often refused such licenses in order to protect incumbent firms. Licenses that were granted might not be given to the most efficient potential entrants (McKinsey Global Institute, 2001).

India's overall primary and secondary education is poor in quantity and quality. The caste system relegates many in the lower castes to the poorest education and limits their employment opportunities and upward mobility. A sharp division separates the lower castes from the fortunate who attend excellent universities. Each of India's many political parties sees its role as promoting the special interests of its particular group of supporters. More than 650 dialects are spoken; there are 18 official languages and numerous religions. India's states have constitutional rights and responsibilities separate from the federal government. Rather than having a coherent and unified social capital, India consists of a maze of barriers that separate very different groups, resulting in some outstanding business sectors and geographical regions alongside many that are stuck in traditional business routines. In sharp contrast with India, China's government has been eager to facilitate entrepreneurship and innovation and has developed social capital that can support these achievements. China has invested far more than India in its physical and educational infrastructure to serve all business activities in a unified and coherent national mission. For China, social capital is not geared to the protection of vested business or class interests. Yet the tension surrounding protection of the Communist Party and its political leadership may conceivably create divisions that could impede economic progress in the future.

The Culture of Government: Implications for Entrepreneurship

When a government decides to give grants or loans to individuals or firms in the private sector, then the public service becomes a part of the entrepreneurial process. The public service must possess enough perception and creativity to recognize and support perception and creativity; it must evaluate risk-return outcomes and decide which proposals it will support. Deciding which funding requests should be accepted and which should be rejected are entrepreneurial decisions, and government employees may even attempt to negotiate changes in the applications for funding. However, the creativity and spontaneity, the individual initiative and personal risk taking of the entrepreneur contrast sharply with the obedience to bureaucratic rules, concern for proper process, and reference to chains of authority that mark the government employee. Individuals who seek the financial rewards that accompany successful risk taking and originality may not apply for public service positions, while those citizens who fear risk taking and appreciate an occupation that has clear guidelines may be more inclined to apply for government positions. In describing entrepreneurs, Ronen (1982) states, "Rarely does this individual reside in the large, bureaucratic organization. . . . The entrepreneur and the small firm seek each other out. The managerial-type individuals, preferring the executive suites of large organizations, hardly encourage alert entrepreneurs to cast permanent anchor anywhere near them" (pp. x, 5). Marginal individuals who have been raised outside the established social order—for example, members of minority groups and immigrants—may see private entrepreneurship as their only route to wealth and prestige. Such backgrounds and personalities may not be accepted readily into the elite ranks of civil service leadership.

Arrow (1983) concludes that "entrepreneurial activity, however defined, operates in different ways in large firms than in small ones" (p. 16). Decisions about capital allocation differ because they are based on different decision-making procedures, the internal accounting prices of large firms may not reflect relative costs, and information may not be conveyed as readily within large firms as it is through changes in market prices. In some ways, large firms are in the same position as government bureaucracies in fostering entrepreneurship, but in several very important respects government bureaucracies face much greater barriers. The large firm does respond to market prices; it pursues profit as a clear success criterion, and it is shaped by and interacts with its competitors. By contrast, government bureaucracies may not respond to market prices, they generally do not pursue profit as a criterion of success, and they generally lack competitors.

In order to reach an entrepreneurial decision that involves new production methods, the decision maker must be able to measure, compile, and compare the many aspects of an innovation in some common scale, so as to ascertain whether the new combination of costs and outputs will be more or less favorable than those yielded by the existing production methods. Here the role of prices is absolutely decisive; it is through price comparisons and combinations that the decision maker can anticipate probable results. The price structure sets the guidelines for entrepreneurial decisions.

Simple repetition of traditional production processes need not rely on these guidelines nearly as much as do the deliberations over the advisability of adopting particular innovations. To some degree, government decision makers have been able to refer to free market prices as the basis for their calculations. In some nations, however, governments themselves play a major role in determining the price structure, with the result that prices may be influenced significantly by administrators rather than by the market forces of supply and demand. A major concern is that price relationships determined by government that may have once been appropriate may no longer be so and may be sending the wrong signals for entrepreneurship in both the government and the private sectors.

Each nation's government bears responsibility for determining key elements of the nation's economic development and entrepreneurial capacity. The Organisation for Economic Co-operation and Development (OECD) has published a report on the role of human and social capital in stimulating innovation and enhancing the well-being of nations. This report emphasizes that both human capital and social capital depend on a country's political, institutional, and legal arrangements. The concept of social capital is closely aligned to the concept of social cohesion, where social cohesion depends on a community's shared values and commitment. The level of learning and the acquisition of skills and knowledge depend very much on a community's social capital in the sense of networks and relationships that support these processes. Hence human capital depends on social capital. At the same time, the learning process can cultivate social cohesion and social capital. For the OECD, this strong interaction between human and social capital must underlie government programs for economic development. "Recent work at the World Bank on the role of social capital in reducing poverty and promoting sustainable development has emphasized the role of institutions, social arrangements, trust and networks" (OECD, 2001, p. 40). The OECD report proposes that one way of measuring changes in social capital is through measurement of social dysfunctions or absences of social cooperation. They point to surveys in which people respond to the question whether most people can be trusted.

The OECD report analyzes specific communities where social capital may be seen as enhancing the competitive advantage of the firms located there. Apart from the role of government in such areas as job search and innovation networks, the report points to the impact of trust on a community's risk taking and attitudes toward investment. The OECD emphasizes the role for government to stimulate innovation through linkages between educational and research institutions and the firms located in the community.

Public research facilities have become a modern form of social capital that is necessary for today's entrepreneurship. A precursor was the creation, especially in North America, of agricultural research institutes and the development of linkages between university agricultural science depart-ments and the implementation of new farming techniques, together with the use of new seeds and fertilizers. The modern agricultural revolution with its pervasive entrepreneurial innovation depended very much on pub-lic research facilities. Individual farmers and the businesses supplying those farmers were able to experiment with new production methods based on the research conducted in the publicly funded institutions. Left to them-selves, farmers and businesses could not have afforded this level of institu-tional development, largely because they could not capture all the benefits of the research and because their organizational problems would have been immense. Schultz (1981) has emphasized the importance of externalities in this type of research: "Under competition, the reductions in real costs of producing agricultural products realized as a consequence of agricultural research are transferred in large measure to consumers" (p. 11). Such exter-nalities occur through price reductions, and they cause the social rate of return in research investment to exceed the private rate of return.

The Impacts of Entrepreneurship on Social Forces

Some authors have concluded that entrepreneurship alters social and political relationships, destroying established patterns and replacing them with new arrangements. The editors of *Entrepreneurs in Cultural Context* summarize this argument.

> Cultures are ultimately transformed by the actions and decisions of indi-viduals. Perhaps in no area of social science research is this process more dramatically illustrated than in the study of the entrepreneur.... The entrepreneur is also able to work within the cultural system while con-sciously upsetting its state of equilibrium to his advantage. (Greenfield, Stricken, & Aubey, 1979, p. vii)

Schumpeter (1962) is a prominent proponent of this view. He explains the economic development of capitalist societies as a "process of creative destruction" in which the "fundamental impulse that sets and keeps the capitalist engine in motion comes from the new consumers' goods, the new methods of production or transportation, the new markets, the new forms of industrial organization that capitalist enterprise creates" (p. 83). He describes the "process of industrial mutation . . . that incessantly revo-lutionizes the industrial structure from within, incessantly destroying the old one, incessantly creating a new one. This process of Creative Destruction is the essential fact about capitalism" (p. 83).

Landes (1969) has linked these two perspectives, noting that "economic theory has traditionally been interested in one half of the problem—the determinants of economic change—rather than its non-economic effects; and it has long vitiated that half by holding non-economic variables constant" (p. 545). Referring to specific economic achievements, he has concluded that these "material advances in turn have provoked and promoted a large complex of economic, social, political, and cultural changes, which have reciprocally influenced the rate and course of technological development (p. 544). This combination of the two perspectives suggests the self-reinforcing nature of change and the self-reinforcing nature of ossification. Rapid entrepreneurial advances alter relationships, thereby preventing the codification and regulation of conduct that could hinder future advances. But a society that falters in its economic development may automatically lose the fluidity of structure on which a revival of development depends. The second perspective, which sees social and political structures as being changed by entrepreneurial advances in a cumulative process, strengthens Olson's warning that governmental protection of vested interests can lead a nation into economic decline.

Kanter (2003), points to the opportunities for corporate entrepreneurship in partnerships between public and private enterprise, creating a new kind of social capital. She emphasizes that firms can move beyond CSR to corporate social innovation. Opportunities exist to develop new technologies, serve new markets, and develop new business ideas. The firm can view the needs in a community as opportunities in response to which the firm can develop innovative solutions. Kanter points to education, welfare-to-work programs, and inner-city development as particularly significant areas in this regard.

Jenkins, Akhalkatsi, Roberts, and Gardiner (2007) present analyses of the many relationships developed by MNEs with local firms. In this creation of new partnerships, the MNE is able to play a vital role in stimulating the growth of small and medium-sized enterprises (SMEs) in low-income countries.

> More than ever, companies realize that it is good business to share benefits with the communities in developing countries in which they operate. Enabling small, local firms to supply goods and services to larger enterprises creates more efficient supply chains. At the same time it maximizes development benefits by helping local companies to grow and create jobs. (p. 4)

In its report "Partnering for Success: Business Perspectives on Multistakeholder Partnerships," the World Economic Forum (2005) analyzed the opportunities for innovation by MNEs in less developed countries. They recommend a variety of partnerships between business, government, and society in order to find new solutions to practical issues that confront each community. They see such networks as crucial in the economic development process, and they point to the gains to be made by MNEs in this process.

Some of the world's most successful companies are recognizing the potential to turn innovative solutions to development challenges into profit-making ventures and new forms of social investment. New types of partnerships aimed at expanding economic opportunity, serving unmet social and environmental needs, and improving governance structures are becoming an important approach to address such challenges. (p. 4)

Immigrants as Entrepreneurs

The careers of individual entrepreneurs add another dimension to the relationships between social capital and entrepreneurship. A disproportionate number of entrepreneurs have come from minority groups who are outside the mainstream of society. Wilken (1979) refers to many authors who have concluded

> that entrepreneurship very often is promoted by social marginality.... Individuals or groups on the perimeter of a given social system or between two social systems are believed to provide the personnel to fill entrepreneurial roles. They may be drawn from religious, cultural, ethnic, or migrant minority groups, and their marginal social position is generally believed to have psychological effects which make entrepreneurship a particularly attractive alternative for them. (p. 11)

Hagen (1962) has carried this an additional step by focusing not simply on minorities but on minorities who have suffered "withdrawal of status respect" and, in particular, has noted the importance of self-selection in immigration and nonacceptance in a new society. Other authors examine the ways that social capital develops within immigrant communities and can form the basis for business success.

Immigration entails self-selection in that immigrants generally are aggressive and optimistic risk takers. Furthermore, they may find that avenues to success in their new country are blocked. They are not part of the established culture, and their professional qualifications may not be honored. Their only available route for advancement may be to go into business. Exposure to different production methods in their homeland may spur certain immigrants to take risks and pursue an entrepreneurial career. Wilken (1979) has noted the importance of cohesion within the immigrant community and "the presence of positive attitudes toward entrepreneurship within the group. . . . A high degree of group solidarity or cohesion . . . is necessary to counteract whatever opposition may be forthcoming from mainstream groups within the larger social situation" (p. 12).

Social Capital and Entrepreneurship Within the Firm

Creative and conscientious initiative has become necessary at many different stages of the business process, so management must cultivate entrepreneurial characteristics throughout the firm. Some authors argue that this requires a radically new approach to management-labor relations and group versus individual success criteria within each firm. For employees to work together in joint problem solving requires new decision-making procedures and structures, as well as new social attitudes toward consensus building. Reich (1983), whose views were shaped by Japan's experience, has been a proponent of this theory.

> A social organization premised on equity, security, and participation will generate greater productivity than one premised on greed and fear. Collaboration and collective adaptation are coming to be more important to an industrialized nation's well-being than are personal daring and ambition. (p. 20)

The era of standardized mass production has been disappearing in the economically advanced nations, largely because the newly industrialized countries are able to manufacture with much lower labor costs. Instead, the firms in the advanced nations have come to focus on products and services that are unique or that have small production runs. Such products and services require innovation, as well as special skills. All workers must be involved in the development of a new product or in the creation of product or service modifications. The traditional corporate command structure cannot respond quickly or appropriately enough to the customers' specialized needs. New patterns of corporate organization are necessary—patterns that foster entrepreneurial attitudes among all workers.

In his book *Theory Z: How American Business Can Meet the Japanese Challenge*, Ouchi (1981) has gone so far as to claim that in Japan "nothing of consequence occurs as a result of individual effort" (p. 50). Similarly, Athos and Pascale (1981) state in their book *The Art of Japanese Management: Application for American Executives* that

> for the Japanese, independence in an organization context has negative connotations; it implies disregard for others and self-centeredness. . . . The work group is the basic building block of Japanese organizations. Owing to the central importance of group efforts in their thinking the Japanese are extremely sensitive to and concerned about group interactions and relationships. (p. 125)

The participative approach to decision making requires the exploration of alternative solutions by managers and production workers until a consensus is reached. This process minimizes the role of middle management by bringing senior management into direct contact with the workers.

Firms throughout the world have introduced some elements of the Japanese approach in order to imbue employees with more support for their company's objectives and success. Within "quality circles," for example, groups of employees develop new techniques to improve the quality of the product they are manufacturing. The expansion of profit sharing is based on the expectation that employees will be more conscientious and creative when they receive financial rewards geared to the firm's success and that the firm will benefit from this internal entrepreneurship. Such processes can strengthen the social capital within the firm and enhance its entrepreneurial capability.

The Acer Group struggled to decide whether China's social capital could support the internal entrepreneurship necessary to locate research and development activities in China. The case of Acer adds to the earlier discussions of Hofstede's cultural typologies and of China's social capital. Social capital is not necessary only in the form of physical and educational infrastructure. Social capital also must create a culture that encourages innovation throughout the firm. We explore this in more depth in Chapter 5.

In Practice 4.1	**Differences in Social Capital as Determinants of Investment Locations**

The Acer Group had become one of the world's largest PC and computer component manufacturers. Its production facilities had been concentrated in Taiwan, but it now faced the question whether it should build new facilities in mainland China. The key to Acer's success had been the ability to continually innovate, and Acer management saw this ability as dependent on its organizational structure, with delegated responsibility and employee initiative. However, potential employees in mainland China had developed a very different set of attitudes toward their work as a result of employment in state-owned enterprises where their pay was guaranteed regardless of performance. The system of government ownership had discouraged creativity and initiative, and many thought that these traits could create resentment within the workforce.

Stan Shih, the founder and chairman of the Acer group and widely regarded as a high-tech visionary, had a long-term vision for Acer to transform the Group into a global high-tech corporation. Though fully committed to aggressively pursuing ever-growing segments of the PC market, Acer began to shift a sizable portion of its attention and resources to the "3E" market—education, entertainment, and e-commerce. Newly created ventures in the realm of semiconductors, communications, and consumer electronics were expected to play an integral role in Acer's strategic growth.

(Continued)

(Continued)

Acer's decentralized organizational structure delegated responsibility to management to involve employees in the decision-making process. This was considered their strategic advantage in the fast-moving, ever-changing world of computers. It was expected that this approach would occasionally involve conflicts that would be assuaged through open discussion and persuasion. Head office management recognized that it was unreasonable to ask their managers to follow various courses of action without reason. According to the associate vice-president of the Acer Institute of Education, Alan Chang, management at corporate headquarters were willing to explain and justify policies to local managers, were willing to "take the time to convince the manager, and importantly, were willing to be convinced."

Although there were several advantages in the autonomy of individual business units, senior management's biggest challenge at Acer was to consolidate the strength of the decentralized structure—to find the balance between Acer's core concept of "symbiotic common interest," which fostered personal commitment toward Acer's goals, and another core concept of adopting a highly decentralized, delegated management system that encouraged the head of each business unit to interpret and implement the corporate culture according to their own ideas and to achieve their specific mandates in the way they considered most effective. In this way, it was Shih's belief that Acer would achieve a "global vision with a local touch."

A highly disciplined and flexible workforce was critical for success at any of Acer's manufacturing locations. This meant that during peak production periods, workers would be asked to work diligently and commit to overtime.

The communist doctrine and the environment of the state-owned-enterprise (SOE) had a strong influence on the attitudes of Chinese workers. For example, a worker's pay in an SOE was guaranteed, regardless of the performance of the company or of the individual employee. The SOE system had inherently discouraged creativity and initiative, and indeed, showing these traits could create resentment and hostility among one's peers. Thus, the underlying concept behind incentives or reward programs was not fully understood by Chinese workers. Therefore, Lin felt that creating a disciplined workforce who were willing to "go the extra mile" for Acer when required would be a significant challenge awaiting any management team in mainland China.

SOURCE: Tsai, Everatt, and Cheng (1999).

Critical Thinking Questions

1. Should Acer allocate research and development activities to its plants outside China and place only routine production activities in China?

2. Develop a plan through which Acer will be able to transform China's social capital as it relates to Acer's new investments in China. How many years will be required to achieve an entrepreneurial and innovative environment within their business in China?

References and Suggested Readings

Adler, P., & Kwon, S. (2002). Social capital: Prospects for a new concept. *Academy of Management Review, 27*(1), 17–40.

Arrow, K. J. (1983). Innovation in large and small firms. In J. Ronen (Ed.), *Entrepreneurship: Price institute for entrepreneurial studies* (pp. 15–27). Lexington, MA: Lexington.

Athos, G., & Pascale, R. (1981). *The art of Japanese management: Applications for American executives.* New York: Simon & Schuster.

Baker, T., Gedajlovic, E., & Lubatkin, M. (2005). A framework for comparing entrepreneurial processes across nations. *Journal of International Business Studies, 36,* 492–504.

Baron, R., & Markman, G. (2000). Beyond social capital: How social skills can enhance entrepreneurs' success. *The Academy of Management Executive, 14*(1), 106–116.

Bolino, M., Turnley, W., & Bloodgood, J. (2002). Citizenship behavior and the creation of social capital in organizations. *Academy of Management Review, 27*(4), 505–522.

Greenfield, S., Stricken, A., & Aubey, R. (Eds.). (1979). *Entrepreneurs in cultural context.* Albuquerque: University of New Mexico Press.

Hagen, E. (1962). *On the theory of social change.* Homewood, IL: Dorsey.

Jenkins, B., Akhalkatsi, A., Roberts, B., & Gardiner, A. (2007). *Business linkages: Lessons, opportunities, and challenges.* Boston: International Finance Corporation, International Business Leaders Forum, & Fellows of Harvard College.

Kanter, R. (2003). From spare change to real change: The social sector as beta site for business innovation. *Harvard Business Review on Corporate Responsibility.* Boston: Harvard Business School Press.

Landes, D. (1969). *The unbound Prometheus: Technological change and industrial development in Western Europe from 1750 to the present.* Cambridge, UK: Cambridge University Press.

McKinsey Global Institute. (2001). *India: The growth imperative.* New York: Author.

Nahapiet, J., & Ghoshal, S. (1998). Social capital, intellectual capital, and the organizational advantage. *Academy of Management Review, 23*(2), 242–266.

Olson, M. (1982). *The rise and decline of nations: Economic growth, stagflation and social rigidities.* New Haven, CT: Yale University Press.

Organisation for Economic Co-operation and Development. (2001). *The well-being of nations: The role of human and social capital.* Paris: Author.

Ouchi, W. (1981). *Theory Z: How American business can meet the Japanese challenge.* Reading, MA: Addison-Wesley.

Reich, R. (1983). *The next American frontier.* New York: Times Books.

Ronen, J. (1982). *Entrepreneurship.* Lexington, MA: D. C. Heath.

Schoorman, F., Mayer, R., & Davis, J. (2007). An integrative model of organizational trust: Past, present and future. *Academy of Management Review, 32*(2), 344–354.

Schultz, T. (1981). Knowledge is power in agriculture. *Challenge, 24*(4), 4–13.

Schumpeter, J. (1962). *Capitalism, socialism and democracy* (3rd ed.). New York: Harper & Row.

Tsai, T., Everatt, D., Cheng, B. (1999). *Acer group's China manufacturing decision.* London: Ivey. (Ivey Case No. 9A99M009)

Wilken, P. (1979). *Entrepreneurship: A comparative and historical study.* Norwood, NJ: ABLEX.

Wolf, M. (2005, February 23). India and China part 1: On the move: Asia's giants take different routes in pursuit of economic greatness. *Financial Times*, p. 13.

World Economic Forum. (2005). *Partnering for success: Business perspectives on multistakeholder partnerships.* Geneva, Switzerland: Author.

Strengthening the Firm's Knowledge Capabilities 5

CHAPTER LEARNING OBJECTIVES

On completion of this chapter, students should be able to

- understand the significance for strategies and management of the new "knowledge economy,"

- recognize the impacts of a nation's innovation culture and technological advances on the firm's international competitiveness,

- describe how technological advances may be transferred among nations,

- understand how the innovation process may be strengthened within the firm,

- evaluate the importance and forms of the "triple helix" and each nation's "innovation system,"

- assess the success of alternative financial systems in supporting a nation's knowledge economy,

- relate these issues to the advantages and disadvantages for the firm of alternative investment location decisions.

The key message is that the new knowledge-networked economy requires a totally different strategic management mindset and toolbox. The traditional approaches are not completely obsolete, but used on their own they are inappropriate for sustainable organizational performance and survival in today's knowledge-networked economy. (Leibold, Probst, & Gibbert, 2002, p. 5)

D ramatic shifts in strategies and management are occurring as a result of the growth of the knowledge economy. To a major degree, these shifts relate to the greatly increased pace of change with a need for ongoing innovation in the context of heightened international competition. Within each firm, traditional strategies and management were relatively static compared with what is necessary today. In the knowledge economy, new niche firms are continually seizing opportunities that had not been imagined in the past. The complexity of decision making has also increased in response to continual technological change. At the same time, innovation is now increasingly based on partnerships among firms and also between firms, governments, and universities.

What is involved in the knowledge economy is much more than the compilation of information. Rather, the focus is on new ways to analyze data in order to better understand the factors that are relevant for strategies and management. The firm needs to search continually for the implications underlying the data that it can now collect and analyze, and it must develop systems for continually creating new insights and sound judgments in regard to these implications. Consequently, knowledge has become a new factor of production, quite apart from the traditional factors of land, labor, and capital. This shift requires that the firm develop a new sense of purpose and mission that involves ongoing innovation to achieve new types of unique value-added attributes that create a competitive advantage for the firm—a competitive advantage that may well be temporary. This perspective emphasizes the importance of creating a learning organization that is structured so as to stimulate and facilitate the development of knowledge that is relevant for that organization.

Traditionally, management placed specific functions within "silos." Interrelationships among these silos were structured and were limited to standard procedures of communication. Innovation was the responsibility of the research and development (R&D) department. Management was the central hub for coordinating information and establishing plans and procedures. Today, managerial structures must be subject to change in response to new opportunities and challenges, so there must be a new flexibility in organizational structures. Rather than simply reacting to competitive forces, the firm must now focus on what may happen and must collaborate with other organizations in order to deal most effectively with what may lie ahead. These partnerships create flexibility beyond that of the traditional hierarchical organization. The firm must seek to stimulate creative thought and new ideas throughout all of its employees rather than concentrating this process within certain departments or groups of a hierarchical bureaucracy.

The knowledge economy has introduced a heightened uncertainty since innovations may occur at any point in the value chain—at any time and in any place. This increasingly turbulent environment means that a firm's competitive advantage must rest on its capability in regard to continual adaptation to new realities. Consumers have a new degree of freedom and power in demanding unique value-added attributes from both products and services. For the firm, success requires procedures for continually creating these value-added attributes—as well as cost reductions—that will support its competitiveness.

Leibold et al. (2002) suggest that in the knowledge economy the traditional strategy process confronts three major deficiencies. First, the process of strategy analysis and formulation was traditionally analytical and rational. Today, what a firm requires is not just specific strategies but rather strategic thinking. Second, in the past the process for analyzing strategic options involved sequential steps, moving from the comparison of strategic options through strategy formulation into strategy implementation. In the knowledge economy, these elements in strategy development are linked together in ways that involve the emergence of strategies as the result of various forms of interaction. Third, traditionally a new strategy was implemented throughout an organization at a single point in time. In the knowledge economy, an important theme is experimentation; so various strategies may be in the process of implementation and evaluation on an ongoing basis, often in response to significant changes in the environment.

The boundaries of the firm should now be seen as variable and subject to management decisions. Rather than focusing on structure and order, the firm must focus on entrepreneurial adjustments. Management must create an atmosphere that is collaborative and personally fulfilling. Decision-making practices must change from "direction and control" to decentralized initiatives. The creation of new business units and the elimination of certain traditional business units must be an ongoing process. This involves a preparedness to change rapidly and to redeploy capabilities as necessary.

New strategic management tools have been developed for the knowledge economy. Customer knowledge management (CKM) enables the firm to sense emerging market opportunities. Communities of practice (COPs) link groups informally across traditional organizational boundaries in order to bring together expertise, interests, and passions. Network incubators foster partnerships that can be important for start-up firms. The organizational knowledge audit is helpful in delineating gaps that must be filled in order for the firm to understand its environment more clearly. Knowledge creation can be encouraged through formal procedures. As part of the process for creating strategy, the firm can engage in play or make-believe situations that stimulate the imagination and creativity of its employees and partners and so lead to new ideas and insights.

Knowledge Transfers Among Nations

One of the recurring themes in the literature on multinational enterprises (MNEs) concerns the role of technology in determining international trade and investment decisions. The issue of technological advantage is one of the main types of firm-specific advantages that allows the firm to overcome the costs of producing in a foreign country. Vernon's (1966) international product cycle theory describes the links between trade and investment and emphasizes that MNE production and trade are determined to a great extent by innovation and the international diffusion of new technology. In the first stage, a new product is developed and produced exclusively for the market where the innovation has occurred. If the product is successful, it is exported and foreign direct investment is required to establish distribution and service facilities abroad. In the second stage, the world market for the product has grown and the product becomes standardized, but the technology and scale of production continue to create barriers to entry. At this point, the firm may shift production to foreign subsidiaries to take advantage of cost differentials or, as a defensive measure, to retain its share in a market where local competitors could gain an advantage from local production. In the third stage, when the product has become completely standardized, production will be carried out where it can be least expensive, and the home market may be served from abroad. From the perspective of the product cycle theory, the corporate structure of the MNE provides a nearly automatic shift of business activities out of high-wage more developed countries to less developed countries that have lower wage rates. Consequently, the development of global mandates for new products and components is a continual necessity if employment levels in economically advanced nations are to be maintained. This "product cycle" process underlies the potential volatility of profits and mobility of capital.

The "appropriability theory" of direct investment focuses on the returns to specific information. MNEs specialize in the production of information that is most efficiently transmitted intrafirm. The incentive is for MNEs to produce returns from these. The optimum size of a firm will be determined by the appropriability of the returns from and the complementarities among different types of information. An MNE can gain more from an innovation than can firms in a single country because it can apply the innovation globally. In addition, the imperfection of markets in intermediate goods such as technical and entrepreneurial expertise can lead MNEs to internalize these activities as part of its international expansion strategies.

David Teece (1998) emphasizes the difference between what he terms codified knowledge that stands apart from any particular organizational structure and uncodified or tacit knowledge that requires interpersonal relationships and direct communications. Teece relates tacit knowledge to the example of the traditional apprenticeship system where a master craftsman works with an apprentice over a long period of time. Those who are learning have to be involved in time-consuming repetition. In this process, various elements of a procedure will be modified by each individual, and a personal style becomes part of the learning process.

This analogy is helpful in understanding the process of transferring tacit knowledge from one firm or subsidiary to another. The need for direct person-to-person involvement in the transfer process places particularly severe obstacles in the path of transferring tacit knowledge across national boundaries.

Teece (1998) also emphasizes the dichotomy between product technologies that can be examined closely and reverse engineered and process technologies that involve a lengthy time component that cannot easily be observed in detail. Consequently, product technologies can be transferred internationally more readily than process technologies. Teece also points to a dichotomy between positive and negative knowledge. He suggests that a firm's knowledge of failures is valuable since it limits future inquiries and experimentations in ways that avoid blind alleys. Here as well, the knowledge of failures cannot be transferred internationally as readily as knowledge of specific successes. Finally, Teece points to the dichotomy between autonomous and systemic knowledge. Autonomous knowledge can be transferred without requiring significant modifications in organizational systems. Systemic knowledge requires that systems within the firm must be changed in order to implement the new knowledge. Consequently, Teece emphasizes that knowledge assets may be difficult to replicate without changes to organizational routines. Autonomous knowledge may be transferred internationally far more readily than systemic knowledge.

Taken together, many of these realities combine to impact the appropriability of new technologies. The ease of appropriability differs among sectors. In particular, chemicals and pharmaceuticals may rest on specific formulae that can be copied quite readily. On the other hand, the use of new information technologies depends on the creation of new software and systems that may involve modifications of a firm's organizational structure, as well as new electronics components; so the appropriability of new knowledge in this sector is more challenging. The successful use of knowledge assets may rest on complementary assets, perhaps provided by a particular supplier. Challenges in transferring complementary assets may also hinder international replication.

Competitive Advantage Versus Comparative Advantage

Traditional economic analyses of international trade have focused on the "law of comparative advantage" with static cost comparisons at a particular point in time. The production costs for a certain product are compared between two jurisdictions. Each nation is expected to specialize in those products in which it has a comparative advantage in production costs. Even if a country has higher production costs than another for everything it produces, it will nevertheless gain from trade by specializing in those products where the interjurisdictional differences in costs are smallest. The higher-cost country will specialize in those goods and services for which it has a comparative advantage.

In recent years, business analysts have increased their use of the phrase "competitive advantage" in their explanations of trade patterns. Instead of comparing current costs among countries, as if these were static or permanent, they focus on the ability of firms to change their cost structure and the nature of their products. Their analyses often look to the future with predictions about changes in trade patterns, sometimes with recommendations for government action to strengthen a jurisdiction's future competitiveness. They examine the ability of businesses to change the way they operate. In particular, they emphasize the ability of businesses to undertake product innovation and quality improvements. They discuss the ability of businesses to provide better customer service in which production is continually modified to suit the particular needs of each customer. And they examine the ability of businesses to shift from one product or component to another as the demand for each changes. The latter feature is often referred to as "economies of scope," and it deals with the efficiency with which a business can alter its products to suit particular customers, thereby satisfying limited market demands for each version of its products.

Many authors discuss the theory of competitive advantage from the positive perspective of how this ability can be strengthened. Some authors believe that each nation will be able to develop a competitive advantage within only specific sectors or types of activities. A nation will not be able to develop businesses in every sector that can compete internationally. The competitive advantage perspective has led many firms to recognize the importance of "employee empowerment" and of new alternative procedures for stimulating the positive involvement of all the employees in the achievement of corporate objectives. Profit sharing and employee ownership of shares have received new attention and are an important aspect of this labor empowerment.

The competitive advantage perspective analyzes potential trade patterns in the context of a firm's continual success in changing the cost realities it faces and in modifying the products and services it provides. Competitive advantage has to be won again and again; it is not a feature that is determined at a single point in time and that holds for the indefinite future. Competitive advantage may involve higher unit costs, yet the customer may be prepared to pay higher prices for the more complete and more appropriate satisfaction of its needs. The traditional focus on cost minimization may be replaced with a focus on the value to the customer of product modifications and better service. For example, consumers today have new concerns about their health. They know that their health can be affected by what they eat and drink, so they are concerned about calorie intake and diets. At the same time, the population is ageing. Many consumers also have a greater concern for the safety features of products.

These developments are altering the pattern of market demand and are creating opportunities for new businesses. This paradigm shift is leading to shorter production runs since each customer wishes to have unique product or service features; so the traditional perspectives of comparative advantage and economies of scale may no longer be appropriate. Product cycle studies such as Vernon's (1966) demonstrate that firms in high-wage, more developed nations must continually innovate if they are to maintain jobs there. Each firm will face creative competition from other firms. On a continuing basis, each firm will find that its new products, production processes, and customer services are being challenged by the achievements of its competitors. Each advance is likely to have a short lifespan, so the firm must become a learning organization.

The Learning Firm

The learning firm continually creates new knowledge assets in order to maintain a competitive advantage. A firm may achieve a unique dynamic capability in the process of knowledge creation based on a sense of opportunity and recognition of the potential for value creation. Many authors have built on this perspective in seeking to understand the entrepreneurship process within firms. Chapter 4 discusses some of these authors under the theme of social capital, where entrepreneurship is linked to certain attributes of a particular nation or region or ethnic group. Here, it is useful to consider several additional aspects of entrepreneurship.

Beugré, Acar, and Braun (2006) focus on the importance of transformational leadership in the knowledge economy. In order for an organization to develop a culture of continual knowledge development, it is necessary for the organization to have transformational leadership.

> Transformational leadership refers to a leadership type in which leaders possess charisma and provide intellectual stimulation, individualized consideration and inspirational motivation to followers. Transformational leaders create a dynamic organizational vision that often necessitates a metamorphosis in cultural values to reflect greater innovation. Transformational leadership also seeks a bonding between individual and collective interests allowing subordinates to work for transcendental goals. (p. 54)

A firm's competitive advantage rests on the ability of its management to bring all employees, suppliers, and customers into an awareness of the need for ongoing knowledge creation. This is a particularly important aspect of a firm's competitiveness in situations where the environment is changing quickly in significant ways that reduce predictability. The knowledge economy has greatly heightened this environmental volatility.

A report on innovation by *The Economist* ("Something New," 2007) presents a summary of innovation strategies, suggesting that there are a number of ways in which conscious efforts can stimulate innovation. The report suggests that at the level of the firm, "innovation is turning from an art into a science" (p. 10). The report refers to a number of academics who have focused on processes that can stimulate innovation. The concept of "open innovation" recommends that the firm not rely solely on its own creativity but should be continually searching for ideas that it can appropriate either directly or indirectly from others. GE has focused on a structured process within GE that can continuously result in innovation. Here, the process of execution may be seen as more important than the process of creating new knowledge itself since the latter can often be obtained from outside the firm.

The Economist report notes that North America is a global leader in regard to R&D, having a 43.7% share of the world's aggregate R&D. Europe has a 28.9% share and Japan a 21.5% share, while other countries seem to have been largely left out of the R&D process. The U.S. dominance in R&D may to some degree underlie the exceptional success of the U.S. economy in regard to productivity growth, which in recent decades has far exceeded the achievement of other nations. While increases in capital may account for a major portion of U.S. economic growth in the past 50 years, it appears that productivity growth may account for an even greater component. However, *The Economist* suggests that the past success of the United States relative to Asia may not automatically continue in the future. Apart from the investments currently being made by other nations in the knowledge process, there may be innovations in business models that can stimulate innovation. As an example, the report points to a business model of motorcycle assemblers in China. In their purchasing decisions, the assemblers indicate only the important features of the components that they will purchase, while the supplier firms are encouraged to improvise in how they achieve these features.

New indicators have been developed to reflect a firm's knowledge management. There may be a growing difference between a firm's market value on the stock exchanges and a firm's book value, and it may be appropriate to use various indicators to reflect this gap. The "balanced scorecard" focuses on the firm's competitive strategy, where the objective is to build a competitive value chain, and indicators should reflect performance management in this regard. With the balanced scorecard, new indicators may relate to several alternative perspectives, including financial, customer, internal processes, and learning and growth. The balanced scorecard provides indicators that reflect the firm's market position and its internal organization related to its competitiveness. The balanced scorecard involves the delineation by management of procedures that can strengthen the firm's knowledge capability, and it involves communication to ensure that employees execute the strategy. Management can use the balanced scorecard to help design a value chain and to clarify the implications for employee performance.

The intellectual capital concept focuses on enhancing the knowledge competency of the firm through the skills and capabilities of its employees. This perspective emphasizes "competency-based strategy" that will strengthen the unique knowledge capability of the firm. Indicators relate to various aspects that describe the organization's capability in this regard. The concepts of the balanced scorecard and intellectual capital lead to the use of nonfinancial indicators. For the balanced scorecard, these indicators may be more precise and so may offer employees clearer direction from management. With intellectual capital, the focus is on the firm's strategy for managing knowledge. For intellectual capital, ongoing competitiveness depends on this capability to manage knowledge. The objective of each set of indicators is to understand the firm's progress in becoming a more capable organization in the knowledge economy.

Traditional management tools must be used in new ways in the knowledge economy. The firm creates value for its customers by solving problems, and this may include delineating problems, presenting alternative solutions, and assisting in implementation and follow-up. Firms throughout a value chain must interact in the innovation process among themselves and also with final customers. A firm in the knowledge economy depends to a greater extent on the expertise of individual employees, who therefore have higher bargaining power with the firm than employees traditionally had. Consequently, a major concern of today's firm is the process for obtaining and retaining the best experts. The learning firm presents a number of new paradigms for management decisions.

The Triple Helix: Universities, Governments, and Businesses

With technological capability increasingly becoming the touchstone of competitiveness in an open and integrated world environment, the role of universities in economic growth is taking on a greater salience. Not only do they impart education but also they are coming to be viewed as sources of industrially valuable technical skills, innovations and entrepreneurship. (Yusuf & Nabeshima, 2006, back cover)

In a World Bank publication titled *How Universities Promote Economic Growth* (Yusuf & Nabeshima, 2006), several authors analyze the "triple helix" in nations throughout the world. During the first half of the 20th century, a small number of universities in the United States and Western Europe engaged in research and technology development through various types of relationships with businesses. However, most of the world's universities were not involved in this process. In the second half of the 20th century, a general recognition developed that knowledge has a major impact on economic growth and that increasingly intense international competition is based on knowledge and innovation. Meanwhile, the cost of new technologies has been rising, and many new technologies are being created at the intersection of several disciplines. In response to these realities, governments throughout the world are now encouraging their universities to create technologies that will be useful in domestic businesses and to create new kinds of relationships that will facilitate technology transfer. Governments have instituted programs of direct grants for selected activities such as laboratory facilities and incubators and have provided tax incentives and scholarships. Subnational governments have provided serviced land and infrastructure adjacent to universities, have subsidized the training of industrial workers, and have developed public services geared to local firms. For governments, there is now a competition to attract and retain industries, especially those that provide localized synergies and increase employment, exports, and value added.

> Virtually every industrial country is moving to make university-industry links a centerpiece of its innovation systems, and the notion of a triple helix—representing the symbiotic relations yoking together the government, the universities, and the business community—has acquired wide currency. (p. 7)

Firms have responded to varying degrees, with responses differing among nations. Yusuf concludes that in Japan such ties have generally been informal. In the United States, contractual arrangements have become common, including the outsourcing of entire research projects to universities (Yusuf & Nabeshima, 2006). The growth of alliances and collaborative arrangements has been rapid. This growth has been most dramatic between large firms and the leading universities and research institutes, especially Stanford, MIT, and the University of California, San Diego. Many universities still focus only on teaching, and in the past, small and medium-sized firms have not generally participated actively. The result of these changes is that certain universities, particularly in the United States, now see themselves as "entrepreneurial universities." Meanwhile, many of the newly created university "science parks" have not yet achieved financial success, and the trends noted above are still evolving in terms of structure and processes.

The World Bank publication (Yusuf & Nabeshima, 2006) concludes that each nation, as well as each region within a nation, has a distinct "innovation system." The success of university-industry linkages (UILs) depends on the strength of this innovation system as a whole. Luc Soete, a contributor to the publication, analyzes the process through which nations that have lagged behind in regard to technologies may be able to catch up. Technological advances depend on the "absorptive capacity" of latecomers, including factors such as market size and factor supply. Another major determinant is "social capability," which refers to the ability of lagging countries to improve their education and infrastructure. A number of such factors determine the success of UILs in any particular nation, including the nature of "social capital," the extent of higher education, the research capacity of a country or region, geographical proximity or clusters, and general absorptive capacity of firms and their customers. Other authors in this World Bank publication also emphasize the role of each nation's innovation system as a whole, including the degree to which the financial structure facilitates commercialization in start-ups through venture capital.

In the World Bank publication (Yusuf & Nabeshima, 2006), Alan Hughes presents the results of an extensive survey of innovation at firms in the United Kingdom and the United States. University-industry interactions that have contributed to innovation have in both countries included informal contacts, employee recruitment, publications, and conferences. Hughes concludes that U.S. firms have experienced a greater depth and achievement in their UILs. This difference is particularly striking for small and medium-sized firms. U.S. firms in all size classes are more likely to rank universities as sources of knowledge than are U.K. firms. Furthermore, U.S. firms pursue an open innovation system in which they actively pursue innovations outside their immediate industrial context.

In analyzing technology transfer in Asia for the World Bank publication (Yusuf & Nabeshima, 2006), John Mathews and Mei-Chih Hu emphasize that prior to 1950, Asian countries did not regard universities as agents of innovation. Only recently have governments begun to pursue the encouragement of technology transfers from universities and government-funded public research institutes (PRIs). In recent years, PRIs have been created specifically for this purpose. In general, success has been most noteworthy in information technology, electronics, communications, and semiconductors. In the United States, the Bayh-Dole Act allows universities and research institutes to patent intellectual property rights from their discoveries and to negotiate terms and conditions for the technology transfer of these patents to firms. Mathews and Hu conclude that the Bayh-Dole Act has been a key factor in growing the entrepreneurial university; so many Asian nations have recently attempted to implement similar legislation.

Municipal governments can play a key role in the technology transfer process, particularly in assisting the entrepreneurial university. The successful firm in the knowledge economy is a learning organization, so geographical proximity to a university is helpful in terms of ongoing advances. Proximity also fosters an entrepreneurial culture that can permeate all the related firms and the university. Hence, the municipal government may be in a better position than other levels of government to strengthen and facilitate technology transfers.

Financing the Knowledge Economy

The startup and growth of a firm based in the knowledge economy depends on a financial system that can provide it with adequate funding. Traditionally, a firm could borrow with fixed assets as security for a loan, and the firm's book value could provide some guidance in valuing its stock. With the knowledge economy, the firm has to borrow against knowledge assets that are far more difficult to value. Hence, the traditional banking system—where a bank borrows from depositors, charges a spread in interest rates, and lends to borrowers—may become a severe limitation in the knowledge economy. Supplementing the traditional banking system is the process of "disintermediation" in which the firm obtains funding directly from investors. This process involves a wide range of new financial intermediaries, including venture capitalists, angel investors, investment bankers, private equity funds, "bought deals," and initial public offerings. The availability of these supplementary financial activities and the terms and conditions that they present to the firm for raising capital have differed significantly among nations. Consequently, the extent and nature of the knowledge economy differs significantly among nations. At the forefront has been the United States. In recent years, U.S. financial institutions have extended these new financial activities to other countries, but the gap remains an important determinant of relative productivity growth among nations.

Even within the realm of venture capital, the decision-making processes can differ significantly among nations. In the United States, venture capitalists make decisions on the basis of financial projections related to a "rules-based logic of arms-length transactions." The venture capitalists focus on their analyses of market factors and profit potential. Relevant information includes market size and growth prospects, proprietary technology of the client, and the analysis of competitors and their likely reactions. Consequently, an entrepreneur attempting to fund a start-up must present a clear analysis of market opportunities. In contrast with this approach, in South Korea and China the focus of venture capitalists is the capability of the entrepreneurial team. The traditional emphasis on relationship-based transactions that are the norm within such economies has been carried over to the financing process. Venture capitalists in such economies do not rely on the complex analyses that are required in the United States. Hofstede's typologies are relevant in comparing venture capitalists across countries. As Zacharakis, McMullen, and Shepherd (2007) suggest, "Therefore, even though a shared profession may, through normative pressure, lead venture capitalists across countries to use the same information, differences in economic institutions may introduce variation regarding which information is relied on most heavily" (p. 12).

Wright, Pruthi, and Lockett (2005) compare venture capital markets in a large number of countries, and they emphasize the importance of postinvestment involvement by the investors in the firm's progress.

Literature concerning venture capital has tended to focus on new venture start-ups, with less analysis of later-stage investments. Later stages are seen as distinct segments of the financial market, such as the private equity segment or management buyouts, yet these later stages can also be crucial elements of the venture capital process. A wide range of cultural and institutional factors determine the success of the venture capital process.

> Gompers and Lerner (2001), in Wright, Pruthi, and Lockett (2005), note that until recently, efforts to transplant the VC [venture capital] model internationally were rare and that many recent efforts to stimulate VC have met with mixed success. They suggest that, for a VC market to be successful, there is need for an ample supply of promising new technologies, a set of knowledgeable managers willing to take risks, helpful regulatory and tax conditions, and robust markets in order to exit investments. (p. 160)

The government of Malaysia feared that low-wage competition from China would reduce the labor-intensive business activities on which Malaysia's growth had depended. The government's solution was to create a huge high-tech corridor that it hoped would attract value-added activities. The case of Malaysia's Multimedia Development Corporation illustrates the limitations of physical infrastructure alone in creating a knowledge economy.

In Practice 5.1	How Can a Government Strengthen the Knowledge Capabilities of Firms in Its Jurisdiction?

The Multimedia Super Corridor (MSC) was officially announced by the government of Malaysia in 1995. It was defined as a greenfield project, 15 kilometres long.

The Malaysian government had set a goal to reach developed nation status by 2020. The government had declared that the only way to reach this status was to shift the economy from a labor-based to a service-based economy. The MSC had been selected as the means to achieve this goal. The government would have to target international companies involved in the multimedia industry for assistance. The government committed RM$48 billion towards the physical infrastructure that would be required to make the corridor a success. In 1996, the installation of the telecommunications backbone began with state-of-the-art, fully-digital fibre optics. Located in the heart of Cyberjaya was the Multimedia University. The university, being funded by Telekom Malaysia, would offer educational programs in high-tech fields, as well as conduct research in multimedia areas.

Special incentives were announced to encourage companies to apply for MSC status and to locate within the corridor. They included exemption from local foreign ownership rules, unlimited influx of expatriates, up to 10 years tax holiday or 100% investment tax allowance, duty-free imports on multimedia equipment, special telecommunications rates, and protection of intellectual property rights.

(Continued)

(Continued)

In order to speed up the project's development, the government had identified seven flagship applications that would receive priority; electronic government, smart schools, telemedicine, R&D clusters, national multipurpose cards, borderless marketing centres, and worldwide manufacturing webs. The government also established the Multimedia Development Corporation (MDC) to be the "one-stop shop" for investors.

During the initial phase of the MSC, the preference was for companies referred to as "web shapers." Web shapers were companies that were defining the multimedia industry and its standards throughout the world and included such companies as Intel or Microsoft. The rest were simply web adopters, companies that utilized the existing standards to develop commercialized products.

Five new cyberlaws were introduced for government approval to ensure protection. The laws included the digital signatures cyberlaw, the multimedia intellectual property cyberlaw, the computer crime cyberlaw, the telemedicine development cyberlaw, and the electronic government cyberlaw. In addition, the Multimedia Convergence Act would be established to govern the new communication framework.

SOURCE: Conklin, Thompson, and Weeks (1998).

For the first five years (1996–2001), Malaysia's Multimedia Development Corporation (MDC) pursued its original mission and vision, seeking to create a research and design corridor (Multimedia Super Corridor) that would be at the leading edge of the new economy. However, many analysts criticized key elements of the MDC. Civil servants were attempting to micromanage the corridor's development, but some analysts feared that civil servants lacked the technical capability to predict the emergence of new technologies. Others feared the MDC lacked the ability to encourage a risk-taking culture that would be essential for innovation.

Many pointed to the lack of entrepreneurial activity. Mahathir openly criticized Malaysian banks for failing to support new ventures: "The idea of venture capitalists is still something many Malaysian financiers and bankers find difficulty in doing" ("Investment to Heat Up," 2000). To meet these criticisms, Malaysia created a venture capital stock exchange, modeled after the NASDAQ, in order to attract high-tech start-ups, but it was not successful.

Stan Shih, chairman of Taiwan's Acer computer company, concluded that there were simply not enough knowledge workers in Malaysia to achieve the vision of global leadership in Multimedia research and design.

After 2001, the MDC began to shift its focus to the development of labor-intensive IT-related activities at the low end of value chains, taking advantage of Malaysia's low costs and its geographical position as a potential Asian hub. Data processing centers and customer service centers proliferated. This expansion came at the right time for Malaysia's economy, as its traditional computer-related manufacturing suffered in the face of new, lower-cost competition from China.

Another important development was the creation of similar programs in other countries. Many, such as Canada, offered substantial R&D tax credits. Hong Kong had created the "Cyberport" as Hong Kong's "information technology flagship" aimed at creating an interactive environment that would be home to a strategic cluster of about 100 IT companies. Kerala State in India had created a "Smart City" focused on the Internet. Israel was attempting to become a "second Silicon Valley," attracting twice the number of venture capital investments as the whole of Europe. The MDC now faced many competitors, all seeking to attract high-tech investments.

SOURCE: Conklin and Cadieux (2006).

Critical Thinking Questions

1. Evaluate the challenges faced by Malaysia in trying to create a high-tech corridor. Consider the pros and cons for a high-tech firm in choosing to locate there.

2. Evaluate the 2001 decision to shift the MDC focus to the development of labor-intensive IT-related activities at the low end of value chains. Was this just a stage on the way to the ultimate MDC high-tech mission? Or does it represent a failure of that mission?

3. Is there any alternative growth model that less developed countries can use in order to participate more actively in the knowledge economy?

References and Suggested Readings

Beugré, C., Acar, W., & Braun, W. (2006). Transformational leadership in organizations: An environment-induced model. *International Journal of Manpower, 27*(1), 52–62.

Conklin, D. W., & Cadieux, D. (2006). *Malaysia's Multimedia Development Corporation (B).* London: Ivey. (Ivey Case No. 9B06M057)

Conklin, D. W., Thompson, J., & Weeks, S. (1998). *Malaysia's Multimedia Development Corporation (A).* London: Ivey. (Ivey Case No. 9A98G001)

Investment to heat up at hi-tech super zone. (2000, September 9). *Business Post,* p. 4.

Leibold, M., Probst, G., Gibbert, M. (2002). *Strategic management in the knowledge economy.* Germany: Publicis & Wiley.

Something new under the sun: A special report on innovation. (2007). *The Economist, 385*(8550), 1–20.

Teece, D. (1998). Capturing value from assets: The new economy, markets for know-how, and intangible assets. *California Management Review, 40*(3), 55–79.

Vernon, R. (1966, May). International investment and international trade in the product cycle. *Quarterly Journal of Economics, 80*(2), 190–207.

Wright, M., Pruthi, S., & Lockett, A. (2005). International venture capital research: From cross-country comparisons to crossing borders. *International Journal of Management Reviews, 7*(3), 135–165.

Yusuf, S., & Nabeshima, K. (Eds.). (2006). *How universities promote economic growth.* Washington, DC: World Bank.

Zacharakis, A., McMullen, J., & Shepherd, D. (2007). Venture capitalists' decision policies across three countries: An institutional theory perspective. *Journal of International Business Studies, 38*(5), 1–18.

Investing in New Technologies 6

CHAPTER LEARNING OBJECTIVES

On completion of this chapter, students should be able to

- understand the impacts of new technologies on traditional industry structures, creating new investment opportunities,

- appreciate the value of new forms of interfirm relationships in the innovation process,

- assess differences among nations in the degree to which they offer investment opportunities in new technologies,

- recognize ethical and social issues related to new technologies, especially technologies in e-business, biotech, and sustainability,

- evaluate differences in the role of governments in supporting investments in research and development (R&D) and the implementation of new technologies,

- relate these issues to the advantages and disadvantages for the firm of alternative investment locations.

Several business sectors illustrate the dramatic changes in management paradigms as a result of the development of significant new technologies. This chapter analyzes new management paradigms in e-business, biotech, and environmentally sustainable technologies. The convergence of information technologies and microelectronics has permeated business activities and has led to the proliferation of e-business. Office automation rests on innovation in information storage, retrieval, and analyses through local area networks (LANs), as well as through electronic outsourcing of office activities. A revolution in telecom technologies and in combinations of these technologies facilitates interfirm transfer of information and business functions. Point-of-sale scanning equipment permits the implementation of increasingly sophisticated systems for reordering and controlling inventory. Computer-aided design and engineering have transformed the exchange of information and instructions between computer systems and manufacturing equipment. CAD/CAM integration and robotics have led to flexible manufacturing technologies, often with a reduction in economies of scale. These changes—and others related to them—have radically altered the environment of business. In their book *E-Commerce*, Rayport and Jaworski (2001) analyze the impacts of the information technology revolution on the traditional paradigms for strategies and management. As they emphasize,

> The application of new media and information technology to business— which, of course, includes the Internet and the World Wide Web—has not only changed what we know about management, strategy, and business design, but also has assured us of a continuing and unfolding impact in what managers do and how businesses operate in the foreseeable future. All hype aside, there is truly a revolution here, and we have little choice but to embrace it. (p. xi)

Information technologies have created new opportunities for collecting, analyzing, and distributing a myriad of types of information. These processes now enable management to develop insights and relationships that they were not able to achieve in the past. Management now has the capability to become more sophisticated in its decision making. These processes also mean that management of the firm has become congruent with management of technologies, and strategic decisions are increasingly based on the firm's technologies. These new realities are prominent in the biotech sector. "Biotechnology represents the convergence of biology, computer science, chemistry, physics, and engineering. These component technologies work in synergy, and they are each advancing rapidly" (Rowley, 2002, p. 4).

A new understanding of the molecular pathways for disease is leading to specific therapies through "rational drug design." Medicines can now be customized to suit the needs of specific subgroups of people. New diagnostic tests for a wide range of health issues utilize this knowledge, together with computer technology, physics, and biochemistry. Biotechnology is also developing more effective vaccines, such as DNA vaccines that can stimulate immunity to diseases for which no vaccines had previously existed. Creating ways to manipulate genetic processes enables the bioengineering of new characteristics into existing species. Genetically modified bacteria, plants, and animals can play a new role in the creation of pharmaceutical products. Agricultural biotechnology is leading to a host of new plant and animal characteristics that can improve yields.

Genetically modified food, with the inclusion of genes from other species, can improve a variety of characteristics.

Increasingly, firms are developing new strategies and management systems in order to facilitate the adoption of new technologies that can improve environmental performance. Often referred to as Environmental Management Systems (EMS), these new approaches seek to integrate new environmental technologies more completely into traditional business goals. Objectives include reductions in usage of materials and energy, improvements in efficiency of production processes, expansion of recycling practices, and improvements in end-of-life product management. Not surprisingly, firms that have been at the forefront of this movement are firms that can be classified as high adopters of new technologies in general.

Innovation is the key element in the transformation of a firm into a sustainable enterprise. The achievements of a firm depend largely on management practices that encourage employees to participate actively in the development of innovative solutions to the environmental challenges that they perceive. Each firm must demonstrate that it wants employees to undertake eco-initiatives. The firm should allocate time and resources to supporting employee experimentation with new ideas, and it should reward successful improvements. Management practices should demonstrate openness to employee ideas, and supervisory behavior toward employees in this regard plays a key role.

Investing in E-Business Innovations

E-BUSINESS AND THE TRANSFORMATION OF BUSINESS CULTURE

The dimension of time has changed dramatically in relations among businesses and between businesses and customers. Real-time decisions are now required more often, and the ability to delay decisions is being reduced. Dialogues among market participants occur more frequently and can shape management decisions and strategies to the needs and wishes of customers and suppliers in a more responsive manner. This shift to real-time decision making has altered the nature of competition, resulting in a continual need to improve and change simply to remain competitive. For most firms, an e-business strategy involves Web site-to-face interaction with much less opportunity for direct human contact. Further, customers have a new capability to control their relationships with the businesses with whom they are relating. It is the customer who controls his or her comparisons among firms, in many cases leading to a more precise comparison of prices and products. Traditionally, businesses were built on the basis of supply factors, with distribution and marketing to follow. Today, businesses are increasingly built on the basis of demand factors in direct response to customer preferences.

Once the firm has created a Web site and distribution system, marginal costs may be much lower than in the past. Inventory control can be far more sophisticated, often with the elimination of warehousing and with the direct shipment from suppliers to customers. As larger numbers of firms and potential customers have become involved in e-business, existing Web sites have the potential to increase in value on the basis of a growing number of contacts. Traditional industry boundaries have become blurred, as a single Web site may now offer sets of related products beyond the firm's traditional inventories. For each firm, an extended set of relationships can link all technologies and decisions within the value chain. Furthermore, new product development can be created through an integrated process within this value chain. A firm can more easily expand its geographic scope, and the concept of a global presence has now become more realistic for a larger number of firms.

Business culture in a broad sense is being transformed, and firms must adjust their strategies and management procedures in response to these new realities. Rayport and Jaworski (2001) describe "the transformative effect of the New Economy on how children learn, how work groups communicate across time zones, how scientific interchange occurs, and more generally, how we function as a society" (p. 11). A time profile of this process forms a series of waves, beginning with technology and networks; extending through e-commerce, learning, and entertainment; and finally becoming a way of life. These various waves are each creating new business opportunities and are eliminating traditional business practices. In many cases, telecom carriers are actively encouraging the development of new value-added activities that can provide them with additional revenue to cover their huge initial fixed costs.

The multinational enterprise (MNE) must now consider alternative business models in which the firm delineates a new value proposition, new marketing procedures for this value proposition, a new distribution system, and a new financial structure. The "virtual" nature of business relationships has created a new freedom and flexibility in the design of business models. E-business creates the opportunity to develop more complex pricing structures and introduces new payment systems, including fees and subscriptions. Traditionally, firms focused on specific products and services. Today, firms are creating opportunities that are based on activities that are closely related. As a result of these changes, a host of new potential niche strategies has developed.

Relationships with suppliers have also been dramatically transformed. New information systems have created opportunities to control inventories more effectively and to link suppliers' shipments directly to current sales volumes. In a sense, there is now an integration of suppliers' businesses with retail businesses, where management decisions within the supplier and within the customer are more closely integrated. In this process, it may be necessary to change elements of the delivery system, with the possibility of combining Web site relations with traditional brick-and-mortar establishments. As a result, competition has become more intense among suppliers, and transaction costs have been reduced. Traditional metrics to measure success must in many cases be replaced with revised scorecards in which each firm must determine its unique balance of success criteria. Overall, many would argue that the ultimate consumers have been made much better off, having easier access to a wider variety of offers at a lower level of prices.

Information technology (IT) has enabled firms to access a vast range of digital partnership options, and these options can add flexibility to the firm's strategies and activities. Electronic partnerships can provide access to new markets and technologies, improve product quality, develop new products and services, and achieve greater economies of scale and scope. Partnerships may involve coordination of information, as well as collaboration in the analysis of that information to develop business knowledge. A challenge for the firm is to establish an appropriate level of control within various aspects of the partnerships while at the same time achieving the appropriate degree of flexibility. Each firm may decide to pursue multiple electronic partnering options in the context of varying needs. This challenge introduces a complexity in aligning IT facilities and usage with business strategies. The firm must adjust its partnerships in response to the development of new technologies. Meanwhile, the firm faces an ongoing opportunity to innovate in initiatives throughout all of its activities, including external transactions through the analysis of information and product planning and design and development. There is an advantage in maintaining flexibility in partnerships, with a preparedness to disband, modify, or reconfigure in response to new developments.

The greater integration and collaboration among supply chain partners is changing the face of the logistics market. Trade agreements have stimulated the creation of integrated international distribution networks with more efficient and automated customs procedures. Country-of-origin provisions require documentation that can demonstrate the achievement of certain value-added percentages within the signatories. New national security concerns have elevated the need to guarantee the integrity of the loading and shipping procedures. The new third party logistics (3PL) sector offers to provide this international integration and documentation. 3PL firms address the comprehensive logistics needs of their clients by integrating transportation, warehousing, inventory control, order processing, customs brokerage, and other logistics activities into a seamless supply chain management system. Their emergence and strong growth underlies the increasing trend to outsource supply chain management activities.

THE DIGITAL DIVIDE

The "digital divide" is a challenge for both governments and businesses as governments seek to establish nationwide standards and to achieve international competitiveness for their economies. For low-income people in any country, insufficient educational opportunities, as well as insufficient capital, may prevent full access to information technologies and services. For many less developed countries, the economy as a whole may lack the opportunity to benefit from the increased efficiencies and productivity improvements that rest on new information technologies. For firms, the potential expansion of e-business must be related to a series of national and regional characteristics. As Javalgi and Ramsey (2001) emphasize, these characteristics impact the ability to develop new e-business opportunities.

> To embrace e-commerce potential, countries need to have well-established infrastructure of various kinds in various forms. E-commerce depends on key infrastructure such as information technology and telecommunications, social/cultural, commercial and legal. (p. 376)

Telecommunications systems, computers, and new software programs have become the new infrastructure on which businesses rely. Apart from the infrastructure, a series of cultural elements determine the rate of expansion of e-business. These include the education and technical skills of the population, beliefs and value systems, language, and entrepreneurial attitudes. Many of these cultural variables relate to the discussions of social capital in Chapter 4 of this text. Success for any individual firm in creating an e-business depends very much on the active presence of other e-business firms. Consequently, e-business opportunities in many nations remain somewhat limited.

There are several other factors that explain some nations' relatively slow pace of investment in e-business.

- *Risk taking.* Management may be more risk averse.

- *Difficulties in calculating return on investment (ROI).* Calculating the ROI for information technology investments is notoriously difficult. Higher risk aversion makes this process less likely by setting higher hurdle rates for e-business projects.

- *Legacy brick-and-mortar facilities.* Investments in e-business often make traditional infrastructure obsolete, yet this infrastructure cannot be erased from balance sheets for financial and tax reasons. Moreover, a shift to e-business can often involve layoffs or expensive organizational restructuring, both of which can have important consequences for company morale and profitability.

- *Lack of immediacy.* Local firms are often sheltered from international competition. The imperative for change will become apparent only as time passes.

- *Access to capital.* Many nations have not benefited from the exceptional capitalization of U.S. e-business activities. Lower debt/equity and price/equity ratios mean less capital for investing in e-commerce technologies. Access to capital is made more difficult due to the reluctance of banks to lend for investments in which there is little or no physical capital to serve as collateral.

- *Customer demand and critical mass.* In order for e-business to be successful, a firm's suppliers and customers must be online. A critical mass of companies must therefore be connected for investments to pay off. Many nations have not yet reached this point. Furthermore, low demand reduces the need for companies to change. The result can be a state of inertia.

- *Brain drain.* Higher salaries, lower taxes, and more rewarding career opportunities are drawing some of the best and brightest to work in the United States or Western Europe. This is a loss of entrepreneurial talent and a drain on the capacity to innovate.

- *Economies of scale and scope (EOS/S).* EOS/S are extremely important in e-business because infrastructures are easily scalable; minimal additional investments can handle 100,000 customers as easily as 100. The size of the U.S. economy, higher population densities, and the tendency of U.S. Internet users to spend more online can result in significant relative savings and higher profits.

- *Lower prices in the United States.* U.S. businesses are often willing to operate on lower margins than businesses in other nations. As long as local businesses do not provide Internet shoppers with reasons to shop domestically—and price is the most-often quoted reason for purchasing online—they may pursue the lower prices, better service, and greater variety on U.S. Web sites.

- *The lack of a strong presence in catalogue shopping.* Catalogue shopping has similar infrastructure needs as Internet shopping. The most important are a customer service infrastructure (such as call centers) and delivery capacity (which may be underdeveloped due to low population density or the relative lack of competition in parcel delivery). Parallel networks have allowed U.S. firms to get into the e-business market faster.

The recent mobile phone technology has the ability to bypass existing marketing institutions. E-marketing and Web 2.0 will not only change marketing practices but will also change customer behavior. Customers will increasingly play an active role in modifying product features. Such a role will likely differ across geographic regions, depending on incomes and access to infrastructure. Meanwhile, shopping times will be extended as consumers access marketing opportunities 24-7. E-business has changed traditional patterns of internationalization, particularly in facilitating the creation of international cooperative networks. No longer does a firm have to own and operate a facility in another country in order to ensure that it can control that subsidiary's production. Of particular importance is the ability of firms to link business decisions with suppliers located anywhere in the world. These linkages may be achieved in a very brief time period; so the time profile of internationalization is changed, as well as the organizational structure. Instead of following a sequential country-by-country process, internationalization of the firm may follow a far more rapid and pervasive pattern. E-business has facilitated the rapid expansion of services exports and has reduced the need for the creation of a physical presence in whatever countries one wishes to do business. As e-business in the United States becomes more competitive, American firms look to other countries as a land of opportunity. A host of new entrepreneurial U.S. corporations are now offering e-business services globally.

In discussing social forces, Javalgi, Martin, and Todd (2004) use Hofstede's five cultural dimensions to explain the differences in basic adoption of e-business among nations. Japan, for example, is described as a collectivist culture with high uncertainty avoidance and large power-distance. Consequently, the greater risks that are involved in e-business would lead one to expect that the adoption of e-business will be slower in Japan than in some other countries. The dependence of e-business on human capital in general and various skills in particular can also explain differences among countries in the adoption of e-business. Related to this social capital perspective is the need to engage in organizational adaptation, which itself requires leadership and vision, as well as the entrepreneurial spirit necessary for ongoing changes. As one considers this wide variety of issues underlying the digital divide, one can see that for a nation and its government to create an e-business economy requires a widespread set of changes in business culture and public policies.

E-MARKET SEGMENTATION

In this new business environment, firms confront a series of issues that must be addressed in new and different ways. Among these are questions in regard to market segmentation. A clearer differentiation among customers may be possible on the basis of various factors such as demographics, the process of consumer buying decisions, specific situations related to specific purchases, and qualities related to products. In this process, customers can be targeted more precisely with a set of offers geared directly to their previous consumption patterns and their individual interests. Rather than a traditional uniform presentation to all customers entering a physical store, a firm's Web site today can offer what each customer wants. Consumers can take the initiative in accessing exactly what they want and in joining the "fan" base of certain firms. These new realities require that the firm significantly change its advertising and marketing strategy.

For e-business, differences in the speed and capacity of the local loop also create distinctive market segments that require different strategies. The degree of e-business success may therefore differ among geographical regions: urban versus rural, large business versus small- and medium-sized business, and differing preferences among consumers. Other forces add to the market segmentation created by the disparities in speed and capacity of the local loop among cities and regions. Higher-income households are much more likely to use computer communications than lower-income households. Internet usage also increases with the educational level of households. The under-55 age group uses the Internet much more than older people. People who live in cities make greater use of the Internet than do people in rural areas. Usage rates may also vary according to one's ethnic and cultural background. Developing an appropriate e-business strategy therefore requires a detailed study of these market segmentations. A blanket approach will fail to maximize profits, as some potential e-consumers are left out of reach or are targeted with inappropriate advertising. To be most effective, advertising messages—and even the range of products offered—will have to vary depending on a wide range of population characteristics. Since economies of scale and scope are critical for generating a satisfactory return on investment in e-commerce infrastructure, it is likely that e-business will concentrate on areas with higher population densities and higher incomes, leaving some regions behind in this transformation.

ETHICAL AND SOCIAL ISSUES

Information technologies enhance capabilities to collect data and to store it, analyze it, and then disseminate it. At the same time, the value of information has been increasing. Consequently, new information technologies have created new ethical issues that all businesses must now confront, and the resolution of these issues is in many cases not straightforward. Increasingly, individuals are voluntarily providing information about themselves, their purchases, their interests, and their finances to a host of businesses. Furthermore, businesses have the ability today to gather information without individuals being aware of this process. In particular, "cookies" can provide a means for monitoring consumer preferences over time, as well as user names and passwords. Businesses now have the opportunity to sell information that they have collected to other businesses. As a result of these new IT capabilities, there are new risks of invasion of individual privacy. As part of the privacy challenges, the question of ethics is joined by the concept of trust, as businesses may enhance their success through policies that encourage individuals to trust them in regard to the use of information gathered from them. Furthermore, transactions conducted over the Internet require trust that all parties will perform their part of the bargain. Peace, Weber, Hartzel, and Nightingale (2002) conclude that

> It is imperative that individual, organization, and social ethical concerns are considered, to preempt a serious breach of society's ethics and norms. Many businesses and organizations may simply act on the profit motive, with little consideration of the long-term ethical considerations of their actions. (p. 58)

Stead and Gilbert (2001) add a more detailed examination of a series of social issues, including

> Security concerns, spamming, Web sites that do not carry an "advertising" label, cyber squatters, online marketing to children, conflicts of interest, manufacturers competing with intermediaries online, and "dinosaurs." (p. 75)

There is a need to be clear with customers that information gained from them will not be used for purposes other than those that have been specifically indicated. The individual has a basic right to information security that prevents other uses. From this perspective, each business has an obligation to receive explicit permission for specific uses. Furthermore, each business has an obligation to ensure that information that it has obtained is not stolen and used by others. Generally, businesses do not label Web sites as advertising, nor do they identify the source of their content. This may confuse users in regard to the evaluation of material that they see, so businesses have a new responsibility in terms of clarifying the honesty and truthfulness of the information that they convey. The practice of "spamming" raises the ethical issue of whether individuals should be sent unsolicited information and the terms and conditions under which a business may engage in such activities. An individual has a right to "freedom from intrusion." Here again, each business should ask customers' permission to communicate further with them.

In recent years, "identity theft" has become an increasing concern. With so much information about an individual having been put on databases, it is now possible for criminals to collect and compile enough information to create new credit cards and other forms of identification. The individual may suddenly find that he or she has been billed for products and services that they never ordered.

The Clinton administration advocated self-regulation for the Internet. At a minimum, it suggested that (1) business must develop and post prominent, clearly written policies that inform consumers about the identity of the collector of their personal information, along with intended uses of this information; and (2) consumers must have a readily available, simple and affordable opportunity for exercising choice with respect to whether and how their personal information is used. (Stead & Gilbert, 2001, p. 80)

Individuals have often registered familiar names in order to own a domain address, and they may offer to sell the address to a particular organization. The rights of existing firms to domain names has become a significant legal issue with ethical implications. Web sites have created new ethical challenges in regard to access by children. The concept of censorship, either by the government or by parents, has become an important subject. Apart from this, a Web site operator may attempt to collect personal information from a child, so the use and disclosure of information has become more challenging. These issues relate in particular to Web sites that contain violence or pornography, but they also relate to the temptations created for children in relating with a commercial Web site.

THE ROLE OF GOVERNMENT IN FACILITATING E-BUSINESS

The success of Internet marketing depends on the degree to which each nation has been able to institute and enforce legislation that deals successfully with the challenges noted in the above section concerning ethical and social issues. Consumer protection must rest on legislation that punishes unfair and deceptive trade practices. Legislation must protect the privacy of consumers, restricting the use of data that are obtained from online business transactions. The subject of damage to brand reputation becomes more complex when an individual with a complaint can communicate with thousands of other potential customers in ways that may defame or disparage a particular firm. Other legal issues include the terms and conditions for linking among Web sites and for advertising on such linked Web sites. The protection of intellectual property also becomes more important and more complex in an e-business world. Trademark infringement becomes more difficult to trace. These issues place new burdens on management to set high standards for the firm and to recognize the rights of others, quite apart from the legal provisions.

It is evident that the evolution of international Internet marketing is years ahead of the law's ability to handle it. Current law subjects marketers to a patchwork of domestic and international laws, standards, and regulations, many of which are inconsistent and contradictory. This status of the law, combined with the increasing use of e-commerce, especially in emerging and transitional economies, implies legal uncertainty is likely to increase in the future for Internet marketers. (Zugelder, Flaherty, & Johnson, 2000, p. 271)

In many nations, it is necessary that regulatory procedures and legal frameworks be changed. Internet access varies significantly in terms of speed and capacity across nations and regions within them. Most governments have regulatory structures that impact or determine various aspects of costs and prices, such as the connection fees that new entrants must pay to the owners of the main telecom or cable trunk systems. Availability and price can create distinct market segments that may limit the overall success of e-business. Most nations compare unfavorably with the United States and Europe in regard to e-business infrastructure. In understanding the need for new government policies, one must consider the differences among countries on many dimensions—for example, the relative lack of venture capital when compared to the United States. With these issues as well, government policies will have to play an important role if a nation is to become e-business competitive.

A key question concerns how governments can enhance competition in the telecom infrastructure to further reduce prices and foster more rapid innovation. The expansion and success of all e-business will depend on the creation of viable competition in the telecom market. For many countries, a serious bottleneck in the e-business revolution occurs in the local loop, making capacity enhancement in the local loop an important issue for all countries in the 21st century. The lack of local loop bandwidth represents a severe constraint. Advertisements with a high multimedia content take longer to download, often annoying users. Advertisers and marketers must keep these issues in mind when developing online promotions, creating online ads that consumers will be able to download with slower modems. The unfortunate reality is that ads without high multimedia content, though easier to download, are not as effective.

At this point in time, it is not clear how the constriction in the local loop can best be overcome. For traditional telecoms, DSL (digital subscriber line) offers more carrying capacity on existing copper wires. However, it deteriorates with distance, and signals interfere with one another if more than a limited number of customers are covered in each neighborhood. Wireless and satellite technologies may encounter weather difficulties and may need "line-of-sight" with customers. In all likelihood, there will be a variety of solutions, each geared to certain market niches. One important emerging alternative is the Internet on cable. However, the long-term prospects of this medium are uncertain. Most nations' cable industries cover only a portion of the population and require huge capital outlays in order to provide optimal "broadband" access. Despite the attraction of cable modems, current take-up rates remain low in many countries, and prices may still be expensive compared to (albeit slow) telephone Internet access. For many, affordability remains a key issue.

Investing in Biotech Innovations

THE BIOTECH REVOLUTION

The biotech sector illustrates an additional set of management issues that accompany the new knowledge economy. The R&D process in the pharmaceutical industry is changing dramatically. Whereas blockbuster drugs were developed as general treatments for common conditions, it is becoming increasingly apparent that not all patients react in the same ways to these drugs, and some—although a very small percentage—suffer serious side effects. Advances in medical science reveal that illnesses that look identical under the microscope can be very different when examined at the molecular and genetic level. This perspective is leading to the creation of a much larger number of niche drugs, each targeted at a narrower group of patients. Related to this development is the growth of biopharma, in which new biotech companies are creating drugs that can attack specific cells that are diseased or specific cell characteristics that make a cell vulnerable to a disease. A new industry sector has developed that is called biopharmaceutical, consisting of both biotechnology and pharmaceutical firms. The sequencing of the human genome is expected to facilitate the development of new drugs, although the relationship between genes and disease remains a complexity that has delayed the application of this new body of knowledge. There has also been a shift toward direct-to-customer (DTC) advertising, including the proliferation of information on the Internet, in addition to the traditional sales process of visits to family doctors.

The new biological individualized therapy model contrasts sharply with the chemical-based, blockbuster, trial-and-error testing model of traditional Big Pharma. The biotech model involves a shift to more precise disease segmentation in order to understand differences among patients and the development of drugs targeting subpopulations with specific disease states. Successful biotechs focus on narrow portfolios. They retain an entrepreneurial culture with the innovative features of a small company.

THE NEED FOR STRATEGIC ALLIANCES IN NEW BIOTECH VENTURES

Drug discovery has become more science-intensive, with increased emphasis on understanding physiology at the molecular level that can lead to rational drug design. Consequently, the nature of biotechnology research increases the importance of business relationships with publicly funded institutes and university researchers. In these partnerships, governments are providing funding that can aid the private sector's R&D and hence can increase future profits. Countries have struggled with the question of designing the optimal financial arrangements for these public-private partnerships. In the United States, formal contracts have become increasingly common, in which cost sharing is specified and the rights to patent the innovations from the collaborative research are also specified. Many firms straddle the divide between for-profit research and not-for-profit research, with academic scientists playing an important role in the founding of these companies. In the United States, the Bayh-Dole Act has relaxed barriers to licensing of successful discoveries by universities and others who have participated in government-sponsored research. Most biotech firms specialize in selling their innovations in leading-edge specialty technology to Big Pharma firms. By the year 2005, seven anti-cancer drugs that had originated in biotechnology research had achieved blockbuster status: MabThera, Gilvec, Eloxatine, Gemzar, Casodex, Taxotere, and Zometa.

In the United States, the government-owned National Institutes of Health (NIH) have funded over one third of biomedical research, while nonprofit organizations have funded 5% to 10%, and private sector firms have funded less than 60%. The NIH is composed of 27 institutes and centers, and these provide financial support to researchers in every U.S. state and also researchers in other countries (www.nih.gov). The Foundation of the NIH (FNIH) is an additional government agency that fosters collaborative relationships between the NIH, industry, academia, and nonprofit organizations. The FNIH also supports research, training, and educational programs.

The first public biotech firm, Genentech, was created for the purpose of commercializing scientific advances at Stanford University and the University of California. The rapidly expanding use of university-biotechnology firm alliances has posed a dilemma in regard to the allocation of ownership and control rights in regard to an innovation. Within this struggle, firms that are financially constrained may tend to surrender more ownership of the innovation to alliance partners than might otherwise be justified. At the same time, there can be serious instances of information asymmetry where one alliance partner may take advantage of another simply on the basis that it has more accurate information about the innovation. As a result of these challenges concerning ownership and control, Rothaermel and Deeds (2004) suggest that there seems to be a gradual tendency to substitute internal resources for external resources. However, participation in alliances enables a firm to have more products in development, as well as more products on the market, than it could have on its own. A firm requires different types of knowledge at different stages of the commercialization process, and this can explain the need for multiple partnerships. Nevertheless, considerable transaction costs exist in identifying a suitable alliance partner and in negotiating, managing, and monitoring an alliance. The authors also conclude that "different types of alliances are motivated by different goals, achieve different outcomes, and are best employed at different stages of development" (p. 220).

GOVERNMENT FINANCIAL ASSISTANCE

Many governments within Europe and North America offer programs of financial assistance to pharmaceutical firms, generally related to their R&D expenditures. For some countries, widely available R&D tax credits are of substantial value to pharmaceutical firms. A particular concern of governments has to do with the encouragement of R&D for illnesses that afflict only a small number of patients. It might not be in the interests of a pharmaceutical firm to undertake R&D for such illnesses based on financial analyses alone. However, many of these so-called "orphan drugs" have become blockbusters when it has been found that they could benefit a much wider array of patients than had originally been thought. In the United States, for example,

> The U.S. Orphan Drug Act gives tax benefits and exclusive marketing privileges to applicants for new drug approvals related to products that would otherwise be uneconomic to discover and bring to market. It identified qualifying products as those with expected patient populations of less than 200,000. It has been suggested that industry has incorrectly obtained orphan drug designations on more prevalent forms of cancer, AIDS, and asthma. . . . In light of "blockbuster orphans," Congressman Waxman, sponsor of the original legislation, sought amendments to limit benefits for profitable orphans. (Lanjouw, 2002, p. 5)

GOVERNMENT PRICE REGULATION

There is clearly a tradeoff between two important public health goals: public access to existing drugs and the maintenance of financial incentives and capital to create new drugs. Big Pharma has defended its high prices and profits on the basis that only these prices and profits can fund the necessary R&D. However, many stakeholders have become critical of this argument. While global spending on R&D has risen substantially in recent years, the number of new drugs being approved each year has fallen. In most countries, governments have assumed major responsibility for repayment of the cost of drugs, so they have developed various programs for limiting their total expenditure on drugs. Most important is the establishment of approved drug lists with the requirement that doctors prescribe only the medications on that list. In deciding which drugs should be included in its list for repayment, a government examines the benefits and costs of various competing medications. These calculations may change over time as more data become available concerning health outcomes and negative side effects. In deciding whether to include a particular drug on its list, a government calculates the cost to the health care system if the patient does not receive this particular medication. Government approval requires not just evidence of successful outcomes but also detailed financial analyses indicating that overall government health care expenditures could be reduced if it adds the drug to its approved list.

In the process of price setting, many governments divide drugs into therapeutic groups or categories and assign a single reference price to all drugs falling into each therapeutic group or category. Increasingly, governments are including both patented and generic medications in the same category with the same reference price. Germany and the Netherlands have established pricing systems that are regarded as most disadvantageous for patented drugs, with each therapeutic group being relatively large. In contrast, many other European countries such as Denmark, France, Portugal, Spain, and Sweden have established more narrowly defined therapeutic groups that permit less price competition from generics. Differences in price regulation among nations have led to substantial "parallel trade" in which drugs manufactured in the United States or Europe have been exported and then imported back into the United States or Europe at the lower prices established by other governments.

THE DRUG DIVIDE

Globally, an issue of increasing concern has been the failure of Big Pharma to assist the residents of less developed countries in coping with their health problems. The United States, Western Europe, and Japan consume more than 85% of the world's total production of pharmaceuticals. Consequently, the large pharmaceutical firms focus on the health issues of greatest concern to people living in the rich, advanced nations, ignoring the widespread diseases of less developed countries. Vaccines to prevent common diseases are readily available to children in the rich nations but have been scarce in the less developed countries. Big Pharma have concentrated their marketing efforts on medical doctors and created distribution networks through pharmacies in the rich nations.

The less developed countries (LDCs) contain most of the world's population, but their illnesses are the focus of relatively little R&D. It has been estimated that 18% of the total global disease burden is accounted for by pneumonia, diarrheal disease, and tuberculosis (TB)—widespread illnesses in less developed countries—but only 0.2% of global health-related expenditures are devoted to these afflictions. Vaccines are not readily available in LDCs to provide protection against common illnesses, and problems of storage and distribution have created barriers to widespread usage. There is a need for better drugs and vaccines to treat HIV/AIDS, TB, and malaria. A major concern of LDCs is the fact that their residents cannot afford the high prices of patented drugs. Income levels are simply too low. Recognizing this reality, some pharmaceutical firms charge substantially lower prices in the LDCs. Many nations are permitting local generic production in an effort to reduce prices. For managers in the knowledge economy, the biotech sector illustrates many new challenges that complicate international trade and investment decisions.

Investing in Environmental Innovations

BECOMING A SUSTAINABLE ENTERPRISE

In their book *The Green Capitalists: Industry's Search for Environmental Excellence*, Elkington and Burke (1987) discuss a wide range of products that manufacturers have dramatically changed in response to sustainable development concerns. They indicate how such innovations and modifications have benefited the organizations that have introduced them.

> From lighter cans to jet engines which are cleaner, quieter and more fuel-efficient, industry is coming up with new generations of products which are beginning to win significant shares of existing markets and also look set to open up enormous new markets. In the age of the microchip, too, a degree of "intelligence" can be built into many products, cutting their energy consumption and pollution output. (p. 130)

Porter and van der Linde (1995) argue that "properly designed environmental standards can trigger innovations that lower the total cost of a product or improve its value" (p. 120). A government can play an important role in enhancing the international competitiveness of firms in its jurisdiction by implementing regulations that impose increasingly more stringent requirements for environmental performance. There need not be a trade-off between ecology and the economy. "Policy makers, business leaders, and environmentalists have focused on the static cost impacts of environmental regulation and have ignored the more important offsetting productivity benefits from innovation" (p. 121). Government regulation should be designed to encourage risk taking and experimentation rather than being based on a particular existing technology. Pollution is a sign that a firm has used its resources "incompletely, inefficiently, or ineffectively," (p. 122) so the reduction of pollution can increase the firm's profits.

ANALYZING OPPORTUNITIES FOR SUSTAINABILITY

Porter and van der Linde (1995) present three sets of recommendations for managers. First, managers should carefully measure the firm's environmental impacts, both directly in its production processes and indirectly throughout its life cycle, from activities of its suppliers through usage by its customers to the ultimate disposal of its products. Second, managers should calculate the cost of the firm's waste throughout its life cycle and the profit increases that may be achieved through waste reduction. Third, managers should create systems that encourage environmental management within the firm. With the increasing intensity of international competition, this paradigm shift has become essential for all nations. "Developing countries that stick with reserve-wasting methods and forgo environmental standards because they are 'too expensive' will remain uncompetitive, relegating themselves to poverty" (p. 133).

Geyer and Jackson (2004) have presented a supply loop framework as a new management tool for assessing both the environmental impacts and the economic potential of value-recovery activities. They argue that "forward-looking firms should regard end-of-life management not as a form of organized product disposal but as supply loops, i.e. as strategies to recover economic and environmental value from end-of-life products" (p. 70). Their supply loop analytical framework integrates a series of previously advocated approaches, including reverse logistics, closed-loop supply chains, industrial ecology, and life-cycle assessment. End-of-life management strategies divert products from landfill sites or incineration. Reprocessing these end-of-life products can replace primary resources, often within the firm's supply chain itself. Several constraints exist in the creation of successful supply loops. The firm may have limited access to end-of-life products, there may be limited flexibility of reprocessing, and there may be limited demand for the secondary output. The firm should focus on innovations that may release these constraints through the redesign of the products or through modifications in the processes within the supply loop. Xerox's recovery program for copier cartridges is an example, where "redesign of the cartridge was a key step in this process" (p. 60). A supply chain often consists of many firms, so the supply loop framework must consist of ongoing and active partnerships in the analysis of possible constraints and the subsequent innovation process.

Orsato (2006) argues that eco-efficiency practices, such as the reduction and reuse of waste, byproducts, and energy, can be achieved in virtually every firm. Orsato's recommended category of strategies involves "beyond compliance leadership" that continually seeks to create new advances that can maintain a firm's differentiation from its competitors. Many customers will come to appreciate the firm's ongoing dedication to this objective. Orsato advocates strategies that relate to eco-branding that aims at specific market niches. Customers must be able to see a clear benefit, such as cost savings or better performance. Innovations may also achieve cost leadership. He cites the example of a firm that manufactures packaging. Its innovations in packaging involve substituting calcium carbonate or chalk for polyolefins or plastics, making the packaging potentially degradable. These innovations have greatly reduced the environmental impact and also have reduced costs to a level 25% less than competitors' packaging.

Most MNEs now perform environmental audits that can indicate the firm's success in achieving environmental objectives, providing both shareholders and the general public with an array of environmental reports on a regular basis. However, conceptual problems, as well as practical measurement problems, may still cloud many of the reports. For example, the cost of closing and restoring a mine site or an oil field at some uncertain time in the future is difficult to predict. Consequently, provisions for the future costs cannot be entered with much precision in the firm's annual financial statements. For some activities, an environmental audit provides quantities of emissions such as tons of sulphur dioxide or liters of liquid effluent. Yet science may not yet be able to conclude what levels could create a specific degree of risk to human health. Because of reasons such as these, managers may confront a series of moving targets in regard to evaluating progress toward the firm's environmental objectives.

THE KYOTO PROTOCOL

When it featured the Kyoto Protocol, *Time* magazine dramatically warned that "except for nuclear war or a collision with an asteroid, no force has more potential to damage our planet's web of life than global warming" ("Feeling the Heat," 2001, p. 16). In 1997, representatives from more than 160 nations met in Kyoto, Japan, to negotiate an agreement that would limit greenhouse gas emissions in the developed nations, pursuant to the objectives of the Framework Convention on Climate Change of 1992. The result of this meeting was the Kyoto Protocol—an agreement among the developed nations to limit their greenhouse gas emissions, relative to the levels emitted in 1990. Under the protocol, 38 industrialized countries—but not the less developed countries—agreed to reduce their overall emissions to between 6% and 8% below 1990 levels by 2012, with a range of specific reduction requirements for different countries. The United States signed the protocol in 1998 but by 2001 refused to ratify it. Since the United States generates 20% of the world's global warming gases, without U.S. ratification many have feared the protocol has been limited in effectiveness.

For the objectives of the Kyoto Protocol to be achieved, a greater emphasis on renewable energy sources will be required since fossil fuels are a major contributor to global warming. Kolk and Pinkse (2008) analyze a range of business responses to new government and customer pressures concerning greenhouse gas emissions. In Europe, the creation of emission trading schemes has provided managers with the opportunity to choose between various kinds of innovation and investments and the purchase of certified emission reduction (CER) credits. Kolk and Pinkse have studied the responses to a survey of the world's 500 largest companies, where measurement scales relate to six kinds of strategies. "Process improvement" responses range from not mentioning the subject to achieving concrete results. "Internal transfer of emission reductions" range from not mentioning internal reduction targets to having targets for the whole organization and procedures for transferring emission credits between business units as a way of reaching the overall targets. "Product development" ranges from not mentioning the subject to having a product innovation policy, together with concrete examples. "Supply-chain measures" range from no measures to get suppliers to reduce their emissions to specific emission evaluation and/or targets for the supply chain. "New product/market combinations" range from no mention of the subject to actual partnerships having been established or new markets having been entered. "Acquisition of emission credits" ranges from opposition to the concept of emission trading to actual involvement in this market mechanism. Kolk and Pinkse conclude that there are many dimensions along which new management paradigms are being created and that firms differ significantly in their progress along each dimension.

"GREEN ELECTRICITY": NEW RENEWABLES

Electricity generation has become a central focus for all who are concerned about global warming and about government regulations and consumer preferences related to global warming. Traditional generation technologies have been major contributors to greenhouse gas emissions, but new technologies promise substantial reductions. Consequently, the choice among alternative generation technologies has become a vibrant public issue in many countries, as has the innovation process that may result in ongoing improvements. In many jurisdictions, both firms and individuals now face choices concerning the purchase of electricity from alternative generation technologies, and increasingly they face investment opportunities in new types of "green energy." This electricity revolution is impacting all managers as they consider these choices and opportunities.

While combustion of coal is used in many different industrial processes, combustion for the purpose of generating electricity is the single-largest contributor to the emission of global warming gases into the atmosphere. Concerns about pollution and global warming in particular have created a market for the so-called "new renewables," including solar, wind, biomass, and geothermal. Although these technologies have formed only a miniscule percentage of global electrical generating capacity in the past, they are the most rapidly growing. Solar energy technology consists of thermal applications for home heating and photovoltaic (PV), which is used to generate electricity. While the cost of energy generated by solar PV has decreased substantially since the 1970s, it is still not competitive with wind energy on a kWh basis. Like wind energy, solar PV is particularly attractive in developing regions of the world, where there is a need for electrical capacity that can be implemented rapidly.

In 2007, Credit Suisse and the Economist Intelligence Unit collaborated in writing a series of articles on renewable energy. These articles point to wind as the lowest-cost renewable energy, with costs of 4 to 7 U.S. cents per kilowatt-hour. A series of innovations has reduced wind energy costs from as much as 30 U.S. cents per kilowatt-hour just 10 years previous. It is expected that further innovations will continue to reduce these costs and extend the geographical limitations of wind energy. While several experimental wind turbines were developed for electricity generation throughout the mid-1900s, large-scale government R&D efforts did not begin until the global oil crisis of 1973. These R&D efforts focused on developing larger wind turbines with the aim of achieving greater economies of scale. In the late 1970s, governments began to develop incentives for wind-generated electricity. In the United States, this took the form of the National Energy Act, which encouraged the conservation and development of domestic energy resources. Federal tax credits combined with California state tax incentives spawned a California wind energy boom of the early 1980s.

Political support for wind energy development also exists in many other countries. In Canada, the Canadian Renewable and Conservation Expense regulations give wind energy developers preferential tax treatment on expenses related to the development of projects, as well as accelerated depreciation on installed equipment. The German government in 1991 instituted its Renewable Energy Feed-In Tariff, which guaranteed a set price for electricity generated from wind. In the United Kingdom, wind energy development has been driven by the Non-Fossil Fuel Obligation, a law passed under the 1989 Electricity Act. This legislation obligates Regional Electricity Companies to purchase specified amounts of renewable energy.

A further environmental driver of wind energy is that of market demand. The deregulation of the power generation industry worldwide is leading consumers to increase their knowledge of how electricity is generated. Where consumers have increased knowledge of generation sources and a choice between those sources, some are more likely to choose clean electricity from renewable sources such as wind. In North

America, this has spawned green-power marketing programs—in the United States by 2000, there were more than 150 utilities offering consumers wind-generated electricity at a premium price (*Wind Energy Weekly*, 2000). The high demand for green power places further demands on utilities for new wind-generating capacity.

Another significant force is the prevailing interest rate. The upfront capital cost of a wind energy project is about twice as high as that of an equal capacity gas-fired power plant. This means that an increase in the interest rate would adversely affect the cost of electricity from a wind power facility compared with a gas-fired plant. Wind energy advocates argue that a "social discount rate" should be used when comparing the costs of various forms of electricity-generating capacity, rather than the market rate of interest. While it cannot be calculated precisely, the social discount rate would be no higher than the rate a government would pay on long-term bonds. Some believe that the interest rate used in cost comparisons should be even less than the government rate to reflect the heavy costs future generations will incur as a result of the global warming caused by fossil fuels.

Deregulation has complicated the profitability of energy investments. In 1998, California, like many other American states and other countries, opened its electricity industry to competition. The resulting industry uncertainty inhibited investment in new power capacity, which—combined with the severe increase in the price of natural gas, used in many electricity-generating plants—caused cost spikes and blackouts in California. In addition, price regulation placed California's two largest electricity utilities on the verge of bankruptcy, causing many to reconsider the rationale behind breaking up the traditional power monopoly. Deregulation of electricity markets has not been confined to the United States. In the European Union for example, the United Kingdom was the first country to deregulate its electricity market, beginning in 1989. By 1996, Sweden, Norway, and Finland had all initiated the deregulation process and had the intention of integrating their electrical systems. The ultimate goal in the European Union is to create a unified internal electricity market, which will be open to competition and allow for cross-border electricity sales among all member countries.

Deregulation and privatization are opening new opportunities for investors, although the California experience demonstrates the new risks that can accompany this shift toward free markets. Yet the proclaimed goal of California to generate 20% of its power from renewable sources by 2010 provides significant incentives for investors. Meanwhile, the government of China has passed a Law on Renewable Energy which includes the goal of increasing the use of renewable energy to 10% of the national electricity generation by 2010. China's action indicates that investment opportunities for new technologies will be expanding even in countries that are not bound by the Kyoto Protocol.

The three business sectors of e-business, biotech, and environmental illustrate the importance and the challenges of new technologies. The following case focuses on the key role of the telecom sector and e-business in transforming traditional management paradigms to operate within the new economy. Many governments confront the need for new public policies to facilitate this transformation. Yet the ability of firms and governments to move into the new economy can be held back by the social and cultural realities discussed in Part I of this text.

In Practice 6.1	Investing in Telecom and E-Business in a Less Developed Economy

As it entered the 21st century, the Polish government faced the dilemma of how to develop an optimal telecom structure and related services. For decades, a government-owned and operated telecom, TPSA (Telekomunikacja Polska S.A.), had held a monopoly, but in the late 1990s the Polish government gradually allowed the entry of some competitors, many of whom brought new technologies. The government had undertaken a major privatization program throughout the economy, and it faced the question of whether and how it should privatize TPSA. Yet privatization would have to be accompanied by ongoing regulation in order to ensure that managerial decisions were made in the interests of the nation as a whole.

This challenge of continual government intervention could reduce the attractiveness of acquiring TPSA, in spite of its market dominance. For potential foreign investors, a host of additional difficulties appeared to be so severe that perhaps the privatization bidding process should be ignored. Existing infrastructure was largely obsolete, and employees lacked the skills and motivation to transform TPSA into a modern, competitive entity. Meanwhile, alternative modes of entry into the telecom sector might be pursued, and some, like wireless and the Internet, could threaten TPSA's future.

In the new era of e-business, would Poland be able to retain the economic momentum that its 1990s market reforms had created? A new investor could be very discouraged about the prospects for the "new economy" and e-business. The future success of the Polish economy as a whole would depend very much on a transformation in Poland's telecom industry, but would this transformation occur soon? A special report on Poland in "Computer World Top 2000" emphasized that

Another threat is looming on the horizon—the new model of the economy. The development of electronic business, which will most likely become an economic standard in the developed parts of the world, puts Poland in the dramatic pursuit after escaping leaders. Every Polish enterprise must take a long and hard look at itself once again and answer the question: "to which part of the chain of value creation does it want to belong?" How well Poland adopts e-business solutions will dictate whether it will belong to the part of the world that engages in costly production or the part that carries out lucrative distribution.

(Continued)

(Continued)

Poland's leaders had been shifting the nation successfully from communism to free enterprise, and analysts expected that they would continue along the path of transferring decision making to the private sector. Many potential investors recognized the key role to be played by the telecom structure and e-business. Perhaps now was the time to achieve a "first mover advantage." The very low level of Poland's involvement in the new economy and e-business might be seen as an ideal business environment for developing market share and attaining extraordinary profits.

The company generated over US$200 million a year in net profit (TPSA, 1998). The telecom market in Poland could be characterized as extremely underdeveloped, with under 30 fixed lines per 100 inhabitants. TPSA held about 96% of the fixed line telecom service market in Poland (nine million subscribers). But so far TPSA operated uncontested and no company other than TPSA even had a permit to build a true alternative infrastructure. In the future this situation would likely change. The entire Polish market might open up to competition without restrictions. Given that alternative networks existed, such as cable TV, or were in the planning stage, could the company sustain its profitability in the long run?

The Internet market in Poland was still in its infancy. The size of the market was estimated to be between US$50 million and US$55 million annually. E-business was almost nonexistent in Poland. Even though there were more than 300 Web sites offering products and services, their average turnover amounted to only US$12,500 per year. According to Arthur Anderson Consulting, the total turnover on the Internet in 1998 was between US$1 and US$1.50 per person compared to US$30 in the United States ("Computer World," 2000). Most users quoted lack of trust in an online payment security system as a reason for not shopping on the Internet. Fraud seemed to be quite widespread in everyday life and the lack of an efficient legal system to deal with the problem would likely remain a major stumbling block to e-business evolution in Poland.

The attitude toward shopping in general was quite different from that in North America. It was strongly embedded in the Polish culture to shop in person with the possibility to touch and see the products. Catalogue sales did not exist in the past, and so there was no tradition to shop this way either ("Computer World," 2000). Furthermore, for e-business to develop properly, an efficient payment system had to exist. Only 6% of Poland's population had a credit card. The great majority of cardholders did not use them because of the interest charges and widespread fraud involving credit cards.

In addition, only 35% of the country's population had a bank account and almost everyone preferred to pay cash for products and services ("Computer World," 2000). Moreover, the banking system in Poland was insufficient to support online transactions.

On the 22nd of May, 2000, the government of Poland named France Telecom as a winner of the bidding process. Analysts estimated that France Telecom paid approximately US$5 billion for a 35% stake in TPSA. France Telecom had an option to buy an additional 16% of the company, thus eventually achieving a controlling stake in the Polish national carrier.

SOURCE: Conklin and Siwak (2001).

Critical Thinking Questions

1. Evaluate the likely time profile for the future adoption of e-business in the Polish economy.

2. What should the Polish government do to stimulate and facilitate e-business?

3. Assess the future competitive position of TPSA in the context of potential new entrants with new technologies. Did France Telecom pay too high a price, at $5 billion for a 35% stake?

References and Suggested Readings

Computer world Polska, top 2000. (2000, May). *Polski Rynek Informatyczny i Telekomunikacyjny.*

Conklin, D. W., & Siwak, M. (2001). *Privatizing Poland's telecom industry: Opportunities and challenges in the new economy of e-business (A).* London: Ivey. (Ivey Case No. 9B00M023)

Elkington, J., & Burke, T. (1987). *The green capitalists: Industry's search for environmental excellence.* London: Victor Gollancz.

Feeling the heat: Global warming. (2001, April 9). *Time,* 16.

Geyer, R., & Jackson, T. (2004). Supply loops and their constraints: The industrial ecology of recycling and reuse. *California Management Review, 46,* 55–73.

Javalgi, R., Martin, C., & Todd, P. (2004). The export of e-services in the age of technology transformation: Challenges and implications for international service providers. *Journal of Services Marketing, 18*(7), 560–573.

Javalgi, R., & Ramsey, R. (2001). Strategic issues of e-commerce as an alternative global distribution system. *International Marketing Review, 18*(4), 376–391.

Kolk, A., & Pinkse, J. (2008). A perspective on multinational enterprises and climate change: Learning from "an inconvenient truth"? *Journal of International Business Studies, 39*(8), 1359–1378.

Lanjouw, J. (2002, July). *Beyond TRIPS: A new global patent regime* (Policy Brief No. 3). Washington, DC: Center for Global Development.

Orsato, R. (2006). Competitive environmental strategies: When does it pay to be green? *California Management Review, 48*(2), 127–143.

Peace, A., Weber, J., Hartzel, K., & Nightingale, J. (2002). Ethical issues in e-business: A proposal for creating the e-business principles. *Business and Society Review, 107*(1), 41–60.

Porter, M. E., & van der Linde, C. (1995). Green and competitive: Ending the stalemate. *Harvard Business Review, 73*(45), 120–134.

Rayport, J., & Jaworski, B. (2001). *E-commerce.* New York: McGraw-Hill Higher Education.

Rothaermel, F., & Deeds, D. (2004). Exploration and exploitation alliances in biotechnology: A system of new product development. *Strategic Management Journal, 25,* 201–221.

Rowley, W. (2002). Biotechnology overview: Applications and forecasts. *Foresight, 4*(4), 4–12.

Stead, B., & Gilbert, J. (2001). Ethical issues in electronic commerce. *Journal of Business Ethics, 34*(2), 75–85.

Telekomunikacja Polska S.A. (1998). *TPSA annual report.* Poland: Author.

Wind Energy Weekly. (2000, June 30). *19*(903).

Zugelder, M., Flaherty, T., & Johnson, J. (2000). Legal issues associated with international Internet marketing. *International Marketing Review, 17*(3), 253–271.

Part III

Economic Forces

Industry Structure as a Determinant of Profitability

7

CHAPTER LEARNING OBJECTIVES

On completion of this chapter, students should be able to

- analyze each business sector in any nation from the perspective of its industry structure and likely profitability due to this structure,

- evaluate the advantages and disadvantages of outsourcing and offshoring various firm activities,

- analyze the firm's relationships with customers and suppliers from the perspective of how best to stimulate innovation,

- suggest appropriate interfirm governance procedures with suppliers and customers,

- apply these perspectives to the firm's investment decisions.

Managers make decisions concerning investment, prices, and output levels in the context of their industry structure, which can vary from many competitors to just a few competitors or even none. Technological change may be directed toward the ongoing modification of product or service features, quality, and cost, thereby altering an industry structure. Governments can also play a key role in determining industry structures, intervening for a host of reasons. Many of the reasons for government intervention are referred to as "market failures." For example, governments seek to limit negative "externalities" while stimulating activities that could have positive externalities through regulation, taxes, and subsidies, as well as through government ownership. Consequently, the industry structure within which the firm operates may change significantly over time, continually impacting managers' decisions.

As firms and markets extend across national boundaries, the industry structures become more complex, often differing among nations in important dimensions. The degree of competition in a firm's home country market may be more intense than the degree of competition in certain other nations. The asymmetry of information among market participants may differ. The level of costs and the relationships between cost and output may differ. The nature and degree of government intervention may differ. Nations differ in the factors that underlie international competitiveness, such as skills and education, university research, and infrastructure. Social preferences differ, resulting in varying demand conditions. These realities mean that management faces potential profitability that depends on the particular industry structure in a particular nation. Hence, globalization compels managers to analyze differences among nations in an industry's structure in order for them to make optimal investment choices among nations.

Until recently, the size of a firm was largely determined by the transaction costs and transportation costs that would arise if activities were conducted in separate firms. As Chapter 6 discusses, the telecommunications revolution has reduced transaction costs among firms and has facilitated the interfirm flow of information. The transportation revolution has reduced shipment costs, as has the decrease in physical components as a percentage of the final value of a good or service. The nature of economies of scale has changed as a result of these transformations. While final assembly and marketing still leave a role for large corporations, autonomous business units are now able to integrate their planning without the need to be part of a single firm. Increasingly, managers must decide whether to outsource certain activities to a vendor, perhaps located in a different nation. For such interrelated firms, profits depend on stimulating and coordinating continuous improvement among a wide array of individual business units located in various nations.

The simplest traditional value chain was one in which a firm supplied parts to an assembler who then sold to a retailer or an end user. However, increasingly, the multinational connections a firm has with its suppliers, their suppliers, and its customers is more like an interconnected web rather than a sequential chain. A chain implies a unidirectional exchange along a distinct flow, whereas a web suggests the interconnectedness and multidirectional, multilevel relationships that can lead to better and faster innovations. For many firms, innovation today requires that all parties interact on an ongoing, extended basis. If the initial producers of components know the needs of the ultimate users of their products, they can better design for those purposes. If there is an ongoing exchange of information, all parties can benefit from decreased development times and assured market acceptance. For these reasons as well, the nature and boundaries of an industry can change continually.

Competition

In a highly competitive market, new entrants increase the industry's output until price decreases to a level where profit tends to be eliminated. Firms achieve a return on their capital and incomes for their employees and managers, but profits above these levels tend to be competed away. There are so many competitors that any individual firm cannot alter the market price through its decisions. In these markets, management decisions do not alter the behavior of competitors, so decisions are made independently of competitors' possible reactions. In the perfectly competitive market, firms ignore their competitors' strategies; a firm cares only about the price, and since any given competitor is small relative to the market, the action of any one competitor is irrelevant for a firm.

In "destructive competition," each firm faces declining marginal costs and the market price may be below the firm's costs at each output level up to full capacity. The firm would leave the industry if it expected that this situation would continue. However, the firm may have reason to believe that the price will rise at some point. Often this situation may occur for certain periods of time or hours of the day. The taxi industry illustrates this type of market situation. With the departure of some firms or a change in demand over time, the price may rise and new firms may enter. This kind of cycle can also lead to arguments for government intervention to set prices or to restrict the number of firms, as it has in the taxi industry in many cities.

In an industry with many competitors, each firm has an incentive to create unique attributes. The firm may strive to reduce costs through the adoption of new technologies, the enhancement of labor efficiency, or the improved sourcing of supplies. Wal-Mart, for example, has created much of its competitive advantage through cost-cutting innovations. An increase in profits depends on the new enhancement of efficiency being unique. If all competitors can copy the cost reduction, then their competition will tend to reduce prices, leaving the profits of each unchanged. Hence, each firm has an ongoing incentive to develop unique methods for cost cutting. If a firm can offer unique products and services, it may be able to raise prices and profit margins above the level that its competitors can achieve. Where service and quality can consist of a range and can be enhanced by adding value, or where attributes such as delivery time, after-sales support, technical assistance, and advice can be important, each firm has an incentive to develop a unique combination of these attributes. Many companies have succeeded in transforming "commodity" products to "value-added" products by changing their characteristics. Each firm strives to create a brand image—a collection of perceived attributes of a product or service that are immediately associated with a particular brand name. The sensitivity of profits to prices means that the successful firm in a competitive industry structure will continually strive to create the impression among consumers that its products and services warrant a higher price. Consequently, the pursuit of innovation and product modification is a central reality in determining the industry structure.

Monopoly

As a single firm in a particular industry, a firm can impact the market price directly by altering the quantity that it supplies to the market. This monopoly power enables the firm to set a price that will maximize its profit without fear of competitors undercutting its price and reducing its market share. From the perspective of profit maximization, a monopoly offers the optimal type of industry structure but brings with it the threat of government regulation. Consumers and the governments that represent them realize that a monopoly structure, with its monopoly prices, should perhaps face regulations in regard to price setting. Hence, for many managers, an ongoing conflict exists between the desire to create a unique product that can result in price increases and the threat of government price regulation that would limit the extra profits derived from this uniqueness. An increasing concern among many governments is that mergers and acquisitions may create monopolies that can raise prices. Chapter 10 examines the attempts by governments to create "competition policies" or "antitrust laws" to place limits on these corporate actions.

Monopoly situations may exist for several reasons:

• Governments may grant monopolies to private firms as an incentive for making investments that are considered to be of strategic interest to the nation. Many hydroelectric companies, telephone networks, and railroads have required monopoly status to ensure the certainty of recouping the enormous investments required to establish them. In such cases, governments have often controlled prices by regulating them directly or by limiting the rate of return that such monopolies can earn.

• A firm may develop monopoly status by dint of its own successes in research and development or in marketing. Government patent and copyright systems may support such monopolies in that they grant the exclusive right for a certain number of years to exploit the development of innovations and/or brand image.

- An industry as a whole may have declining marginal costs over the entire range of industry demand. This might occur, for example, in a transportation sector with high initial fixed costs but low ongoing costs. In this case, it is possible that the entire industry output can be produced at the lowest possible cost by a single firm. Consequently, declining marginal costs can be the basis for a monopoly. Any prospective entrant facing high initial costs might decide not to enter. If it did enter, the existing firm with its larger production would experience lower average and marginal costs than the new entrant and could under price its new rival, presumably driving it out of the industry.

- Governments and their agencies may own and operate monopolies in order to achieve objectives related to national strategic interest or to create an indirect form of taxation or to capture monopoly profits for the society as a whole.

"Oligopoly" and Game Theory

Many industries service a limited geographic scope, so within a particular city or region there may be only a few competitors. In an industry that consists of only a few competitors, referred to as an oligopoly, business decisions can be viewed as a game in the sense that the actions of one participant will impact the profitability of other participants. Decisions must be undertaken based on an evaluation of a series of possible outcomes, where each outcome depends on the reaction of others in the industry. Participants within an industry may be able to increase their firm's added value, or at least its financial profits, by collaborating rather than competing. An integral part of the business environment is shaped by interactions between firms and rival firms, clients, government, contractors, employees, and other economic entities. What all of these entities have in common is that their actions can significantly affect the performance of the firm, and they, in turn, may benefit according to the actions of the firm. Consider the firm and these other entities as players in a game or sequence of games. When the interests of these entities diverge from those of the firm, all of these other players are unlikely to act the way the firm would like them to if it could choose their actions. For example, rival firms may sell at lower prices or government may increase taxes. As a result, the firm must modify its own actions in order to change the actions of the other players, who in turn will choose their own actions to do as well as possible in their game "against" the firm. We can also use this model to think of industries where there are a few large firms or "leaders" and a "competitive fringe" of many small firms.

Even in the early development of the microeconomics literature, some theorists developed simple models where two firms realize that each will react to the price that the other sets. In such models, Firm A observes Firm B's price behavior and may set a price such that B's expected reaction will maximize A's profit. A price war may erupt, but in some models there may be an equilibrium price. Other theorists have focused on "imperfect competition," in which each firm seeks to differentiate its products or services so as to warrant a higher price in the eyes of customers.

In 1994, the Nobel Prize in economics was awarded jointly to John Nash, John Harsanyi, and Richard Selten for their advances in game theory. While insights from their work could be applied in many fields— international politics or military conflicts, for example—industry structure was an obvious subject for the application of their analyses. By developing and using numerous mathematical theorems, they have generalized the set of problems that economists examined earlier in much simpler models based on narrow assumptions. These Nobel Prize winners analyzed games in which there were no predetermined rules to guide decisions. Players could pursue a wide range of possible strategies in response to one another's decisions. Of importance was the ability of one player to see through its rival's strategies. This led the authors to develop a formal theory of bargaining with the possibility of what became known as the "Nash equilibrium." In "cooperative games," firms might discuss the decisions that each might make, and they might even agree on a rational joint plan of action. Under a particular set of assumptions, one firm could make "side payments" to the other in order to encourage certain decisions. However, it might be impossible or illegal for the firms to communicate or collaborate, so each might rely on its observance of the other's reactions.

In 1995, the Nobel Prize in economics was awarded to Robert Aumann and Thomas Schelling for developing extensions of game theory with particular applications in microeconomics. In their work, they analyzed the impacts on outcomes of games when the players adopt strategies of threats and brinkmanship. Some threats might be "credible," while other threats might not. To be credible, a threat generally has to be seen by the opposing firm as being in the best interests of the opponent. If a game consists of situations that are repeated over time, as pricing decisions are, then the firms might adopt a strategy to encourage the opponent to cooperate. One firm might repeatedly punish its opponent for taking a certain position, and over time the opponent's fear of retaliation might ultimately lead to cooperation. A firm might limit its own options as a way of increasing the likelihood that the opponent will back down. A series of credible threats could be a precursor to a situation of brinkmanship. For these theorists, the subject of "repeated games," in which firms have to deal with one another over an indefinite time period, leads to new insights in regard to conflict and cooperation.

The literature of game theory focuses on the many relationships between the decisions of each individual firm, the reactions of competitors, and the implications of these decisions and reactions for the industry as a whole. While game theory deals largely with the reactions among competitors, this analytical framework has been applied to negotiations with suppliers and customers in situations where the number of firms is small enough that the decisions of one may impact the outcomes experienced by others. It has also been applied to relationships between business and government, in which business tries to shape government intervention so as to minimize negative impacts on its profit while government tries to shape its intervention so as to achieve its political objectives.

Changing the Industry Structure

Brandenburger and Nalebuff (1995) have suggested Figure 7.1 as a useful game framework for the analysis of how firms can change the structure of their industries in order to increase their profits.

Figure 7.1   The Value Net

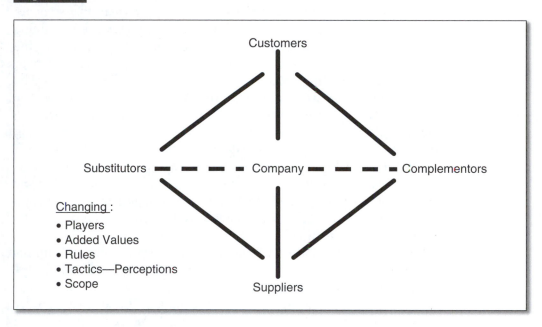

Participants may alter potential outcomes by changing the industry structure in any one or more of a variety of ways. In particular, Brandenburger and Nalebuff (1995) suggest that each firm should use what they refer to as "PARTS as a comprehensive, theory-based set of levers" (p. 71) to help generate strategies. Each letter in the acronym "PARTS" represents a lever for changing the industry structure. A firm may threaten to change the number of players (P) by indicating that it intends to enter an industry. The mere threat may result in compensation being paid to it, thereby altering the allocation of the value added among the participants. A firm may change the "added values" (A) by lowering the perceived added value of others, as well as by increasing its own added value. Advertising may be designed to achieve these changes. A firm may change the rules (R), for example, by developing new pricing policies. A firm may change tactics (T) in ways that alter other player's perceptions and therefore their decisions. A firm may change the scope (S) of the game by severing linkages with other companies or by building new alliances. Unlike analytical frameworks that focus on an existing industry structure, game theory examines the ways that a firm can change the industry structure.

Porter's Five Forces Model

Michael Porter (1980) has created an analytical framework, illustrated in Figure 7.2, through which managers can analyze their industries from the perspective of profitability and how the profit is divided among the firms in the industry. Each firm occupies a link in a value chain that stretches from its suppliers to its customers. For any firm, its relative bargaining power is a key determinant in how the created value is divided among the firm, its suppliers, and its customers. Customers differ in their ability to negotiate lower prices, a process that could reduce the firm's profits. The nature and degree of rivalry among existing competitors can impact the firm's profits, as the firm may have to lower its selling prices in order to compete or raise the prices it pays its suppliers. The relative bargaining power of customers depends on whether substitute products exist such that customers could purchase them instead. It also depends on the likelihood that additional firms could enter the industry to compete. For any firm, its success in negotiating higher profits through paying lower costs to suppliers or through charging higher prices to its customers may not be sustainable if the threat of new entrants is strong.

For Porter (1980), industry structure is not a static concept. With his Five Forces Model, Porter goes beyond the traditional microeconomics literature to focus on the forces that underlie demand and supply. He analyzes how a firm can choose strategies to manipulate these forces in order to maximize its profits. With his Five Forces Model, Porter places more emphasis than microeconomics traditionally has on the role of changes in industry structure over time.

Porter (1980) emphasizes that "the collective strength of these forces determines the ultimate profit potential of an industry" (p. 21). In some industries, these forces are "intense," so the profits of all firms are low, while in other industries, these forces are "mild," so the firm can earn high returns on its investments. Nevertheless, a firm is able to find a position in

Figure 7.2   Porter's Five Forces Model

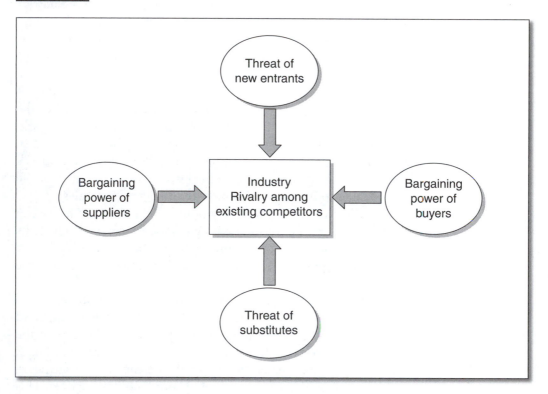

an industry where it can "best defend itself against these forces or can influence them in its favor" (p. 88). Porter's Five Forces Model is a framework for analyzing an industry for the purpose of choosing optimal strategies in order to maximize profits. The following summary points to a number of the features that Porter has discussed in regard to his Five Forces Model.

The intensity of the threat of new entrants to the industry depends on many features of the industry. Economies of scale in required activities from research to production to marketing can deter potential entrants since they will have to make large investments and experience critical losses in order to expand to a volume where their costs will be as low as existing firms. Strong brand identity and loyalty can deter potential entrants since they will require time and expenditures to create an alternative brand. The need for high initial investments can deter all but the largest firms. Incumbents may possess cost advantages for many unique reasons such as the possession of patents or simply due to knowledge gained from experience. The need to create new distribution channels may require time and expenditures. Certain government regulations may also serve as a barrier to entry. Some of these industry features may change over time, altering the threat of new entrants.

The relative bargaining power of the firm vis-à-vis its suppliers also depends on many features of the industry. Suppliers may be more powerful depending on whether they are few in number, whether they offer a unique or differentiated product, whether they compete with substitutes, whether they threaten to integrate forward into the firm's activities, and whether the firm is a major customer.

The relative bargaining power of the firm vis-à-vis its customers depends on whether the buyer is a large-volume customer, whether the product is unique or differentiated, whether the product forms a major component of the buyer's costs, whether the buyer earns low profits, whether the product is important in determining the quality of the buyer's products, whether the product reduces the buyer's costs, and whether the buyer can threaten to integrate backward into the firm's activities.

Substitutes can reduce the bargaining power of the firm and hence can limit its profits. The nature of the existing competition can also limit its profits, depending on whether the products are differentiated, whether competitors can expand their capacity in small increments, or whether the products are perishable.

Porter (1980) argues that each firm should choose its strategies in the context of his Five Forces Model. Over time, the five forces do change, and acquisitions may create discontinuities in the pace of change. Hence, the firm must anticipate relevant trends and adjust its strategies accordingly. For Porter, an important subject in regard to the choice of strategies is whether the firm should diversify into other products and services. This perspective can be extended to the subject of diversification geographically into other countries. Porter's Five Forces differ significantly from one country to another, and these differences in industry structure form an important component of each firm's investment location decisions. Hence, managers must analyze each industry structure in many nations in order to determine where they can maximize their profitability. The analysis of industry structure is essential in developing a global strategy.

When and What Should the Firm Outsource?

A major change in industry structures has involved the outsourcing of certain activities to a vendor that specializes in them and that may offer to undertake these activities for many firms at the same time. In the "make or buy" literature, a core versus noncore dichotomy has suggested that unique activities essential to a firm's competitive advantage are core activities and should not be outsourced, while all other activities should be candidates for outsourcing. A separate argument is that firms that need to cope quickly with strategic impediments may outsource in order to gain certain management expertise that the vendor possesses. In analyzing potential candidates for outsourcing, a common conceptual framework emphasizes transaction costs, asset specificity, and incomplete contracts. Business activities differ in regard to these features, so the outsourcing evaluation will differ among business activities. In particular, if a deliverable can be quantified with certainty, then the contract may be precise enough that risk becomes a minor factor. However, to the degree that an activity cannot be quantified precisely in terms of deliverables, then the risk of uncertain outcomes becomes important, together with ways to mitigate this risk.

Many believe that the activities that define a firm's competitive advantage may be too important to outsource. This view is linked to the resource-based theory of the firm, which argues that the capabilities of a firm are dependent on resources within the firm; so to outsource certain resources might limit any capabilities that depend on them. Some analysts of the outsourcing decision point to other features of importance in choosing activities that could be outsourced. Lepak and Snell (1998) discuss the new role for which they named their book, *Virtual HR: Strategic Human Resource Management in the 21st Century*, a role in which in-house human resources (HR) personnel should focus on organizational change and should work with senior management in business strategy. This role is strengthened if traditional functions are outsourced. In their analysis of various business activities, Lepak and Snell extend the core/noncore focus to include uniqueness. Activities should be categorized both in accordance with their contribution to the firm's core competencies and competitive advantages and also in accordance with the extent to which they are rare in the external market. All activities are candidates for outsourcing except for those possessing both core competence and uniqueness. Other authors focus on the degree to which certain activities entail an interactive relationship with employees and other business units in the firm. Activities with both high strategic value and high relationship features should be kept in-house, while all the remainder are candidates for outsourcing. Also of importance is whether the firm wants to achieve substantial and rapid change in its business processes. A firm- and time-specific need to remove a strategic impediment may be a central determinant in considering "transformational" outsourcing.

Managers have to undertake a dynamic analysis with projections of future circumstances. For example, the nature and extent of projected economies of scale and scope should be analyzed in order to negotiate fair pricing. The number and strength of alternative vendors should be considered in order to determine the possibilities for switching vendors if the buyer becomes dissatisfied with its initial choice of vendor, and also from the perspective of the future negotiating power of the buyer. The outsourcing process itself may improve a firm's benchmarking and target setting—benefits that should be included in the analysis. Finally, a vendor may be able to cope more efficiently with fluctuations in a buyer's demand, enabling a buyer to lay off this risk and turn fixed costs into variable costs—another benefit whose value may differ among firms.

Mitigation of risks emphasizes the importance in the outsourcing decision of factors in addition to price. An International Data Corporation (IDC) white paper sponsored by Cap Gemini Ernst & Young has reported on IDC surveys of 65 senior decision makers in large companies that opted for what they termed "transformational outsourcing." These surveys have found that "customers are evaluating their service providers on much more than price. . . . While price is a factor, it is not among the top reasons for working with one service provider over another" (Goepfert, 2002, p. 19). The white paper concludes that more important issues include responsiveness and customer service, guarantees and service level agreements, ability to enable future business strategies, and expertise within the specific industry.

Buyer and vendor may anticipate ongoing innovation that will improve technologies and practices. Strategy authors recommend that if ongoing innovation is necessary for an outsourced product, then the outsourcing relationship should take the form of a strategic alliance. Product development necessarily entails incomplete contracts with uncertainty and risk, so the issue of trust is emphasized in this context. Related concerns include how best to stimulate innovation and how best to direct innovation in the interests of the firm purchasing the good or service. Ongoing innovation has been significant in information technology (IT), so literature dealing with IT outsourcing has analyzed this partnership perspective and the need for "trust." Both product development and IT literature have studied the nature of the intercorporate governance structure as a crucial determinant of outsourcing success. Consequently, risk mitigation focuses to a large degree on the interfirm processes and structures for joint decision making and dispute resolution and the cultures and capabilities that are necessary for a successful strategic alliance.

A considerable literature has developed in regard to "clusters" that are geographically concentrated in particular regions, and some authors have focused on the advantages of geographic proximity. For example, Mick Carney (1998) in the article "The Competitiveness of Networked Production: The Role of Trust and Asset Specificity" has suggested that "proximity fosters norms of trust because there is a greater probability of future interaction among neighbouring businesses and because reputation signals are more reliably transmitted over short distances" (p. 460). With the 21st century, an important subject will be the development of interfirm organizational structures that can achieve such trust without geographical concentration.

Future needs are uncertain, as are future technologies to meet those needs. The buyer must depend on the vendor and their relationship to institute the most appropriate changes, but vendors differ in their ability to innovate in a specific activity. Furthermore, success depends on whether there is a strategic fit between buyer and vendor in regard to the innovation process. Some analysts have emphasized that outsourcing, if organized properly so as to manage strategic risk, may improve innovation to the extent that it may become a firm's "new engine of growth" (Quinn, 2000, p. 13). Many of these issues will differ in importance among firms, among activities, and over time, emphasizing that each management team will have to study its own situation in considerable detail before reaching a make or buy decision. The complexity of issues concerning outsourcing has led to the creation of consulting firms that specialize in providing advice in analyzing whether to outsource, how to design a contract, and what governance structures to establish.

New Interfirm Governance Procedures in Outsourcing

The outsourcing contract can delineate performance benchmarks for each activity, and here it is important to specify carefully as far as is possible. This initial phase will differ among firms and among activities. Some firms may have established performance benchmarks internally, while others may not. Some activities may be specified precisely, while others may involve objectives that cannot be quantified as clearly and where both firms expect changes over time, especially as a result of innovations and continuous improvement. Consequently, interfirm governance can be very important.

Fulfilling a contract is not enough since the contract is necessarily incomplete; there must also be a social process of give and take. This involves a change in focus from contractual to "embeddedness," with interfirm processes that foster social structures among many individuals in different firms and facilitate dispute resolution. The buyer's vision must be shared by the vendor, including relevant cultural attributes and values. Over time, the relationship may improve with the strengthening of these attributes and a clearer understanding of each other's organizations. However, McFarlan and Nolan (1995) have noted that with the passage of time "the contract payment stream becomes less and less tied to the initial set of planned outputs (as the world changes) and, thus, more subject to negotiation and misunderstanding" (p. 9). Their interviews reveal the biggest challenge is the continuous commitment to the spirit of a flexible partnership, so culture and fit are crucial.

Many theorists have examined the relationships between risk and trust. Das and Teng (1998, 2004) have presented three perspectives from this literature. First, uncertainty that hinges on decisions of others requires trust. Second, a sense of trust encourages risk taking. Third, trust relates to risk perceptions of outcome possibilities. Some authors have recently applied these risk-trust relationships to the subject of success in outsourcing. Successful outsourcing requires a trust-based pattern of control rather than either a market-based or a bureaucratic-based pattern. Paauwe, Farndale, and Williams (2004) emphasize the climate of trust that is required for change and innovation. They refer to a similar dichotomy in trust: "cognition-based trust" related to the vendor's technical abilities and "affect-based trust" dependent on personal relationships.

Research by Grugulis and Hebson (2003) demonstrates that "work that was outsourced was managed very differently to that undertaken in-house" (p. 45). In particular, informal contacts and interfirm tacit knowledge play a new role. A successful outsourcing relationship rests on interfirm processes and structures that foster collaboration and trust in order to deal with issues beyond those specified in the contract. Useem and Harder (2000) point to certain management capabilities required for "Leading Laterally in Company Outsourcing": strategic thinking, deal making, partnership governing, and managing change. For a particular firm, these leadership qualities may be different from skills used in traditional management, so the choice of personnel to participate in interfirm, cross-functional committees becomes an important determinant of success. At the same time, Useem and Harder's management interviews indicate that outsourcing will be doomed without top management support for the outsourcing mission.

For outsourcing, with the need for ongoing innovation and the consequent inability to include all relevant specifications in the contract, a central issue concerns the choice of personnel, processes, and structures that can strengthen trust over time. How can interfirm decisions best be made? How can interfirm disputes best be resolved? Again, the right answers will differ among firms and over time. The extent and nature of economies of scale in interfirm governance structures is also an important subject. For managers evaluating outsourcing, careful consideration of new governance costs is an important issue. Issues that should be considered in achieving interfirm governance include

- the ability to delineate performance benchmarks,
- similar corporate culture and vision between buyer and vendor,
- prospects for developing goodwill trust,
- the ability to put in place processes and structures that can best foster collaboration and resolve problems and disputes,
- the availability of management capabilities to lead laterally with interfirm, cross-functional teams,
- the strength of top management support for outsourcing the activity, and
- the cost of interfirm governance structures.

Achieving Ongoing Innovation in the Globalization Process

For many firms, a key success factor is the ability to innovate on a continual basis. Outsourcing has added a complexity to this challenge. "Offshoring" of activities to vendors in another nation has added further complexity. Today, managers in many separate firms and subsidiaries must develop ways of collaborating to increase the profits of all participants in an international "creative web." Each member of the group may still attempt to negotiate a particular share of the total value created by the group, but the success of the group requires that all participants receive compensation that they consider to be satisfactory in return for their contribution to the success of the group as a whole.

The creative web involves dynamic rather than static analyses. The best "answers" to managerial questions will change over time. In fact, a purpose of the group is to create change. While the game theory perspective focuses on a particular firm achieving success vis-à-vis other firms by changing one or more of the PARTS, the creative web focuses on the group as a whole changing the PARTS. There is continual collaboration in regard to the group's production processes. In terms of the game analogy, all members of the group are on the same side for purposes of increasing innovation. To a greater degree than game theory analysis, this perspective emphasizes the dependence of each member of the group on the creativity of the group as a whole. This radically changes the traditional customer-supplier concepts.

The creative web generally has a central organizer. There is a concentration of decision-making power in the hands of a single corporation near the center of the web. Coordination is necessary for success, and a central question in the creative web is "Who will do the coordinating?" Often this will be a retailer or a final assembler, each of whom seeks to develop a differentiated set of goods and services that give the coordinator—and hence the web—a unique place from the perspective of the ultimate customer. Neither the retailer nor the final assembler can achieve success by itself. Each such coordinator relies on a web of relationships. The success of the web must be a shared success, and in this sense there is an ongoing and permanent mutual dependence even on the part of those farthest removed from the central coordinator. The nature of the relationships involves much more than a unidirectional flow of components or partially completed materials. The reverse flow involves decisions concerning the objectives and procedures of R&D&M (research, development, and marketing) and often financial assistance toward achievement of these objectives and procedures. Hence, dependence runs in many directions throughout the web.

The above perspectives are also relevant for the internal organization of large and complex multinational enterprises (MNEs). A substantial body of literature has discussed recent modifications of traditional business hierarchies. Many firms have recognized the importance of "employee empowerment" and of new managerial techniques for stimulating the positive involvement of all the employees in the achievement of corporate objectives. As noted in Chapter 4, many authors have pointed to Japan as a nation that pioneered such concepts as "quality circles," where employees participate actively in discussing how they can modify their procedures to better satisfy the company's customers. The incentives of profit sharing and employee ownership of shares, together with the process for creating profit centers within the corporate structure have become common. These shifts in organizational structure have resulted in decentralized decision-making units, often in different countries, operating with some independence within the overall corporate structure. For such organizations, strengthening the creative web is an internal challenge. With the shift of responsibility from a hierarchical corporate structure to separate but related work groups, a central issue is the organizational structure that can best foster "intrapreneurship," the practice of entrepreneurship by employees within an organization.

A vast array of journal articles examines corporate experiences in regard to international joint ventures and strategic alliances. Much research has focused on technical "how to" issues, such as those involving cross-cultural challenges and the development of "trust" in business relationships. Part I of this book presents many such issues in the context of differences in social forces among countries and cultures. The creative web brings with it a series of new management issues. Each firm must decide which web to join and whether it should join more than one. The joining decision is similar to an investment decision in the sense that there will be a commitment of resources to the success of the new organizational structure. For some firms, entry into a creative web may require the establishment of new subsidiaries that do not carry the baggage of the past. The creative web requires a mindset very different from that of the traditional hierarchical corporation, and it may simply be impossible to include the latter in the former. Conversely, the web must make decisions about whom to accept into the web, and in this regard an important criterion for acceptance is innovative capability. Another set of issues concerns the criteria and terms and conditions for leaving a particular creative web or for dismissing a member. The degree to which the creative web should devote resources to R&D&M is crucial for the success of each member of the group. A decision to join one group as opposed to another may be impacted by a firm's evaluation of the creativity of the web.

For the decisions described above, an additional aspect of trust is crucial. Here the concept of trust involves an evaluation of the ability of the various participants to work together in order to achieve effective R&D&M

in the long term. The outcomes are uncertain, and trust concerns the faith that one's fellow participants will be able to achieve success. For many social scientists, such as Fukuyama (1995), the degree of trust drives organizational structure. For Fukuyama, organizational structures differ among countries because the degree of trust differs among nations.

Of central concern will be the nature of financial relationships in the context of substantial R&D commitments with uncertain outcomes, or the need for effective marketing in order to maximize these outcomes. Incentives for successful innovation must be offered to each member of the web. It is in the interest of all members that each member should feel appropriately compensated. How should the success of a particular member be evaluated in the context of group success? Derivatives may be used to gear compensation at one moment in time to outcomes that will occur later in time.

Figure 7.3 illustrates a continuum involving the degree of hierarchy and cooperation, where firms may shift from a lower left quadrant toward the upper right quadrant, from A to B.

Figure 7.3   The Shift in Organizational Structure

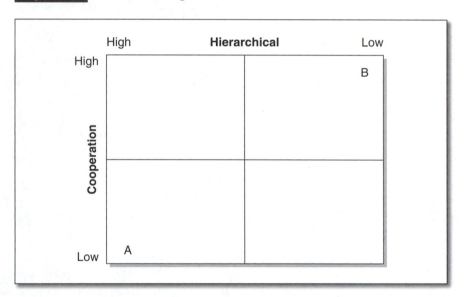

The Canadian Imperial Bank of Commerce (CIBC), a major Canadian bank, sought to evaluate the benefits and risks that it might face if it outsourced its HR business processes to the IT firm, Electronic Data Systems (EDS). A key focus was the need for the creation of interfirm governance procedures to resolve disagreements and to foster ongoing improvements and innovations. These interfirm procedures rested on changes in organizational structure, as illustrated in Figure 7.3.

| In Practice 7.1 | Challenges and Rewards of Outsourcing the HR Department |

CIBC's Human Resources (HR) department was about to take a significant step forward. Over the past year, CIBC's HR department had been in discussion on how to further develop CIBC's HR capabilities. They knew that they wanted to improve the way that they were delivering services to their employees, but the question was how to do this. The CIBC HR team knew that they wanted to reinvent HR service delivery and that greater automation and increased self-service operations were a necessity. However, the way in which to go about doing this was a difficult question to answer.

Over the past year, a number of options were brought forward and analyzed. These included continuing with the status quo but performing some patchwork operations to develop new HR capabilities and also exploring the new opportunity to outsource entire functions to be managed and implemented by another company, through Business Process Outsourcing (BPO).

There were also risks in pursuing such a new venture. Employees who were currently performing the necessary HR operations would either be eliminated or transferred to the vendor, and there would be a risk of losing corporate knowledge. There would also be no means of answering questions or performing any analyses internally.

Patterson highlighted the potential difficulties of implementing the HR BPO option.

> Businesses within CIBC would see "internal" as more flexible and nimble. Some in the business are concerned that every time you want to go and do something, you would have to pay for it. Of course, they are paying for it now, but they just don't see it because it isn't tracked or reported in a disciplined and laid out process.

There was also the difficulty of trying to persuade HR management to let go of their positions of power within the firm. Chris Klus, a consultant with Klynveld Peat Marwick Goerdeler's (KPMG's) strategic HR practice noted:

> Aside from a lack of providers (vendors), many HR directors and vice-presidents continue to feel threatened by the notion of handing over so much of their department. For many HR leaders it is a case of the more people they have reporting to them, the more powerful they feel. While they may know they could outsource the transactional work, they choose instead to hold on to it and end up bringing in consultants to handle the strategic issues. (Brown, 2001)

In addition, the vendor (EDS) would be required to produce a number of reports on a regular basis with key performance measurements. These reports would include metrics such as number of payroll records completed on time without error and call center statistics (i.e. number of calls answered within a given period of time). Other reports would include status reports on the project progress and financial reports that were used to ensure that the vendor did not miss any service levels. These reports, although necessary, would cause problems from an optics perspective. Since the vendor would have sets of reports that they would produce, bad news would become glaring in those reports. Thus, the perception may be that the service today is worse than when it was performed internally since there were no measures of the same caliber in CIBC HR prior to HR BPO.

Finally, being the first mover also posed a risk. The number of vendors with expertise in this field was limited, and thus, the selection was less competitive and might not result in the best vendor selection. As many of the vendors were IT companies, they had limited HR expertise and thus, while they would be able to meet the technological needs, they would have limited resources and knowledge in terms of the delivery of high quality HR services and thought leadership.

SOURCE: Conklin and Pun (2002a).

There were a number of issues that arose before and after the transition that required MacDonald and the rest of the Alliance Management Team's (AMT's) attention.

The Transfer

MacDonald contemplated the challenge of working with individuals who were once his employees but who were now members of a third-party vendor.

Asking someone to do something as a colleague is different from asking a third-party vendor. When you're dealing with a vendor, one expects to be treated like a customer. You expect, if anything, a higher more formal standard of performance.

Also, all of a sudden, some (CIBC) units expected services that they never had before. We had to remember that EDS could not fix everything that needed improvement all at once.

Process and Payment Details

There were also many smaller issues that arose such as legal fees, communication memos, and translation cost, which required joint problem solving. In terms of legal fees, EDS expected CIBC's legal department to handle problems and make decisions, but CIBC expected EDS to take care of certain issues. In regard to some communication materials and memo translations, when CIBC issued or translated memos to employees regarding HR operations, it was thought that EDS would pay for these items. EDS thought otherwise.

Management Styles

While an initial cultural assessment during the request for proposal (RFP) process indicated that the two companies (CIBC and EDS) were very similar, in reality, there were many differences. There were differences in terms of management styles and in the degree to which CIBC and EDS engaged in hands-on management. There were also different attitudes regarding customer service.

(Continued)

(Continued)

CIBC had maintained a large HR department and a long history of developing and maintaining best practices in HR operations. EDS (in Canada) by comparison was much smaller and had access to fewer HR thought leaders and subject matter experts.

MacDonald discussed the delicate nature of impeding on the vendor's management style.

The issues around management of people were not built into the contract because what you don't want to do in these contracts is tell them (EDS) how to do the business because you might as well have kept it (in-house). They need to get the efficiencies up in a way that they deem necessary while still managing the service levels that they signed up for.

SOURCE: Conklin and Pun (2002b).

Critical Thinking Questions

1. Analyze the pros and cons of CIBC outsourcing its HR business processes.

2. Evaluate the appropriate responses to the outsourcing challenges encountered by CIBC.

3. What concerns would you have about offshoring the various HR activities to another nation?

References and Suggested Readings

Brandenburger, A. M., & Nalebuff, B. J. (1995, July/August). The right game: Use game theory to shape strategy. *Harvard Business Review*, 57–71.

Brown, D. (2001). Measuring the value of HR. *Canadian HR Reporter, 14*(6), 1–5.

Carney, M. (1998). The competitiveness of networked production: The role of trust and asset specificity. *Journal of Management Studies, 35*(4), 460.

Conklin, D. W., & Pun, J. (2002a). *CIBC: Outsourcing the human resources department (A)*. London: Ivey. (Ivey Case No. 9B02C062)

Conklin, D. W., & Pun, J. (2002b). *CIBC: Outsourcing the human resources department (B)*. London: Ivey. (Ivey Case No. 9B02C063)

Das, T. K., & Teng, B. S. (1998). Between trust and control: Developing confidence in partner cooperation in alliances. *Academy of Management Review, 23*(3), 491–512.

Das, T. K., & Teng, B. S. (2004). The risk-based view of trust: A conceptual framework. *Journal of Business and Psychology, 19*(1).

Fukuyama, F. (1995). *Trust: The social virtues and the creation of prosperity.* New York: Free Press.

Goepfert, J. (2002). *Transformational outsourcing: Helping companies adapt to a volatile future* (International Data Corporation White Paper, p. 19). Framingham, MA: IDC.

Grugulis, S. V., & Hebson, G. (2003). The rise of the "network organisation" and the decline of discretion. *Human Resource Management Journal, 13*(2), 45–59.

Lepak, D. P., & Snell, S. A. (1998). Virtual HR: Strategic human resource management in the 21st century. *Human Resource Management Review, 8*(3), 215–234.

McFarlan, F. W., & Nolan, R. L. (1995). How to manage an IT outsourcing alliance. *MIT Sloan Management Review, 36*(2), 9–22.

Paauwe, J., Farndale, E., & Williams, A. R. T. (2004). Web-based organizing in traditional brick-and-mortar companies: The impact on HR. *ERIM Report Series: Research in Management* (pp. 1–45). Netherlands: Rotterdam University.

Porter, M. (1990). *The competitive advantage of nations.* New York: Free Press.

Porter, M. E. (1980). *Competitive strategy.* New York: Free Press.

Quinn, J. B. (2000). Outsourcing innovation: The new engine of growth. *Sloan Management Review, 41*(4), 13–27.

Useem, M., & Harder, J. (2000). Leading laterally in company outsourcing. *MIT Sloan Management Review, 41*(2), 25–36.

Comparing Nations as Investment Locations 8

CHAPTER LEARNING OBJECTIVES

On completion of this chapter, students should be able to

- evaluate the wide range of economic forces that impact the advantages and dis-advantages of each nation as an investment location for each type of business activity,

- discuss the impact of tax rates and tax havens on the firm's investment location decisions,

- recognize the social and ethical issues in using a legal tax haven,

- assess alternative types of subsidies and Special Economic Zones (SEZs) as invest-ment location determinants.

In his book *The Competitive Advantage of Nations,* Michael Porter (1990) examines the dependence of a firm's success on certain features of the national economy where the firm is located. Each nation has a unique configuration of these determinants, so a nation has characteristics that can support the international competitiveness of firms in only certain industries. Porter focuses on understanding why nations have developed clusters of industries in which firms have attained global success. He begins his book by referring to the success of specific industries based in specific nations: printing presses, luxury cars, and chemicals in Germany; pharmaceuticals, chocolate, and trading in Switzerland; heavy trucks and mining equipment in Sweden; and personal computers, software, credit cards, and movies in the United States. He analyzes success criteria under four headings, which he illustrates as the four points in his diamond framework, as illustrated in Figure 8.1.

Figure 8.1   Analyzing International Competitiveness

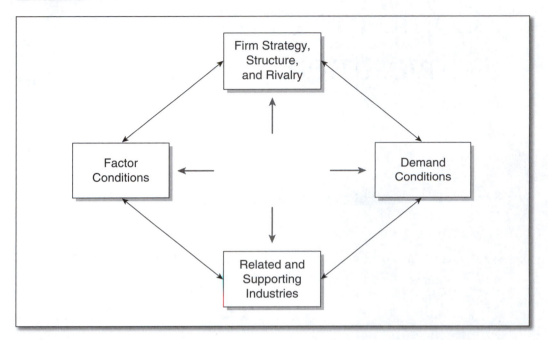

While he developed his analyses in order to advance our understanding of the competitive advantage of nations, Porter's (1990) diamond model also provides an analytical framework for a firm to decide where geographically to locate each of its activities. For each activity, there will be a limited number of nations that offer an optimal diamond, and international investment decisions should focus on these nations. Consequently, it is important for managers to consider Porter's diamond in considerable detail and to relate his determinants of success to their specific industry and business activities.

Porter's (1990) analyses also emphasize that each nation's growth potential will depend on appropriate government policies. Of particular importance are attempts by governments to "engineer a competitive advantage" through programs such as tax incentives and subsidies. Tax design is one of the few location determinants that can be influenced in the short term by government. For example, programs that are designed to attract businesses by improving education and retraining and by stimulating innovation require considerably more time to be effective. The design of the tax structure can become a competition among jurisdictions for the pursuit of new investments and, hence, more jobs and perhaps, ultimately, more aggregate tax revenue. Tax concessions include various exemptions from the payment of sales and property taxes, as well as exemptions from the payment of corporate income taxes, or special provisions such as accelerated depreciation or tax-exempt bonds. In many cases, these exemptions are "tax holidays" for a stipulated number of years. Often these exemptions are combined with other incentives such as city- or county-revenue bond financing, employee training programs, industrial parks, and research and development (R&D) assistance. Personal income tax provisions may encourage the individual taxpayer to invest in certain types of corporations, and this greater access to capital may also play a role in business location decisions.

Investment by a private firm may provide benefits that cannot be appropriated by the firm but that are significant for others within the country where the investment is located. Consequently, governments offer a wide variety of subsidies to attract and retain investment. However, subsidies for new investments may have a negative impact on existing manufacturers. Subsidized investment will increase the supply of a product, and existing manufacturers of that product may consequently suffer reductions in prices, output, employment, and profits. For a government, the calculation of net externalities and appropriate subsidies involves complexities, and for managers, the negotiation of subsidies involves considerable uncertainties concerning the amount that a government may be willing to offer. Many nations have created geographically distinct areas with special features designed to attract foreign investment. In deciding where to locate various operations, businesses today must investigate the benefits and subsidies offered by a plethora of SEZs throughout the world. The business location decision involves a comparison of many alternative sites, each with its own set of incentives. This chapter begins with an examination of Porter's (1990) diamond framework and then extends the comparisons among nations that include tax policies, subsidy programs, and SEZs.

Porter's Diamond Framework as a Manager's Investment Guide

FACTOR CONDITIONS

Factors of production include labor, land, natural resources, capital, and infrastructure. The specific factors that are relevant for a particular industry are not inherited but rather have been created, and they can be upgraded over time. The status of human resources depends on educational institutions and industrial training practices. The work ethic depends on cultural features. Each nation has a unique combination of knowledge resources, including research facilities and trade associations. The status of physical resources includes not only the natural features of a nation but also its climate and its geographical position vis-à-vis potential customers and suppliers. Each form of capital, from equity and venture capital to alternative types of debt, may have different degrees of availability and terms and conditions in different nations. The nature and cost of the relevant types of infrastructure impact a firm's costs and its ability to create and deliver its products and services.

In recent years, many of these factors have become mobile and can be upgraded, so international competitiveness has a time dimension. For each industry or business activity, some factors are more important than others. Factors can be tailored to the specific needs of each industry or business activity. Whether a nation possesses such advanced factors that are most relevant for a certain industry will be a major determinant of the international competitiveness of its firms in that industry. This analysis is made more complex in that "innovation to offset selective weakness is more likely than innovation to exploit strengths" (Porter, 1990, p. 83). At issue is how a nation responds to its relative weaknesses. The political process may be one in which the government is actively seeking to create solutions to its nation's weaknesses. Consequently, for a firm considering various nations as alternative investment sites, a central issue is the likelihood of upgrading on an ongoing basis of the specific factors on which its competitiveness will depend.

An industry in the service sector may have a need for a set of specified factors that differ from those required in manufacturing. Language skills, for example, may be essential in determining the ability to compete internationally, as may be the skills in adapting to a wide variety of cultures. Certain management capabilities may be more relevant for the service sector. This service sector perspective emphasizes the need for each firm to analyze for each potential investment site the range of factor conditions most important as the determinants of its international competitiveness.

With the reduction in trade barriers in recent years, one factor of production that has become extremely important is the level of wages for employees in manufacturing. Rather suddenly, manufacturing businesses located in advanced nations have found that their relatively high wage levels now make them unable to compete against labor-intensive imports from low-wage countries. For China, low wages have become a key determinant of international competitiveness, and a growing flood of Chinese exports has caused "deindustrialization" in many countries. For the United States, the issue of relative wage levels has now become important for imports from Mexico, as well as China. Meanwhile, India's low wage level has stimulated the shift of services such as call centers and software development to India.

DEMAND CONDITIONS

The residents of each nation have a unique configuration of what they perceive to be their needs. A firm is guided in many of its strategic decisions by its understanding of these local demand conditions. A firm cannot as readily understand the demand configuration in other nations, since such understanding depends on communication with potential buyers and an appreciation for consumer preferences. Products and services can be designed in a vast array of varieties, and the demand at home for certain varieties will lead a firm to specialize in them. In this sense, demand is segmented and each nation has its own distribution of demand for alternative varieties. "The more significant role of segment structure at home is in shaping the attention and priorities of a nation's firms" (Porter, 1990, p. 87).

In the ever-present search for improvements in product design and service attributes, the nature of domestic demand plays a key role. Furthermore, consumers in some nations may exert continual pressure to develop innovative attributes, while consumers in other nations may not. An industry's international competitiveness will be enhanced if its domestic consumers encourage it to innovate in ways that make it a world leader, anticipating the future preferences of consumers in other nations. Related to this perspective is the rate of growth of domestic demand, supporting the pace of investment and the adoption of technological advances that are embodied in new investments.

For demand conditions as well, the other points on Porter's (1990) diamond play a key role in determining the pace and nature of advances and hence, of the international competitiveness that relies on these ongoing advances. Rivalry among domestic firms can enhance the sensitivity of each competitor to changing nuances in demand conditions, and rivalry can make customers more aware of product and service enhancements. Other nations' residents may come to see this cluster as a leader in innovative design, creating an ongoing focus on this cluster. The strength of related and supporting industries may determine an industry's ability to innovate, while factor conditions may or may not facilitate these continual modifications.

RELATED AND SUPPORTING INDUSTRIES

A firm's ability to achieve international competitiveness is impacted by the degree to which its domestic suppliers are internationally competitive. Suppliers' prices play a key role in determining a firm's costs. Even more important may be the role that suppliers can play in innovation and upgrading. Related industries may purchase similar inputs and so may assist in achieving economies of scale, as well as innovations and upgrading at the supplier level. Suppliers who serve a number of industries may be able to achieve greater specialization than otherwise. Together, the related industries may stimulate investment in activities that are used by each of them and in the factor conditions on which they all depend. Interchanges of information and technologies may strengthen all of the related industries.

Firms may readily expand into industries that are related, bringing heightened competitiveness with the experiences, skills, and technologies that they can transfer. Service sector firms may transfer organizational practices across industries. Industries whose products or services are used in a combined or complementary manner will find their international competitiveness enhanced by the success of one another.

FIRM STRATEGY, STRUCTURE, AND RIVALRY

Each nation has an underlying set of forces that determine the ways in which firms are created and organized. The nature of rivalry plays a key role in this environment. Of particular importance is the extent to which a nation's environment encourages entrepreneurial activities and the formation of new businesses.

Some nations, such as Germany, have a strong history of engineering, and this has supported the competitiveness of industries that depend on technical or engineering content. Some nations have a strong history of certain management practices, perhaps based on domestic educational institutions, as well as industrial experience. Attitudes toward risk taking and international business impact the scope of expansion ambitions. Underlying the strategy and structure of firms are many cultural features such as social norms, professional standards, and the place of family business. The goals and expectations of both employees and shareholders drive the strategy and structure of firms. In some countries, respect for hierarchical decision making may limit employee initiative, while in other countries, the culture may support decentralized decision making and individual initiative. Differences in corporate governance practices, financial practices, and provisions for bonus payments may also impact the nature of corporate structures and their contribution to international competitiveness. A nation as a whole may share a common attitude toward business success and the accumulation of wealth.

Porter (1990) emphasizes the relationship between domestic rivalry and international competitiveness. Ongoing achievement internationally requires not just one or two national champions that achieve economies of scale. Rather, ongoing success requires vigorous competition within the home market, a competition that continually stimulates innovation. Advances by one firm may be copied readily by others as they learn from each other's experiences. Foreign rivalry cannot have the same beneficial impacts since distance reduces this ongoing interaction.

Porter (1990) argues that these diamond characteristics that confront each industry create an environment within which chance events still can play a role. Major inventions or technological breakthroughs can change the realities of international competitiveness. Yet, even here, nations may respond to chance events in different ways. "The nation with the most favorable diamond will be the most likely to convert chance events into competitive advantage" (p. 125).

A government can influence each of the four sets of determinants in the diamond. In this sense, a government can play a significant role in determining an industry's competitive advantage. Most factor conditions require investments in order to remain at the global forefront, and governments can participate in these investments. Governments can stimulate demand through the technical specifications that they require in their procurement polices. Such policies and programs can stimulate clusters of related and supporting industries. A host of regulations bear on firm strategy, structure, and rivalry. Most significant may be regulations and antitrust laws that seek to encourage competition. In particular, regulations, subsidies, and competition policies focus on government intervention that seeks to alter industry structures. Part IV of this text expands on the role of public policies as a key force in the environment of business.

Porter (1990) draws attention to the interrelationships among the four points of the diamond. A nation's demand conditions may create priorities for upgrading of factors. Some factors may be shared with other industries, so the nature of related and supporting industries may determine the pace of upgrading of relevant factors. The strategy, structure, and rivalry of existing firms may stimulate the upgrading process. "The existence of a cluster of several industries that draws on common inputs, skills and infrastructure also further stimulates government bodies, educational institutions, firms, and individuals to invest in relevant factor-creating mechanisms" (p. 135).

Taxation as an Investment Determinant

Taxes form an important determinant of a firm's after-tax profitability, so managers must study tax rates and provisions in alternative location sites as part of their international investment decisions. Taxes, through their impact on the rates of return involved, can alter the supply of labor, the rate of saving, and the rate of investment. Because taxes affect the supply of labor and capital, which are major determinants of growth, governments often attempt to design taxes that will foster the accumulation of these factors of production. Another target of tax policy is the rate of technological progress. By providing R&D tax incentives, preferential tax treatment of small business, and investment tax credits, governments hope to foster innovation and entrepreneurship in such a way as to increase factor productivity and economic growth. By affecting the level of corporate sales, the tax system influences the need for increased capacity and the investment of the firm. By affecting depreciation reserves and retained earnings, the profit's tax influences the availability of internal funds, which is a variable in the investment decision. Managers may be attracted in their location decisions by a reduction in the tax rate or by an acceleration in depreciation or by the provision of investment credits.

Tax incentives may encourage investment in new small businesses. Many believe that new small businesses provide society with special economic benefits. Evidence exists that job creation occurs to a greater degree in new small businesses, rather than in the expansion of older, larger firms in traditional industries, and that innovation occurs to a greater degree in small businesses. It is often argued that shortcomings or "failures" in capital markets make it difficult for small businesses to acquire financing on the terms and conditions that would be socially optimal. Tax concessions to increase the availability of small business capital and decrease its costs may consequently be offered by some governments.

The multinational enterprise (MNE) can alter the transfer prices that it uses internally. By charging higher prices for the goods and services it provides to its business in the high-tax jurisdiction and by paying lower prices for its purchases from its subsidiary there, the MNE is able to reduce its profits in the high-tax jurisdiction as reported for tax purposes. These techniques mean that the MNE's tax base is highly mobile in response to differences in tax rates. To the degree that an MNE can avoid paying the higher tax rates of some jurisdictions, the MNE's location decisions will not be affected by interjurisdictional tax differentials.

Using Tax Havens to Minimize Taxes

Many small nations have put in place minimal corporate tax rates as a way of gaining some revenue by attracting head office functions, particularly those related to finance. This government revenue may be only a very small percentage of a corporation's international profit; nevertheless, it may form a significant portion of the tax haven's government revenue. Many businesses arrange their international location decisions so as to legally accumulate their taxable profits in tax havens. Apart from these zero-tax regimes, countries impose a wide range of corporate profit tax rates. A business can often find a country with a lower tax rate than the country where it was incorporated and also lower than the country where it wishes to invest. By funneling profits to a zero-tax or even a lower-tax jurisdiction, a business is able to minimize its aggregate tax payments. Recent international agreements have sought to limit these practices, but these agreements have left opportunities for tax minimization, so tax havens can still play an important role in business location decisions.

Businesses face the question of whether to include detailed information in their financial statements concerning their use of tax havens. Laws and regulations concerning tax provisions might change, abruptly altering the net profit projections on which investors rely. New tax rulings could impact profits funneled through tax havens. Furthermore, government authorities in tax havens could alter the conditions and rates in their tax regimes in ways that might reduce after-tax profits. Changes in government officials as a result of an election could lead to changes in tax policies. Whether or not to explicitly inform shareholders of these risks may create an ethical dilemma for managers.

The process for funneling profits to a "tax haven" is illustrated in Figure 8.2. A business creates a separate, wholly-owned entity in the low-tax jurisdiction with capital provided to the subsidiary in the form of equity. This subsidiary lends to another subsidiary in a third country where the parent wishes to invest. All or a large portion of the earnings in the third country is returned as interest payments to the entity in the low-tax jurisdiction. In this way, the investment earnings may escape tax at least partially in the third country (where they are tax-deductible expenses), as well as in the country of the parent company (at least until they are repatriated). Furthermore, if the parent borrows in its home country to invest in the tax haven, and thence in the third country, then the interest it pays on these loans could reduce taxable earnings in its home country. The entity in the low-tax jurisdiction can reinvest the tax-free earnings in additional foreign investments. Furthermore, in some countries, distribution of these tax-free earnings as dividends to the home country firm is taxed at a minimal rate. Both the European Union (EU) and the Organisation for Economic Co-operation and Development (OECD) have attempted to create a more level playing field in regard to corporate tax rates.

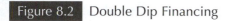

Figure 8.2   Double Dip Financing

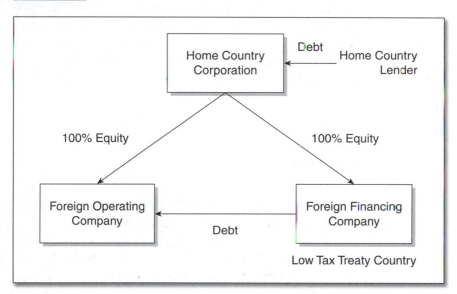

International Codes of Conduct for Taxation

In 1997, the EU Member States agreed a Code of Conduct for Business Taxation aimed at tackling what they regarded as harmful tax competition where certain corporations obtained special tax concessions. The code sought to prevent measures that provided for a significantly lower effective level of taxation than normally applied in the Member State concerned ("ring-fenced tax regimes") and that could significantly impact the location of business activity in the EU. A basic principle underlying the code was that a nation could retain a low corporate tax rate as long as this tax rate was applied across all types of business activities, both foreign owned and domestically owned. A corporation can still legally funnel its profits into one of the lowest tax jurisdictions within the EU, such as Ireland. The diversion of profits within the EU continues to be attractive as long as any EU country has a generally applied corporate tax rate less than that of other EU countries. Hence, tax provisions continue to be an important determinant of business location decisions.

The OECD does not have any formal enforcement tools; the success of its Harmful Tax Competition initiative depends on peer pressure. In 1998, the Committee on Fiscal Affairs of the OECD released a report titled *Harmful Tax Competition: An Emerging Global Issue* (OECD, 1998), dealing with its plans to strengthen international tax enforcement. The 1998 report addressed harmful tax practices in both OECD member and non-member countries. It was the OECD's intention to convince nonmember states to cooperate through a combination of dialogue, weak promises of economic support, hidden threats of economic sanctions, and threats to ostracize noncooperative countries by putting them on a tax haven list. In 2000, the OECD published a progress report. It identified 47 preferential tax regimes of OECD member states as potentially harmful. The 2000 report also identified 35 countries as uncooperative tax havens (listed countries). A small number of listed countries reached bilateral agreements with the OECD to cooperate. A large number of listed countries, however, strongly resisted the OECD harmful tax competition initiative.

Obtaining Subsidies and
Investing in Special Economic Zones

Most governments provide consumption subsidies to reduce the price of certain goods and services below the price that would prevail in a free, competitive market. The production of these goods and services is often left to the marketplace, rather than being undertaken directly by the government. However, the amounts that are produced and their distribution among individuals are affected by the terms and conditions of the subsidy programs. The subsidy programs may be designed so the firm receives financial assistance in return for fulfilling certain requirements. For health care, subsidies may be geared to the number of patients treated and to the nature of each treatment. For education, subsidies may be based on the number of students and the completion of a specified curriculum. For housing, subsidies may depend on renting to people whose incomes are below a stipulated level. With programs such as these, the firm is usually required to adhere to prices set by the government in order to receive the subsidy. Each nation has its unique pattern of subsidies, so managers must develop strategies that differ among nations. Here as well, managers must study the consumption subsidies offered by each government in deciding on international investments.

Many government agencies and programs provide loans, investments, and loan guarantees. Such programs do not involve outright grants but rather the provision of capital on terms more favorable than the recipients could obtain in the market. It is difficult to estimate precisely the extent of the subsidy involved in such programs. The benefit to each firm depends on the terms the recipient would in fact have to accept in the market if these programs did not exist. Many governments have created grant programs to encourage R&D, innovation, and the adoption of new technologies. Export development corporations may offer subsidized export loans at interest rates below market levels, together with government guarantees of commercial bank loans and insurance to cover the risk that foreign buyers will default on their payments. It is important to recognize the large and growing role of subnational governments in the provision of subsidies in some countries. Subnational governments may not be bound by international agreements to limit subsidies.

In many nations, public enterprises produce and sell significant quantities of goods and services. Generally, such government operations do not base their prices on the same market criteria followed by private firms, nor do they always pay the same levels of corporate income taxes as private firms. A market rate of return on capital invested is usually not of the same concern in government as in private business operations. Government provision of capital to such firms at less than market rates and government payments to cover operating losses can provide significant subsidies for the products concerned, and consideration of these subsidies may also enter into a firm's international investment decisions.

Governments throughout the world now direct substantial production subsidies to "high-tech" activities. Much of these subsidies have been developed at the state rather than the federal level. In recent years, another widely used form of subsidy has been the government bailout of firms that are approaching bankruptcy and closure. The bailout is usually advocated as a means of restructuring the organization in order to make it more efficient and, hence, to enable a continuation of the firm. When many employees are involved, the local community and the society as a whole have a strong interest in ensuring that operations continue. If the firm shuts down a plant or lays off workers, society must suffer from the strains of increased unemployment. Many nations have also implemented large-scale regional development programs to provide special investment subsidies to firms willing to locate in depressed regions. For some managers, the availability of subsidies may impact decisions concerning plant closures, as well as investments.

The World Trade Organization (WTO) has attempted to establish a definition of "subsidy," relating this definition to whether the financial contribution is specific to a particular enterprise or industry, as opposed to being offered to all firms in the nation. Based on this definition, the WTO has decreed that certain subsidies are prohibited for its members, and this prohibition has enmeshed many firms in international trade disputes. Prohibited subsidies can take a wide variety of forms, quite apart from grants, loans, or equity. Government revenue that is otherwise due may be foregone or not collected. A government may provide goods or services to firms at below-market prices, or it may purchase from firms at above-market prices. A government may engage in these various activities indirectly through an agency. Furthermore, subsidies are prohibited if a condition of receipt is export performance or use of domestic over imported goods. Any of such benefits can be considered to be a subsidy for the purposes of formal trade disputes. It is acceptable for a government to offer such programs equally to all firms in its jurisdiction. A government may promulgate objective criteria or conditions that govern eligibility, provided that the eligibility is automatic. It is when such programs are aimed at a specific firm or industry or group of firms that the subsidy may distort relative prices and so alter free-market trade and investment flows. Considerable scope for disputes exists over whether a subsidy is "specific" such that it is prohibited, so a firm may accept financial assistance without realizing that its foreign competitors may instigate a trade dispute, claiming "unfair competition." We return to this subject when we examine trade and investment agreements in Chapter 12.

The Attractions of Special Economic Zones as Investment Locations

Thirty years ago, 80 special economic zones (SEZs) in 30 countries generated barely $6 billion in exports and employed about 1 million people. Today (2006), 3,000 SEZs operate in 120 countries and account for $600+ billion in exports and 50 million direct jobs. (Akinci, 2006)

The following list describes common components of SEZs:

1. Parcels of vacant land in various shapes and sizes. A business has the opportunity to purchase or lease a parcel of land that is ideally suited to its needs, and it does not have to incur the expense of tearing down or restructuring buildings. Often an SEZ attempts to attract investment by offering land at prices lower than might be found elsewhere in the nation.

2. Modern public utility infrastructure. A business can be assured that the infrastructure is new and has been built with advanced technologies and efficiencies. Often, an SEZ attempts to attract investment by offering public utility infrastructure at prices lower than might be found elsewhere. This advantage of an SEZ is particularly attractive if a business wishes to invest in a country whose infrastructure is decrepit and may periodically fail. Of importance for many businesses, for example, is the assurance that adequate electricity will be available so as to avoid blackouts or brownouts.

3. Tax Concessions. Many SEZs offer reductions in taxation for speci-fied time periods. A business must calculate the overall cost of each rele-vant SEZ by calculating the costs of land, public utilities, and taxation.

4. Tariff reductions and free trade. Many SEZs permit businesses to import machinery and equipment duty-free. Some zones have gone a step further and offer a tariff-free, export-oriented manufacturing center. Businesses are permitted to import raw materials or components duty-free for fabrication in the zone and then for export outside of the country. These arrangements require that the SEZ be surrounded by a fence with customs officials so that all production will be exported, or if any production is shipped within the country, appropriate customs duties have to be paid. Such businesses do not disrupt the activities of the indigenous firms. Their value-added activities offer jobs, and their net exports add to the country's foreign exchange earnings. Zones that offer this tariff concession are often referred to as "Export Processing Zones" (EPZs) or "Free Trade Zones."

5. Simplified regulations. SEZs generally offer an efficient and rapid process for negotiating terms and conditions for investment. Often this takes the form of a "one-stop" regulatory agency that has the power to deal with the prospective investor, separate from traditional bureaucracies. This attribute is particularly important in countries where regulatory approvals are required from many government agencies, where approvals may depend on bribery, and where the bureaucratic processes involve interminable delays. Many SEZs provide a regulatory oasis, where certain regulations are suspended. For example, many nations have had rules that limited the percentage of equity that could be owned by foreigners, and these foreign ownership restrictions have often been waived within the SEZs. Many nations have had laws that restrict the right to hire and fire employees, and these labor laws have often been waived within the SEZs.

6. Cluster Synergies. By encouraging firms to locate in a consolidated zone, a government can create synergies that might not be available if businesses were scattered geographically. In many zones, a new firm can readily hire various types of skilled labor due to the existence of a large labor pool. Furthermore, some zones provide educational facilities for the training of employees, and some even include universities that may conduct research in collaboration with businesses. As we have discussed earlier in this chapter, Michael Porter has emphasized the importance for a firm of being a member of a cluster in order to enhance its international competitiveness. SEZs provide government with a mechanism to create clusters that may add value to the firms that locate there and consequently assist prospective employees and possibly other firms who receive spin-off benefits, and perhaps even enhance government revenues. From the perspective of cluster synergies, the size of the SEZ is an important determinant with the largest SEZs offering greater advantages.

China's Special Economic Zones

China led the way in attracting international investment by creating SEZs. Mao Ze Dong had espoused the vision of communism in one country with autarky and import substitution as the basis for economic development. Mao is reputed to have stated that "perfect international trade consists of zero imports and zero exports." By 1978, however, China's leaders came to realize that communism had failed in regard to economic development and that foreign investment was necessary to bring managerial capability, new technologies, and growing export markets. There were several reasons for China to create SEZs in order to initiate international investment. With SEZs, the reliance on foreign capitalist firms could be gradual and experimental, without disrupting the traditional government-owned-and-operated business sector. With SEZs, the various provisions and concessions offered to foreign investors could take the form of experiments that could be expanded if successful. If the experiment with foreign investment had been judged unsatisfactory, SEZs could have been reduced or eliminated without disrupting the Chinese economy.

With SEZs, the central government was able to maintain control over the extent and nature of the provisions and concessions, while such control might have not been possible if foreign firms had been free to negotiate with any municipality in China. This degree of control was particularly important in the context of the government's decisions that all foreign direct investment should take the form of joint ventures with Chinese government agencies and that foreign exchange controls should be retained. A purpose of the joint venture requirement was to enhance the managerial capabilities of indigenous Chinese and to ensure that businesses operated in the interests of China. The control, facilitated by concentration in the SEZs, helped to achieve these objectives. For adherents to communist philosophy, the SEZs provided a continuation of a version of the planned economy concept.

China's public utility infrastructure was not geared to the needs of modern businesses, so concentration on improving infrastructure in a few SEZs was a reasonable first step in expanding public sector investment. By placing the SEZs on the coast, the need for new transportation facilities was minimized. Furthermore, the coastal locations facilitated the achievement of a basic government objective, to increase exports and foreign exchange earnings. Many authors have expressed the view that SEZs initiated China's rapid economic growth by successfully attracting enormous volumes of foreign investment.

To illustrate the competitive advantage of nations, we turn to the case of the world watch industry (see In Practice 8.1). The world watch industry has experienced several major shifts in national competitive advantage, from Switzerland to the United States to Asia and finally back to Switzerland. These shifts have been responses to changes in the relative importance of various determinants of competitive advantage. Successful firms were able to create new strategies to profit from these shifts in national competitive advantage.

In Practice 8.1	Changes in the Industry Structure and National Competitive Advantage in the Watch Industry

In the 18th and 19th centuries, English competitors were a constant challenge for the Swiss, who undertook serious efforts to overcome early British supremacy. First, the Swiss invested in education and training, establishing several watchmaking academies at home and watch-repair schools in major foreign markets. Second, and to strengthen their image internationally, they created a "Swiss made" label, which would become by 1920 an important symbol of quality, style, and prestige. Third, the Swiss significantly improved process technology, setting up the world's first mechanized watch factory in 1839. British watchmakers made no attempt to mass manufacture watches until much later. Seeing mass production techniques as a threat to their craft, they persuaded Parliament to pass a law barring the use of specialty production tools in the British watch industry and devoted themselves to the production of very expensive marine chronometers. As a result, the British watch industry steadily declined during the 19th century, while the Swiss industry was on its way to achieving world dominance thanks to significant advances in design, features, standardization, interchangeability of parts, and productivity.

(Continued)

(Continued)

The main source of competition for the Swiss arose from two American watch-makers, Timex and Bulova. Using a combination of automation, precision tooling, and simpler design than that of higher-priced Swiss watches, U.S. Time Corporation introduced in 1951 a line of inexpensive (US$6.95 to US$7.95), disposable, yet stylized and highly durable Timex watches, whose movements had new hard alloy bearings instead of traditional and more expensive jewels. Hard alloy metals allowed for the creation of durable watches at lower costs than jeweled lever timepieces. They also allowed U.S. Time to more effectively automate its production lines, further lowering costs.

Traditional jewelers were very reluctant to carry the Timex brand for a variety of reasons. Its prices and margins were slim compared to those offered by the Swiss, while the watches' riveted cases could not be opened, thereby eliminating the possibility for jewelers to generate after-sales repair revenues. Locked out of jewelry stores, Timex had no choice but to innovate in its marketing and distribution strategy. Its first extensive worldwide advertising campaign on television, "Took a licking and kept on ticking," was to become a legend in marketing history. Consumer demand soared after John Cameron Swazey, a famous U.S. news commentator, was featured in live "torture tests" commercials emphasizing the watch's low cost and incredible durability. The disposable aspect of Timex watches (no local repair involved) pushed the company to develop new distribution channels, including drugstores, discount houses, department stores, catalogue showrooms, military bases, and sporting goods outlets. By 1970, Timex (having changed its name from U.S. Time) had established a manufacturing and/or marketing presence in more than 30 countries and become the world's largest watch manufacturer in terms of units sold.

Bulova was the leading U.S. manufacturer of quality, jeweled-lever watches, integrating the highly accurate tuning fork technology bought from a Swiss engineer in 1959, after the main Swiss companies had turned down the technology. Bulova introduced Accutron in 1962. Five years later, Accutron was the best-selling watch over $100 in the United States. Bulova also formed a partnership with Japan's Citizen Watch Company to produce the movements for the Caravelle line, designed to meet the low-cost/high quality challenge imposed by Timex. By 1970, Bulova had expanded its international presence all around the world and become the largest seller of watches, in revenue terms, in both the United States and the world overall.

Like the U.S. industry, the Japanese watch industry was highly concentrated. In 1950, three main competitors, K. Hattori (which marketed the Seiko brand), Citizen, and Orient accounted for 50%, 30%, and 20% of the Japanese market respectively. Their positions were protected by the 70% tariff and sales tax imposed on all imported watches by the Japanese government.

As the Japanese market became saturated in the 1960s, Hattori and Citizen moved aggressively into other Asia Pacific countries. After first exporting from Japan, Hattori and Citizen established component and assembly operations in low-cost Hong Kong, Singapore, and Malaysia. With hundreds of millions of unserved consumers, the region was also a highly attractive market. From a position of strength in Asia, the Japanese watch companies began in earnest to push into Europe and North America.

The Swiss response to the growing power of U.S. and Japanese competitors was limited. A rising worldwide demand for watches did little to slow the steady decline in the Swiss share on the world market (from 80% in 1946 to 42% in 1970).

The Swatch mania marked the 1980s for the Swiss industry. The Swatch (contraction of "Swiss" and "watch") was conceived as an inexpensive, SFr50 (US$40), yet good quality watch, with quartz accuracy, water and shock resistance, as well as a one-year guarantee. The concept was challenging. Particular efforts were needed to reduce production costs down to Asian levels. Watch engineers slashed the number of individual parts required in the production of a watch from 91 to 51, and housed them in a standardized plastic case that could be produced on a fully automated assembly line. For the first time ever, it became possible to produce cheap watches in high-cost Switzerland. By 1985, production costs were decreased to under SFr10 per unit, and only 130 people were needed to assemble the first eight million Swatch models. By comparison, 350 people were still required to assemble 700,000 Omega watches.

SOURCE: Morrison and Bouquet (1999).

Critical Thinking Questions

1. Use Porter's diamond framework to analyze the initial success of the Swiss watch industry.

2. What changes caused a shift in competitive advantage in watch-making from Switzerland to the United States and then to Asia and finally back to Switzerland?

3. Evaluate each of the new firms that threatened the Swiss watch industry. In what ways was the success of each new firm dependent on its nation's competitive features?

References and Suggested Readings

Akinci, G. (2006). Discussion posting. Retrieved June 30, 2009, from http://rru.worldbank.org/Discussions/Topics/Topic40.aspx

Boskin, M. J., & McLure, C. E. (Eds.). (1990). *World tax reform: Case studies of developed and developing countries.* San Francisco: ICS Press.

Eden, L., & Kudrle, R. (2005). Tax havens: Renegade states in the international tax regime? *Law & Policy, 27*(1), 100–127.

European Union code of conduct for business taxation. (1997). Retrieved October 10, 2009, from http://ec.europa.eu/taxation_customs/taxation/company_tax/harmful_tax_practices/index_en.htm

Feldstein, M., Hines, J., & Hubbard, R. G. (1995a). *The effects of taxation on multinational corporations.* University of Chicago Press.

Feldstein, M., Hines, J., & Hubbard, R. G. (1995b). *Taxing multinational corporations.* University of Chicago Press.

Fernandez, R. A. (1989). *The Mexican-American border region: Issues and trends.* Notre Dame, IN: University of Notre Dame Press.

Hines, J. R., & Rice, E. M. (1994). Fiscal paradise: Foreign tax havens and American business. *Quarterly Journal of Economics, 109*(1), 149–182.

Katzner, D. W. (2001). Explaining the Japanese economic miracle. *Japan and the World Economy, 13,* 303–319.

Kotler, P., & Kartajaya, H. (2000). *Repositioning Asia: From bubble to sustainable economy.* Singapore: John Wiley.

McKenny, K. I. (1993). *An assessment of China's special economic zones* (p. 12). Washington, DC: Industrial College of the Armed Forces, National Defense University.

Morrison, A., & Bouquet, C. (1999). *Swatch and the global watch industry.* London: Ivey. (Ivey Case No. 9A99M023)

Organisation for Economic Co-operation and Development. (1998). *Harmful tax competition: An emerging global issue.* Paris: Author.

Porter, M. (1990). *The competitive advantage of nations.* New York: Free Press.

Slemrod, J. (Ed.). (1990). *Do taxes matter?* Cambridge: MIT Press.

Adjusting to Economic Volatility 9

CHAPTER LEARNING OBJECTIVES

On completion of this chapter, students should be able to

- assess the macroeconomic variables in each nation that can impact the firm's sales and profit projections and so must be considered in designing strategies,

- understand fiscal, monetary, and exchange rate policies in each nation where the firm does business and understand how these policies can impact the macroeconomic variables,

- evaluate the likelihood of encountering severe economic volatility in each nation where the firm does business,

- understand and be able to foresee the inflation/devaluation cycle and exchange rate crises,

- assess the advantages of doing business and investing in a single currency area rather than in nations with separate currencies.

Executives who carefully cultivate financial market and business cycle literacy are likely to manage their companies better than those who do not."
(Navarro, 2004, p. 20)

Managers continually encounter changes in macroeconomic variables that require them to change their strategies. In order to respond to macroeconomic risks, it is necessary for managers to understand government policies that impact macroeconomic variables, particularly rates of unemployment, growth, inflation, and foreign exchange. Here, fiscal, monetary, and exchange rate policies play a central role. Each government chooses a unique set of macroeconomic policies, so managers have to analyze each nation's economic prospects from the perspective of the government policies that may impact them. The recent proliferation of databases and reports available on the Internet facilitates this analysis of current macroeconomic issues in most nations.

Responses of less developed economies to macroeconomic policies are not the same as the responses of the economies of the United States and Western Europe. Impacts depend, for example, on the industry structure and income distribution. Fiscal policy rests on the reactions of consumers and businesses to changes in taxes and government expenditures. These reactions may differ among nations and over time. Monetary policy rests on the strength and resilience of domestic financial institutions. The efficacy of both monetary and fiscal policies depends on the responsiveness of consumption and investment decisions to fluctuations in interest and exchange rates, which again may be country and time specific. Furthermore, the political strength required to implement appropriate macroeconomic policies may simply not be present in many countries. These realities demonstrate the array of potential linkages among macroeconomic variables and public policies and between microeconomics and macroeconomics.

Hyperinflation occurs periodically in many less developed countries and creates new challenges for foreign investors who may not have encountered such rapid price changes in their home countries. Hyperinflation occurs when the money supply has been expanded rapidly and people have lost faith in the ability of a government to maintain a noninflationary policy. At such times, investors can convert their holdings into a foreign currency to avoid the risks that accompany hyperinflation. This capital flight puts pressure on the exchange rate as investors sell domestic currency. If the exchange rate of the domestic currency were to fall, the price of imports would rise, driving up the cost of living and causing further inflation as wages and prices adjust to compensate. This situation can add further complexity to business risks and can lower the return to investments in domestic currency yet further, provoking additional capital flight. Fears of future inflation and devaluation can encourage both businesses and consumers to buy foreign currencies, accelerating the inflation/devaluation spiral. The volatility of exchange rates rapidly alters the relative costs and prices among nations, making it necessary for management to reevaluate its strategies concerning both investment location decisions and its supply chains.

Predicting and Adjusting to the Business Cycle

More broadly, while the predictability of the business cycle remains very much a debate among both academics and managers, it seems quite beyond debate that the line between corporate success and failure is often defined by the decisions that are made around key turning points and movements in that cycle. (Navarro, 2004, p. 24)

Economies are vulnerable to business cycles. Business investment is generally geared to increases in gross domestic product (GDP) since investment is necessary to meet increases in demand. If GDP increases slow down, then investment will fall. When investment falls, GDP growth will fall since investment is a major component of GDP. Then consumption, which is a function of GDP, will also fall, further reducing GDP. From this perspective, recessions are built into the structure of the economy. J. R. Hicks (1950) emphasizes that there is a ceiling to the growth of GDP—full employment. When an economy reaches full employment, then the rate of increase in GDP must fall—and the economy automatically heads toward a recession, with lower investment and then lower consumption. An increase in inflation indicates an economy is close to full employment and is a leading indicator of a stock market crash and recession. For Hicks, there is also a floor to a recession. Depreciation of business assets will eventually require more investment. An increase in investment will increase GDP and consumption. A recovery is then inevitable.

Several forces may impact the timing of a stock market crash and recession. Expansionary fiscal and monetary policies may postpone the downward turning point in a boom. Many analysts point to the dot-com crash, 9/11, and accounting scandals as shocks that could have put the U.S. economy into recession—except for President Bush's tax cuts and the Federal Reserve's loose monetary policies. Productivity improvements serve to raise the full employment ceiling, delaying the decline in GDP growth rates that Hicks predicted. By reducing inflationary pressures, productivity improvements also delay tight monetary policies that central banks might impose in response to inflation, which could slow GDP growth. Meanwhile, consumer confidence can be volatile, responding to a wide variety of events—either positively or negatively. For example, a terrorist attack might precipitate a fall in consumer confidence that could cause a stock market crash and could precipitate a recession. A nation's financial system is particularly important in determining consumer confidence, and the failure of banks can suddenly precipitate a loss of confidence, leading to a recession. The failure of banks can also directly reduce business investment, as some businesses lose their lines of credit. Consequently, the turning points in a business cycle may be determined by events where timing cannot be predicted with much certainty.

Many of these issues indicate a need to exercise judgment and to calculate probabilities and risks in predicting the timing of stock market turns, as well as general macroeconomic conditions. Because of these issues, one cannot count on a 7 to 10 year business cycle as automatic, with clear timing of the cycles. Economists have developed correlations among various indices to determine which are "leading" and which are "lagging" indicators of business cycles. For example, as early as the 1930s, Mitchell and Burns discovered that stock markets were a leading indicator (Shaw, 1947). In recent years, many analysts have developed complex economic models that include many variables in an attempt to predict business cycles. Navarro (2004) has analyzed the strategic reactions of many firms to their economic forecasts. He notes that in response to a widely anticipated recession in 2001, Johnson & Johnson cut its capital expenditures by over $100 million and DuPont reduced its capital expenditures by $400 million. In early 2001, DuPont cut 4,000 jobs, or about 4% of its workforce, besides reducing its contract personnel by another 1,300. "Similarly, energy provider Duke Power, based in Charlotte, North Carolina, attempted to align its acquisition and divestiture strategies with business cycle movements" (p. 24). Southwest Airlines Co. also "relies heavily on macroeconomic forecasting to manage all phases of its business" (p. 23), including reliance on fuel-cost hedging strategies.

Pearce and Michael (2006) have written an article that advocates and describes "Strategies to Prevent Economic Recessions From Causing Business Failure." They note that an average of more than 500,000 U.S. businesses have failed in each of the past 10 recessions. Pearce and Michael recommend that each firm diversify these risks by operating in multiple markets and geographies. The sales of various products move in a cyclical or a counter-cyclical direction, and the firm should seek to offer a combination of such products in order to minimize volatility in its revenue and profits. The firm should have a plan in place during a boom to cope quickly if and when sales decline. During a recession, the firm should continue to promote its products and services and should maintain its advertising. It should attempt to attract new customers. A recession may be a good time to introduce new products as a way of supporting its revenue rather than cutting employees. During a recession, the firm should have a plan in place to quickly take advantage of the inevitable economic recovery.

McKinsey & Company have also emphasized the need to plan ahead for recessions. Their advice focuses on the value to the firm of including flexibility in its strategies. Balance sheet flexibility can create the financing capacity to take advantage of the investment opportunities that accompany a recession. Operating flexibility should enable the firm to preemptively cut its costs as the recession develops. Flexibility in the firm's product offering can help to expand sales to profitable customers and reduce sales to unprofitable customers. Writing during the 2007 boom months, Dobbs, Karakolev, and Raj (2007) state that "impossible as it is to forecast the timing or depth of the next downturn, executives enjoying today's upbeat economy should also be preparing for the recession that will inevitably follow" (p. 23).

Understanding Fiscal Policies

According to Keynes (1936), whose theories form much of the basis for fiscal policies, governments should sustain aggregate demand during recessions by injecting additional spending into the economy, even though this will likely create fiscal deficits. While Keynes focused on an increase in government expenditures as the means to increase aggregate demand, others have been reluctant to accept this greater role for government spending. Rather, "conservative" proponents of a deficit during a recession have focused on reductions in tax rates as the better mechanism to stimulate private sector demand. To the extent that income generated by an increase in government spending or a decrease in taxes is then spent by recipients, a stimulus can have a "multiplier" effect on aggregate demand far greater than the size of the stimulus itself. A recipient of increased government expenditures or a tax rebate may use the extra income to purchase goods or services. These extra purchases will raise the income of the sellers, who in turn may increase their purchases of goods or services—and so on. However, the initial recipients of extra income might simply use this income to reduce their debts, so this fiscal policy might have no direct stimulus for the economy. The society's marginal propensity to consume the extra income determines the size of the multiplier impact. If the marginal propensity to consume is, say, two-thirds of additional income, then the total increase in spending could be three times the initial increase in government expenditures.

Keynesians believe that wage and price rigidities may cause involuntary unemployment of productive resources to persist over long periods of time. Therefore, government action is a necessary means by which the economy can be returned to full employment. Keynesian theory does not recommend a policy of permanent deficit spending. Rather, Keynesians assign a useful role to government deficits only when the level of private spending falls temporarily. By minimizing the contraction in total demand, a deficit helps to restore the level of confidence necessary for an eventual upturn in private expenditures. As income and employment return to their normal levels, the need for the government deficit disappears. Conversely, if full employment leads to inflation, then fiscal surpluses based on cutting government expenditures or raising taxes can reduce aggregate demand and so reduce inflation. Hopefully, the fiscal budget can be balanced over the business cycle so that aggregate government debt can be constrained to manageable levels.

However, Keynesian economics has never commanded universal acceptance. Some opponents of Keynes reject his view that the economy can become stuck at an "under-employment equilibrium." Non-Keynesians tend to have greater faith in the ability of the economy to bounce back from a cyclical downturn without an active fiscal policy. This conflict is essentially over the flexibility of market prices, with non-Keynesians believing that unemployment and lack of adequate demand to clear markets will eventually lead to decreases in wages and prices that will clear both labor and product markets. Non-Keynesians argue that temporary fluctuations in the levels of production and employment are corrected by the automatic adjustment of wages and prices, so fiscal stabilization is unnecessary and may even be counterproductive.

Several additional arguments have been levied against the use of fiscal deficits to expand aggregate demand in a time of high unemployment. It is the possible consequences of government deficits for future economic growth that many opponents find most disturbing. Some economists believe that fiscal deficits lead a government to compete with businesses to obtain the savings of the private sector. Some have opposed fiscal deficits because of a fear that this competition for savings will drive up interest rates, thereby depressing interest-sensitive private sector investments. If a higher government deficit forces interest rates up, the resulting decline in private sector investment will reduce growth potential over the longer run and may even offset any positive impact of the deficit on demand in the short run. This concern about "crowding out" of investment may not hold if capital flows readily among nations. If domestic interest rates rise in a particular country, then foreign investors will shift more of their funds into that country and capital inflows can prevent the crowding out of investment.

As long as no restrictions are placed on capital flows across international boundaries, long-term interest rates are influenced not just by domestic supply of and demand for savings but also by world supply and demand. Nevertheless, ongoing fiscal deficits and an accumulation of debt in a particular country may add to the general perception of "country risk," particularly the risk of default, so the domestic interest rates might rise vis-à-vis world interest rate levels, crowding out domestic investment in spite of international capital flows. In addition, an increase in foreign purchases of domestic bonds may put immediate upward pressure on that country's foreign exchange rate. A higher foreign exchange rate may decrease the nation's exports. This process may reduce to some degree the growth in aggregate demand caused initially by the fiscal deficit. Furthermore, a country may build up a future problem related to servicing this foreign debt as a result of the future impact on its foreign exchange rate. From a different perspective, some expect that fiscal deficits and an accumulation of debt will place an inappropriate and unfair financial burden on future generations, who will have to repay the debt.

Canada illustrates a number of theoretical issues relevant for a "small open economy" that may be considering fiscal deficits to stimulate the economy. Canada's fiscal multiplier is reduced by the fact that a very large portion of both consumer and producer goods are imported from the United States, so part of the impact of a Canadian fiscal deficit may stimulate the U.S. economy rather than the Canadian economy. Furthermore, the Canadian government borrows in the United States to fund part of its debt, so a fiscal deficit may raise the Canadian foreign exchange rate, reducing Canadian exports at a time when aggregate demand needs to be increased. As a result, for a small open economy, fiscal deficits can "crowd out exports" even if domestic investment is not crowded out.

For all countries, some portion of the fiscal stimulus created by a deficit will occur in other countries as the residents spend part of their increased purchasing power on imports. In addition, some residents may fear that current deficits will lead to higher taxes in the future, so they may not react with higher expenditures, rather they may save a portion of their increased purchasing power. For these reasons, the fiscal multiplier may be less than expected. Consequently, the impacts of fiscal policy may vary from one nation to another and may vary over time.

The 2007 to 2009 global financial crisis quickly led to a global recession in which unemployment soared and growth fell. Nations throughout the world debated the nature and extent of appropriate fiscal policies. While aggregate incomes stagnated, profits fell, threatening to reduce tax revenue automatically. Many argued for an active reduction of personal income tax rates in order to leave more purchasing power in the hands of consumers. In addition to these attempts to stimulate aggregate demand, many supported huge "stimulus packages" with increases in government expenditures to replace the void left by consumers' reluctance to spend. The interconnectedness of the global economy meant that each nation's economy would be impacted by the fiscal policies of other countries, so international negotiations took place concerning the need for coordination of fiscal policies. The combination of these fiscal policies threatened enormous fiscal deficits in many countries. The annual U.S. fiscal deficit exceeded $1 trillion, rising to over 10% of the U.S. GDP, while in many other countries the fiscal deficit exceeded 5%.

Some critics of fiscal activism have taken the position that deficit spending can do real harm by adding to inflationary pressures that will follow a recession. This fear rests on the possible links between fiscal deficits and the expansion of the money supply.

Understanding Monetary Policies

Each government, usually acting through the agency of its central bank, can implement monetary policies through the use of several mechanisms. Governments can impose reserve requirements for commercial banks, requiring them to place a certain percentage of their deposits with the central bank. Governments can then lower the reserve ratio in times of recession or raise this ratio in times of inflation. Such action impacts the ability of the banks to extend loans and alters aggregate demand, raising it in recessions and lowering it in times of inflation. Governments can impose certain statutory interest rates. These often include the interest rate charged on interbank loans, particularly on loans from the central bank to commercial banks. In recession, the government can lower these rates to stimulate bank loans and, hence, private sector expenditures. In times of inflation, the government can raise these rates to reduce bank loans and, hence, private sector expenditures. In China, the government even dictates the interest rates paid to depositors and charged to customers. China's government can lower these rates in times of recession or raise them in times of inflation in a more direct manner than most other governments. Government actions to alter reserve requirements or statutory interest rates also serve as a signal to the banks and the public of the government's objectives and intentions in regard to monetary policies.

The 2007 to 2009 recession focused attention on the concept referred to as "quantitative easing." In a recession, a government can buy bonds from the public, thereby directly increasing the money supply since the public receive money in return for their bonds. The reserve ratio system can permit a multiplier impact as banks need to keep only a small fraction of the increase in money supply as reserves. Hence, total bank loans and the expenditures based on bank loans may increase by a multiple of the original government bond purchase. Recipients of revenue from the sale of bonds to the government may deposit this revenue in the banking system, where it may form an increase in bank reserves. If the required reserve ratio is, say, 5%, then the ultimate multiplier impact of increases in bank loans could potentially be 20 times the initial bond purchase. Of course, this money multiplier depends on the desire of consumers or investors to increase their borrowing for the purpose of increasing their expenditures, and it depends on the willingness of the banks to increase their loans in a time of recession. In addition, a government bond purchase tends to increase the general price level of bonds that provide fixed interest payments. As the price of a bond rises, the fixed interest payment falls as a percentage of this price. The interest rate is reduced. Consequently, the bond purchase not only expands the ability of banks to increase loans, it also reduces the level of interest rates, adding further stimulus to aggregate demand. In times of inflation, a government can reverse each of these mechanisms: raising statutory interest rates and selling bonds.

The U.S. Federal Reserve seeks to ensure both full employment and low inflation. The European Central Bank places emphasis on the restraint of inflation. This difference in mandate explains why the United States and Europe may sometimes pursue divergent monetary policies. Monetary policies are also impacted by capital flows, which will respond to a divergence in interest rates between countries. With monetary policies, the openness of the economy may add to a policy stimulus in a recession, since a decrease in interest rates may also decrease the foreign exchange rate, thereby increasing exports.

Central banks have generally served as a "lender of last resort" to banks that experience a temporary cash shortage. Faced with the 2007 to 2009 financial crisis, many central banks extended this concept to lend longer term against bank assets of questionable value. Emerging market countries had engaged in such bank "bailouts" in the past. Asian central banks purchased nonperforming loans from their commercial banks during their 1997 crisis. In 1995, Mexico's government created a separate agency, FOBAPROA, to fill this role, offering government treasury bills in return for nonperforming loans. With the 2007 to 2009 crisis, European and U.S. central banks also adopted this new type of monetary policy. The U.S. Troubled Assets Relief Plan, or TARP, promised to aid banks directly by buying or lending against their nonperforming loans. With this process, monetary policies can become entwined with fiscal policies. The government makes expenditure commitments that will occur in the event of default, thereby threatening to increase the fiscal deficit to an extent that cannot be predicted with much certainty.

The 2007 to 2009 economic recession also brought a new policy of government purchases of shares in banks. At the extreme, a run of depositors on the U.K. bank, Northern Rock, led to the U.K. government acquiring ownership and operating the bank. In the United States, bailouts also included government purchases of bank shares. In some situations where the U.S. government extended emergency loans to banks and to businesses, the loan provisions included the right of the government to be given shares in the event of default on the loans. Here as well, the division between monetary policies and fiscal policies becomes blurred.

While the above discussion points to theoretical limitations of fiscal and monetary policies, analyses of Japan's economy add important practical insights in regard to these limitations. With the onset of recession in the early 1990s, Japan's government created fiscal deficits, but these large ongoing fiscal deficits failed to cause a recovery. Rather, fiscal deficits resulted in a cumulative national debt that was so huge that it became an added burden on Japan's recovery prospects. This situation illustrates the warnings of "rational expectations" economists that a fiscal deficit may be offset by increased savings since taxpayers may fear that taxes will have to be raised in the future to cover the increasing national debt. Meanwhile, Japan implemented loose monetary policies with interest rates below 1%, but these also failed to stimulate aggregate demand. Both consumers and businesses in Japan chose not to increase their expenditures in response to fiscal deficits and low interest rates—at least not enough to lead to a rapid recovery. "Stuck in a depression," the Japanese experience points dramatically to the possibility of both a low fiscal "multiplier" and a low "money multiplier."

Understanding Inflation

The link between fiscal policies and the rate of inflation depends on how a fiscal deficit is financed. If a deficit is financed through bond sales to the country's consumers or businesses, then the money supply may not change. However, government bonds issued to cover a deficit can be purchased by the central bank instead of being sold to consumers or businesses. In the latter situation, aggregate demand is increased by the fiscal deficit and it is also increased by the expansion of the money supply. Our later discussion of hyperinflation emphasizes the impact of fiscal deficit financing on the money supply and, hence, on inflation. While strengthening the impact of the deficit, the purchase by the central bank of the debt to cover the deficit may lead to such a large increase in aggregate demand that inflation can quickly become a threat.

It is important to recognize that there is no necessary connection between government deficits and monetary policies. Central banks in most countries enjoy some degree of independence. When a central bank does buy bonds, it remains free to take other steps that neutralize the effect of its purchases on the money supply, such as raising statutory interest rates or reserve requirements. Nevertheless, many observers attribute the high inflation in many countries during the 1970s to accommodation by the central banks of large government deficits. Some argue that the nominal freedom granted to central banks is, in actual practice, a façade. Government officials, motivated by political concerns, may exert considerable pressure on central banks to finance budget deficits, so inflationary pressures may accumulate.

Some analysts question the direct link between money supply expansion and the rate of inflation. The velocity of circulation of the money supply may vary over time, interrupting this link. Furthermore, in recent years, the definition of money supply has become increasingly complex. Money supply is now analyzed under differing definitions. In the United States, M1 consists of currency held by the public, traveler's checks, and demand and other checkable deposits. M2 consists of M1 plus small denomination time deposits, savings deposits, money market deposit accounts, and retail money market mutual fund balances. Other definitions of money supply include other types of liquid assets. Further confusion has been caused by the expanded use of credit and debit cards, as well as other electronic payment methods. No longer is it clear exactly how the money supply should be calculated. Furthermore, increasingly investment may not depend on traditional bank loans since private equity firms and investment bankers have created new financial instruments for raising capital. Apart from these realities, the impact of monetary policies may be limited by the reluctance of consumers and businesses to increase their borrowing in response to lower interest rates or by the reluctance of banks to increase their loans in response to an increase in their reserves or a reduction in their required reserve ratio.

Price stability is one thing, while expectation of future price stability is another. Stable inflation expectations could theoretically be the basis for a stable inflation rate. However, a government that has once destroyed public trust in price stability must work painfully and hard to restore it. Edmund Phelps (1968) has emphasized the role of inflation expectations in wage determination, through which past inflation is built into higher wages in an attempt to compensate for the decline in purchasing power. These higher wages themselves become an escalating force in the determination of future prices and in the determination of future inflation rates. Phelps has developed hypothetical models of the economy that demonstrate the potential impact of errors in wage or price expectations as a cause of unemployment. In this context, "Equilibrium entails equality between the actual and expected rates of wage change" (p. 706). Phelps argues that wage and price dynamics are such that any economy is almost continuously out of equilibrium, so inflation can be an ever-present threat.

These discussions of monetary policies demonstrate that here, as well as with fiscal policies, the impacts may differ over time and among countries. For example, the expansionary policies that were most appropriate for the United States following 9/11 and the dot-com crash may not have the same impact in less developed countries, or even in Western Europe, when aimed at reducing unemployment. Further, the fiscal deficits and loose monetary policies in response to the 2007 to 2009 financial crisis and recession may have different impacts in different nations.

Anticipating Hyperinflation

Hyperinflation refers to rates of inflation that are so high that money quickly decreases in value and prices may even rise daily. Inflation is often caused by government fiscal deficits, and in some nations the fiscal deficit has sometimes even reached 10% of GDP or more. The two standard options for financing a deficit are to borrow from the public (issue government bonds or get loans from international banks) or to borrow from the central bank, which prints more currency and increases the government's accounts with the bank. The problem with printing more currency is that although there is more money in the economy, there is no change in the amount of real resources that money represents; hence, the value of money is diluted. Anticipating that their money will be worth less in the future, investors are less likely to lend at a given rate of interest, producers of goods and services are less willing to sell at a fixed price, and workers are less willing to work for a given money wage. Assuming that markets for investment, goods and services, and labor were in equilibrium before the money supply was increased, then borrowers should be willing to pay a higher rate of interest, buyers higher prices, and employers higher wages to stay at the same levels of activity where they were originally. Thus, when inflation is high and persistent, expectations of further inflation get built into the system through higher interest rates and continually increasing wages and prices.

Even if inflation is difficult to anticipate because it varies widely, contracts can be "indexed" to the rate of inflation so that wages, prices, and interest rates may all automatically vary according to the inflation rate. While it is easy to see how printing money leads to inflation, it is not so easy to explain why inflation should matter to a business. If all prices are adjusting continuously, the economy may always be in equilibrium. However, prices do not all adjust continuously. For managers, hyperinflation disrupts business strategies and business plans and creates unexpected losses and perhaps unexpected gains. It is no easy task to figure out the inflation rate on a daily basis; even monthly estimates are available only with some delay and are subject to correction as more data become available. Furthermore, for a firm that imports or exports, the domestic prices are not the only issue at stake. Also of concern is the level of domestic prices vis-à-vis foreign prices. Here, the exchange rate plays a key role, so the linkages between hyperinflation and the exchange rate can become crucial.

A long tradition of volatile inflation can erode faith in the currency and in financial markets. People may buy durable goods with their money rather than deposit in banks or invest in other financial instruments. The government may not be able to borrow from domestic financial markets and may have to look abroad for loans. Since foreign loans may be denominated in foreign currencies, the government may be committed to a given rate of payment of interest, principal, and fees that will rise in terms of domestic costs if the domestic currency loses value. Thus, the hyperinflationary spiral generally rests on two structural elements: large and recurrent fiscal deficits and an overwhelming burden of foreign debt. In the short term, a government can implement wage and price controls and influence the foreign exchange rate, but ongoing fiscal deficits and increases in foreign debt inevitably cause a return of the crisis.

Predicting and Responding to Exchange Rate Volatility

Exchange rates are a key determinant of the relative costs and prices that management faces as it considers international investment and supply chains. In order to promise foreign investors long-term stability in its foreign exchange rate, a government can sell its international currency reserves to purchase its own currency on the foreign exchange market. However, the ability of the government to maintain its exchange rate by purchasing domestic currency is limited by the size of its reserves. Even with the support of the International Monetary Fund (IMF), reserves are finite; so unless reform is successful in stopping inflation, an eventual devaluation becomes certain. This prospect provokes further capital flight, increasing the downward pressure on the value of the domestic currency in terms of foreign currencies and accelerating inflation. Another aspect of the inflationary spiral is that when prices are rising rapidly, government tax receipts lose value between the time they are levied and the time they are collected. This aggravates the fiscal deficit and can further increase inflation.

How to operate in a country with extreme exchange rate volatility poses a new set of challenges for firms that traditionally had domestic strategies for a domestic economy. These challenges depend to a major degree on whether the firm is an exporter or an importer. For the exporter, revenues will accrue in foreign currencies and devaluation will increase these revenues when reported in the local currency. For the importer, having expenditures in foreign currencies, devaluation will increase expenditures when reported in the local currency. For each firm, the impact of an inflation/devaluation cycle will depend on its export/import composition, as well as the difference between the rate of inflation in its domestic costs and the rate of devaluation. For some firms, the hedging mechanism may offer some risk reduction as the firm operates in the futures markets to gain certainty about future exchange rates. While hedging can achieve stability for the firm's profit flows in the short run, nevertheless, the hedging process generally involves costs for the firm. Furthermore, it is not possible to hedge the long-term cash flows involved in investments in physical assets. Nevertheless, the following guidelines may be of help for long-term investors.

A firm can restrict capital transfers into a country to times when it believes that the foreign exchange rate is in equilibrium; the timing of investments is important. A firm can borrow domestically to do business domestically, thereby avoiding foreign exchange rate exposure. However, this approach does expose the firm to the possibility of interest rate increases as a result of central bank monetary policy in response to a foreign exchange rate devaluation. For a foreign-owned financial institution, this approach also involves the possibility of a "run" on deposits. Management can spread the purchase price over as long a time period as possible so that domestic currency can be purchased at a lower cost if devaluation occurs. Alternatively, management can gear the purchase price to a weighted average of the exchange rate over future years, with future payments adjusted in accordance with the exchange rate. In choosing among countries as investment sites, management must place heavy emphasis on the relative devaluation risk. In choosing among business activities for investment in a country subject to devaluation risk, management must be concerned with the amount of capital required by the activity, relative to the firm's aggregate equity.

Economists have used "purchasing power parity" as a way of providing some guidance concerning the likely future trend in foreign exchange rates. However, this concept provides an explanation for only a portion of the determinants of a foreign exchange rate, namely those related to exports and imports. Purchasing power parity does not take capital flows into account. Purchasing power parity provides no guidance in regard to the timing of changes in a foreign exchange rate. Changes that are predicted by purchasing power parity will likely take a matter of years, since this analysis relates to the impact of price changes resulting from inflation on the volume of exports and imports, and this process may occur slowly. Let us turn to the calculations that underlie this predictive tool.

If inflation in Country A exceeds inflation in its major trading partner, Country B, then Country A's foreign exchange rate will eventually fall relative to Country B's foreign exchange rate. To calculate the likely percentage fall in Country A's foreign exchange rate, deduct the cumulative inflation in B from the cumulative inflation in A. The theory rests on the fact that as prices in A have risen much more than prices in B, A's exports to B will fall and A's imports from B will rise—causing A's exchange rate to fall relative to B's. This process will continue until the original price ratios are restored; that is, the percentage fall in the exchange rate roughly equals the percentage differential in inflation rates. At this point, the volumes of exports and imports, being sensitive to relative prices, will be restored to their original levels (plus some growth factor).

However, choosing the initial date from which to calculate cumulative inflation is a matter of judgment. One should choose a date when it appears the foreign exchange rate was in equilibrium: Exports equaled imports, or at least the exchange rate was stable without any government intervention to stabilize it. Capital flows may delay the purchasing power parity predictions for many years. For example, NAFTA made investing in Mexico much more attractive than previously. Consequently, capital inflows increased the demand for pesos and sustained the peso at a level high above the purchasing power parity prediction.

An alternative methodology for calculating the equilibrium exchange rate is as follows:

(a) Choose a set of goods and services that reflect the production patterns in countries A and B.

(b) Calculate the price of this set in Country A and the price in Country B.

(c) The ratio of these prices indicates the equilibrium exchange rate.

(d) Compare your calculated equilibrium exchange rate with the actual market exchange rate to determine if A's or B's exchange rate is overvalued or undervalued, and by how much.

For many years, Canada's equilibrium exchange rate was calculated to be 0.80–0.85 U.S. Since the market exchange rate was as low as 0.65 U.S., merchants could gain a profit by buying a set of goods and services in Canada and exporting them to the United States. Hence, one could predict that Canada was poised for an increase in exports that would cause a current account surplus and eventually a rise in the value of the Canadian currency. By 2007, Canada's exchange rate had risen to parity with the U.S. dollar, a situation that would also not be stable long-term.

From time to time, *The Economist* publishes its "Big Mac Index" of equilibrium exchange rates for a large number of countries, with comparisons to actual exchange rates. This approach rests on the assumption that a Big Mac from McDonald's is composed of a representative sample of each country's goods and services. This comparison of prices and market exchange rates offers a quick method for calculating purchasing power parity, although one might question its accuracy, particularly since the assumption of a Big Mac being a representative sample may not be valid for all countries.

Warnings and recommendations discussed above in regard to managing in the context of business cycles can also be relevant for the firm in the context of exchange rate volatility. Scenario planning becomes an ongoing and important part of the firm's strategies. Changes in exchange rates can radically alter the prices that the firm pays for its purchases and the prices it receives for its sales. Anticipating possible exchange rate changes can lead the firm to put in place plans to shift its supply chain geographically to nations with depreciating currencies, to put greater marketing emphasis in nations with escalating exchange rates, and even to shift its pattern of international investments. Here again, building flexibility into strategies is a key recommendation, as is geographical dispersion of suppliers and customers in order to diversify exchange rate risks.

Risks of an Inflation/Devaluation Cycle

The discussions of fiscal and monetary policies have pointed to the relationships between these policies and the exchange rate. For many less developed countries, these relationships have led to repeated inflation/devaluation cycles. Frequently, an inflation/devaluation cycle has become a foreign exchange crisis, often impacting the economy as a whole. This process generally has consisted of the following steps:

1. *Fiscal deficits recur.* Many less developed countries have experienced ongoing fiscal deficits, as opposed to the United States and Western Europe, where deficit reduction has become a major political objective accepted by the general populace. In order to win elections and popular support, leaders may have to promise increases in expenditures and reductions in taxes, making fiscal deficits inevitable.

2. *Money supply is expanded.* Many countries have been reluctant to impose constraints on money supply growth, in contrast to central banks in the United States and Western Europe. It may be too

difficult to sell bonds to cover the fiscal deficits, so "printing currency" may be the only option available to the country's leaders.

3. *Inflation rates become high and volatile.* In some countries, inflation rates have been consistently higher than in other countries. For high-inflation countries, ever-higher prices lead to a decrease in export growth over time and an increase in import growth, putting ongoing and increasing downward pressure on the foreign exchange rate.

4. *Portfolio capital inflows create vulnerability.* In response to fiscal deficits, many countries have issued bonds that have been purchased by foreigners. These ongoing portfolio capital inflows depend on interest rate premiums over other countries. Consequently, there is ongoing vulnerability to interest rate differentials, and changes in these differentials can cause speculative runs against the currency.

5. *Foreign debt service payments become large.* The portfolio capital inflows result in ongoing foreign debt service payments—much payable in foreign currencies (both public and private). These payments place a continuing downward pressure on the foreign exchange rate, a pressure which can increase with a devaluation.

6. *Investor horizons have extended internationally, enhancing volatility.* In recent years, there has been a globalization of investor horizons. Consequently, domestic debt and equity held by domestic investors is vulnerable to speculative runs in which domestic investors suddenly sell their domestic assets to shift their capital abroad. It is no longer just a matter of foreign investors shifting their funds abroad.

7. *Primary products experience price volatility.* Many less developed countries are heavily dependent on exports of primary products. Repeatedly, over time, the prices of primary products have rather suddenly increased substantially and a few years later have decreased substantially. This cycle has impacted export earnings to a significant degree, adding to recurrent foreign-exchange volatility.

8. *Devaluations have "domino" impacts.* For any one nation, certain other nations, particularly in the same geographical region, offer a competing set of exports. Consequently, if one of these nations devalues, there is immediate downward pressure on the other countries' exports, creating a "domino" devaluation effect.

9. *Fixed exchange rates lead to devaluation "crises."* Fixed exchange rates should be devalued gradually over time in accordance with inflation differentials, but often they are not. Consequently, foreign exchange rate devaluation "crises" occur when the foreign exchange rate becomes seriously out of line with the appropriate level.

10. *Weaknesses in international competitiveness create continual drag on the foreign exchange rate.* Some nations continually rank far down the list in terms of international competitiveness. Their exporters may experience ongoing reductions in exports, while imports may tend to increase over time. This increase in the current account deficit requires capital inflows to delay a devaluation that may become inevitable.

11. *Exchange rates may swing like a pendulum.* In devaluations, speculation will often depress the current foreign exchange rate below its equilibrium rates. Later, the exchange rate may move upward.

12. *Interest rates may swing like a pendulum.* In a time of foreign exchange crises, the domestic central bank often raises domestic interest rates above their equilibrium level in order to attract portfolio capital inflows, so as to restrain the decline in the foreign exchange rate. This imposition of monetary restraint and higher interest rates adds to business difficulties, thereby extending the "foreign exchange rate crisis" to become a "financial crisis" and an "economic recession."

13. *Banks face financial crises.* Confronted with business difficulties and "runs" on deposits, many banks experience financial difficulties, sometimes resulting in bank closures.

In order to stop this inflation-devaluation cycle, some countries such as Ecuador have eliminated their own currency, using only U.S. dollars. However, these economies must then accept U.S. monetary policies—which at times may not be appropriate for them. Furthermore, as Ecuador has demonstrated since its "dollarization," ongoing fiscal deficits can still lead to the risk of debt default, with a need to borrow from the IMF to support the domestic financial sector.

The "Single Currency" Debate and the Limits of Economic Integration

Western Europe provides insights into a major theme in regard to exchange rate policies, "the optimal currency area" (Hughes Hallett & Piscitelli, 2002). Many observers hope that the integration of Europe—with the establishment of common standards throughout Europe and the adoption of a single currency—will enhance its attractiveness for investment and will increase growth prospects. Currency risks have been eliminated within the euro area, and previous restrictions on cross-border investments and mergers have been reduced. Beyond these obvious changes, a series of questions remain. Will heightened competition among European-wide financial institutions improve the functioning of capital markets? Will "disintermediation" enable entrepreneurs to raise capital directly from households and institutional investors rather than relying on traditional bank loans that require physical assets as security? Will this transformation of financial practices stimulate innovation and productivity? Many observers believe the creation of the European Monetary Union with a single currency will indeed be a major stimulus for economic growth.

However, each country is being impacted differently by the single currency and European integration. Of particular importance is the shift toward common monetary policies. Countries may have different unemployment and inflation rates and may be hurt rather than helped by monetary policies that are implemented on a Europe-wide basis. The mission of the European Central Bank, focusing on combating inflation, has also become controversial, as it led to relatively tight monetary policy in the face of the 2000 to 2002 recession. Many now believe that the bank's inflation focus should be loosened and its mandate should explicitly include job creation and growth.

Some European countries have wished to be members of the European Union in order to participate in freer trade and investment but have wished to retain substantial decision-making powers at the national level. For the United Kingdom, particular concerns have been acceptance of a European social contract and the possible integration of foreign policy decisions. Denmark has chosen to remain outside the euro, but it has pegged its currency to the euro. Presumably, this gives Denmark the advantages of the single currency and also provides the country with a possible escape valve should it need it. If faced with a recession and declining exports, Denmark could devalue its currency to stimulate job creation. Ireland has experienced exceptionally rapid economic growth over the past decade, and many view this success as dependent on tax concessions offered to multinational enterprises to encourage them to locate in Ireland. Other European countries regard these Irish investment incentives as unfair competition in the international struggle to attract foreign direct investment. This situation illustrates the question whether integration within a single currency area should include tax harmonization. Ireland's relatively high inflation as a result of rapid growth illustrates an additional macroeconomic issue, namely that inflation rates may differ significantly among members of a single currency area, adding to concerns that any single set of macroeconomic policies may not be optimal for all members.

To illustrate the impacts of fiscal deficits, loose monetary policies, and the consequent inflation/devaluation cycle, we turn to the case of Argentina. President Menem managed to halt these cycles through tough fiscal and monetary policies. However, Menem's successors did not have the political strength to continue Menem's policies, so rapid inflation returned. Argentina's decision to peg the peso to the U.S. dollar meant that inflation inevitably resulted in a foreign exchange crisis and debt default.

In Practice 9.1   Economic Risks of the Inflation/Devaluation Cycle

With his 1945 election, Juan Peron rapidly increased the size of the civil service, nationalized many businesses, and imposed detailed regulations throughout the economy. The economic policies pursued by him and his successors led to inefficiency, low growth, budget deficits, trade deficits, hyperinflations, and repeated currency devaluations. The political system became increasingly chaotic, climaxing in a 1976 military coup. In the 1976 to 1983 period, the military killed 15,000 to 20,000 civilians, ruthlessly eradicating all forms of opposition. During this "dirty war," as it was known in Argentina, the foreign debt tripled and economic growth was virtually zero.

By the 1980s, hyperinflation had reached an annual three-digit level. More than 50% of the economy was owned by the government. Foreign investment was stifled by taxation, corruption, and government regulation. Imports of equipment and materials required government permits, and these permits were subject to refusal if local substitutes were available. Import tariffs were as high as 210%. In addition to punitive discrimination in taxation, foreign businesses were prohibited from operating in certain sectors, and they were subject to detailed regulation.

Elected in 1989, Carlos Menem introduced a new reform package. Stabilization of the economy would be combined with immediate fundamental restructuring of the public sector. Menem capitalized on his support immediately, passing reform laws in congress that gave the cabinet the power to privatize state-owned businesses, to reorganize the financial sector, and to conduct economic reforms—all without recourse to the legislature. Menem not only centralized the power to take economic stabilization measures but also implicated the other political parties in a democratic reform process. An immediate goal of the reform was to eliminate the fiscal deficit. In addition to privatizing major state-owned companies, the government increased taxes and the prices charged by public utilities, some by as much as 1,000%, overnight. The currency was stabilized at 650 australs to the dollar, and an informal price "agreement" was made with leading industries (Erro, 1993). On January 1, 1990, the government transformed debt of Argentine banks, in the form of 1-day certificates of deposit, into 10-year bonds denominated in U.S. dollars with interest paid every 6 months. This cut the money supply (M2) by 60% overnight. Aggregate demand was reduced by this loss of personal savings and by a 43% reduction in the federal budget.

All branches of government but one were reduced drastically in size. The exception was not, as one might have expected from past experience, the military, which saw its budget cut 50%, but the tax collection agency. With a large part of the economy underground, tax evasion had become a major threat to deficit control. Companies that were scheduled to be privatized were required to fire employees immediately and to sell off assets in preparation. The biggest state enterprise in Argentina, the petroleum company YPF, was required to auction off many of its oil and gas properties, as well as drastically reduce its workforce of 50,000 employees.

(Continued)

(Continued)

The result of Menem's reforms was unprecedented success. In 1990, monthly inflation fell from 95% in March to 12% in April; by November it was 8%. The austral climbed steadily and dramatically in value throughout the year. Tariffs were removed, exposing local industry to foreign competition. The success of the stabilization plan was certified by the lowering of interest rates and by the return of foreign investment to Argentina, with a surge in private capital inflows. As inflation fell and the economy recovered, deficit reduction was made easier by a resurgence in tax revenue. By September 1991, Menem's economic success was entrenched by success in congressional elections. To consolidate this economic success, the austral was replaced in 1992 with a new peso, which the government pledged to maintain at parity with the dollar. This policy was a powerful commitment by the government, since henceforth it would not have the option of printing money to finance its deficits. No restrictions were placed on privatization bids by foreigners, except in the case of the sale of the national airline. Furthermore, in most cases, the companies were sold for foreign debt bonds and foreign currency, reducing the national debt, as well as that portion of the debt held by foreigners. Hopeful of Argentina's determination to reform, international agencies returned to the country's aid.

It is important to note that Menem's success was short-lived. By 2000, Argentina's fiscal deficit and debt had escalated once again, shifting Argentina into another inflation/devaluation crisis involving a huge debt default.

SOURCE: Conklin and Knowles (2001).

Critical Thinking Questions

1. Evaluate the various components of Menem's reform program. Why was Menem able to succeed where others had failed?

2. Will Argentina's inflation/devaluation cycle recur indefinitely?

3. How can a firm cope with the inflation/devaluation cycle?

4. Do these economic risks differ among business sectors?

References and Suggested Readings

Conklin, D. W., & Knowles, J. (2001). *Chauvco Resources Ltd.: The Argentina decisions (A)*. London: Ivey. (Ivey Case No. 9B01M014)

Dobbs, R., Karakolev, T., & Raj, R. (2007, Spring). Preparing for the next downturn. *McKinsey Quarterly, 23*, 23–27.

Ellis, J. H. (2005). *Ahead of the curve: A commonsense guide to forecasting business and market cycles*. Boston: Harvard Business School Press.

Hicks, J. R. (1950). *A contribution to the theory of the trade cycle.* Oxford: Clarendon Press.

Hughes Hallett, A., & Piscitelli, L. (2002). Does one size fit all? A currency union with asymmetric transmissions and a stability pact. *International Review of Applied Economics, 16*(1), 71–96.

Kennedy, P. (2000). *Macroeconomic essentials: Understanding economics in the news.* Cambridge: MIT Press.

Keynes, J. M. (1936). *The general theory of employment, interest, and money.* New York: Harcourt, Brace.

Krugman, P. (2009). *The return of depression economics and the crisis of 2008.* New York: Norton.

Navarro, P. (2004). Principles of the master cyclist. *MIT Sloan Management Review, 45*(2), 20–24.

Pearce, J. A., & Michael, S. C. (2006). Strategies to prevent economic recessions from causing business failure. *Business Horizons, 49*(3), 201–209.

Phelps, E. S. (1968). Money-wage dynamics and labor-market equilibrium. *Journal of Political Economy, 76*(4), 678–711.

Shaw, E. S. (1947). Burns and Mitchell on business cycles. *Journal of Political Economy, 55*(4), 281–298.

Stiglitz, J. E. (2002). *Globalization and its discontents.* New York: W. W. Norton.

Part IV

Political Forces and the Role of Government

Analyzing and Evaluating Political Risks

10

CHAPTER LEARNING OBJECTIVES

On completion of this chapter, students should be able to

- assess the political risks and opportunities of each nation where the firm may do business,

- make comparisons of systemic political risks from the perspective of different business sectors,

- analyze the market failures that underlie government intervention in specific business sectors,

- analyze political risks caused by competition policies that may impact the growth of the firm,

- suggest the likely direction and speed of change in various government policies that are relevant for the firm,

- prioritize political risks and opportunities,

- integrate nonmarket strategies with market strategies.

The subject of political forces and the role of government appears in each of the chapters in this text, and this subject forms a unifying theme. Managers must continually analyze issues where public policies form a significant determinant of the risks and opportunities. Effective business/government relations are crucial in understanding these issues and how the firm can best deal with them. What makes this subject of special difficulty for international management is that political forces and the role of government differ significantly from one nation to another. In this section, we add a further complexity. Political forces and the role of government are continually changing. Managers must analyze not only the current situation but also the most likely scenarios that lie ahead. In this section, our discussions of political risks focus on the need to analyze and evaluate potential changes and how the firm can seize opportunities and deal with risks created by these potential changes. In considering alternative investment locations, managers must include these analyses and evaluations in their decisions.

Managers have to adjust their strategies to deal most effectively with whatever public policies exist in each nation. Many political leaders have been motivated by ideological objectives in designing a public policy paradigm, so the multinational enterprise (MNE) may face systemic political risks related to a nation's pursuit of such ideological objectives. Meanwhile, all governments intervene in specific business sectors in response to what they perceive to be market failures. Management must understand the motivations that underlie government intervention in order to predict the likely path and extent of future changes in sectoral intervention.

This chapter first considers the rationales for government intervention. Traditionally, the word *capitalist* has generally been applied to those political paradigms where the government protects private property and sanctions the inequalities that accompany this right. The word *socialist* has generally been applied to those paradigms in which government ownership and intervention is extensive in pursuit of equality. Today, however, ownership is not the clear-cut concept that it once was, and this reality adds complexity to political forces and the role of government. A government can continually modify the terms and conditions of private ownership and of personal material gain. Prohibition of certain products due to concerns for consumer health and safety or concerns for the environment may suddenly destroy a successful business just as traditional government expropriation could. In most countries, the individual's freedom to use his or her property is restricted in various ways, while incomes are taxed and subsidized. Recent years have witnessed an increasing emphasis on human capital as a form of property. From this perspective, government policies and programs that alter people's income-earning opportunities can be seen as altering the investment returns from this human capital form of property.

It is important to develop a broad perspective on a nation's public philosophy concerning the role of government in the economy. Initially, in this chapter we discuss the public perceptions, often somewhat unique in each nation, concerning "market failures" as justification for government intervention. Since public perceptions of the seriousness of market failure differ among nations, managers must understand the nation-specific perceptions. Further, since public perceptions of the seriousness of market failure differ among business activities, managers must analyze and evaluate those perceived market failures most relevant for their specific firm's activities. Many nations are in transition from one public policy paradigm to another. This chapter focuses on Venezuela, where Hugo Chavez has led a dramatic shift in the political paradigm toward more government ownership and intervention with greater restrictions on foreign investment and the goal of a more integrated Latin America. In contrast with Venezuela, in China and the formerly communist nations of Eastern Europe, the transition from central planning to free enterprise has involved major limitations in government intervention. Meanwhile many countries' investment impediments are being reduced by international trade and investment agreements that require members to create a level playing field. This chapter sheds light on systemic political risk in the form of regime changes, such as those of Venezuela, China, and Eastern Europe, that significantly alter public policies and the role of government.

This chapter also examines changes in the set of policies and programs that governments use to pursue a particular objective, namely, the maintenance and enhancement of competition. In some countries, these policies and programs are referred to as competition policy and in others as antitrust. Today, we are witnessing many new forces to which governments are responding with new decision criteria for their competition policy. Increasingly, the political risks of competition policy are shifting from the national to the international level and are impacting the firm's plans for growth, particularly through mergers and acquisitions. Changes in competition policy illustrate the ongoing nature of political risks and the difficulties in adjusting strategies in response to alternative scenarios that differ among nations.

Consumption Inefficiencies as Rationales for Government Interventions

Often, governments intervene because they question the concept of consumer rationality. Individuals do not, in general, possess much information about the vast array of potential purchases in a modern economy. In particular, consumers may not have product information that is as complete or accurate as the information possessed by the manufacturer or retailers. The prices and qualities of alternative products from alternative suppliers may be too numerous and complex for consumers to make their purchases in a rational manner. This difficulty is increased by advertising through which consumers can become the pawns of the media, responding blindly to the repetitive nonsense of continual commercials. Apart from this lack of accurate information, consumers may be unable to make wise choices. They are concerned with their social status, and they strive to keep up with the material acquisitions of their friends and neighbors. In this pursuit of one another's social recognition, they prefer particular designs that have momentarily caught the public's fancy. In deciding on purchases that obviously affect one's health, many indulge in alcohol, drugs, and tobacco to a degree that demonstrates their irrationality. Individual investors may be confused by the complexity of financial instruments and may make unwise investment decisions because of their ignorance.

In *The Affluent Society,* John Kenneth Galbraith (1958) questions the adequacy of product information and the wisdom of individuals. His recommendation is to shift a large portion of consumption decisions out of the hands of individuals and into the hands of government. Implicit in Galbraith's argument is the opinion that a wise elite can make better choices than can the mass of individuals. Apart from this consumer irrationality, Galbraith points to particular goods and services that, in his opinion, cannot readily be consumed individually. He believes that a significant portion of society's productive capacity should be shifted to such goods and services. Parks, education, and a cleaner environment should form a much larger share of society's consumption. For this to occur, the decisions about consumption must be shifted from individuals to government.

Each government has implemented policies that alter certain types of consumption decisions, and each government has implemented various kinds of government ownership, subsidies, or regulation in order to improve these particular decisions. Government price setting has been implemented for some products in order to alter the quantities that will be purchased by consumers. Subsidies and tax concessions can also alter market outcomes. Regulations can encourage suppliers to control product safety and quality and to ensure moderation in the consumption of some products. Regulations in the form of rationing and quotas can interfere directly in the consumption of certain products. Public enterprise can provide some products at prices below those that would evolve under free enterprise. A government can deal with different products differently. Some governments attempt to alter the overall consumption-saving decision through the provision of subsidies and tax concessions for additional saving and investment or through the imposition of consumption taxes. Not surprisingly, different countries have decided to deal with consumption inefficiencies differently, adding complexity to managers' strategies. Political risks include the possibility that a nation may suddenly alter its previous decisions concerning how it should deal with consumption inefficiencies.

Production Inefficiencies as Rationales for Government Interventions

In deciding when and how to intervene in a market, a democratic government is motivated by public opinion with regard to the market outcomes that will occur in the absence of such intervention. Members of the public may come to feel that market outcomes are not appropriate and so may seek to change those outcomes through the creation of interest groups that lobby for specific legislation. Government intervention may take a wide variety of forms, including regulation of prices or of any other aspect of production and product features. Consequently, the study of industry structure in Chapter 7 is intimately linked with the study of government intervention to alter industry structures. For managers, the nature of government regulations and the ways that these regulations may impact profits can become a central aspect of decision making. Here, game theory may be useful in analyzing the ways in which a firm may influence government policies.

Chapter 7 points to several types of market failure that, in practice, interfere with the attainment of efficiency. The production conditions of some goods and services may be such that the marginal cost declines over the relevant output range. In such cases, a single supplier may be able to produce at an average cost that will be lower than that of any potential new entrant. The creation of a new product or process can also be the cause of monopoly. Not threatened with competition, the solitary producer will be able to set prices above the marginal cost. Less than the socially optimal amount will be produced and consumed, and society would be better off if it shifted more resources into the production of such items. From society's perspective, this distortion of the production pattern creates inefficiency. In addition, monopoly profits transfer income from consumers of the product to the monopolist.

Some governments believe that these distortions and failures are commonplace in free markets. In many industries, only one or perhaps a few producers supply the bulk of the product. Galbraith (1967), in his book *The New Industrial State,* has presented this view forcefully. Price collusion need not involve verbal or written communication among competitors; price collusion can be achieved simply by observing the pricing decisions of competitors and reacting to these decisions. A price increase by one firm may be observed and copied by another firm. As long as all competitors follow a price leader, implicit collusion will raise prices. How much market consolidation will create the possibility of price collusion? Traditionally economists used a Hirschman-Herfindahl Index (HHI) to answer this question. The HHI is calculated by summing the squares of the market shares of the competitors in a specific market. For example, if there are five competitors, each with a market share of 20%, then the HHI is 2,000. If there are four competitors, each with a market share of 25%, then the HHI is 2,500. Generally, it is believed that if the HHI for a market is greater than 2,000, then market power is substantial and regulatory authorities should consider intervening in the market.

The threat of potential competition may create "contestable markets" and so can limit these distortions. The existing firms, although few in number, are aware that if they set prices too high, others will see this profit opportunity and enter the market. This view is strengthened by the new opportunities created by international trade and investment agreements. Foreign firms may be able to export to any economy where monopolists or oligopolists are charging excessive prices. Furthermore, it can be argued that modern technology is able to create substitutes for most products and that excessively high prices will stimulate this. Monopoly or oligopoly situations are constrained in that the dominance of a few firms will be only temporary, with substitute products always a possibility. Faced with this, a monopolist will be restrained in its price-setting decisions.

The production, consumption, and investment decisions of any particular individual can impact other economic activities. It is true that in some situations, private contracts may be developed to deal with such impacts. However, in other situations, contracts may be too complex; interrelationships may be too numerous, and their quantification may be too difficult. The individual whose decision is causing the third-party effects, or "externalities," will then have no incentive to include these impacts in his or her decision making. Pollution, for example, may severely affect the well-being of others who, without collective regulation through government, may not be able to influence the polluting activity. Positive impacts may occur, as well as negative impacts. Expenditures on research and development for new products or processes may provide benefits to others than the originator. Yet the inability to capture these third-party benefits may limit these expenditures to lower amounts than would be socially desirable. Only subsidies or direct government operation of research facilities may be able to maximize social welfare.

The significance of such third-party effects and the degree to which they can be captured by the private contract process vary among economic activities and over time. Furthermore, people disagree about the ability of governments to deal with such situations, and about the most appropriate techniques for collective intervention. Consequently, as with consumption inefficiencies, production inefficiencies have led to very different patterns of government intervention in different countries. Here as well, political risks include the possibility that a nation may suddenly alter its previous decisions.

Assessing Systemic Political Risks: The Chavez Revolution in Venezuela

While countries throughout the world generally reduced their intervention in industry structures in the 1990s, the case of Hugo Chavez in Venezuela illustrates the possibility of an abrupt reversal in a nation's public policy paradigm. Implementation of liberalization reforms in the 1980s hurt many Venezuelans, particularly the poor. The shift to free and open markets resulted in price increases for previously subsidized consumer goods. The shift from government ownership to private ownership resulted in widespread job losses. Riots in 1989 were followed by two attempted military coups in 1992, one led by Lieutenant Colonel Hugo Chavez. Chavez was sentenced to prison for his leadership role in the attempted coup, but after 2 years he was released. He then focused on building public support for a campaign for the presidency. An ever-increasing number of people wore his flamboyant red beret as a symbol of support. In 1998, Chavez ran in the presidential election on a platform that opposed what he termed "savage neoliberalism." His upbringing in a low-income family placed his sensitivities with the poor, who felt that he cared for their concerns. Like Juan and Evita Peron in Argentina many years earlier, Chavez was able as a demagogue to arouse passionate support. Chavez's speeches in the presidential election campaign emphasized the importance of "national sovereignty" and "economic justice."

In 2001, Chavez passed a new hydrocarbons law to enhance the share of oil revenue that would be owed to the government. Chavez abruptly cancelled 32 oil field operating service agreements (OSAs) that had been awarded in the 1990s. Chavez's position was that the foreign companies would have to negotiate new joint ventures under more favorable conditions for Venezuela.

Prior to 2005, Venezuelan banks had enjoyed a wide spread between deposit rates and the returns that they could receive by investing in the government's domestic debt. Some banks devoted a major portion of their assets to public debt, and state agencies placed substantial amounts in bank deposits. Chavez saw this relatively easy profit accumulation as being inappropriate. In response, he created a new government-owned bank that would take over the deposits of all state agencies. Banks suddenly faced the withdrawal of a large portion of their deposits. Furthermore, the profits that banks could earn on credit and debit cards were suddenly threatened by a new law prohibiting the charging of fees on credit cards. This law also introduced the requirement that banks charge a lower interest rate when consumers purchased "basic goods" as opposed to "nonbasic goods." In addition, the new law required banks to include fingerprint verification devices and video cameras in their automatic teller machines, a shift that would impose substantial new costs.

In 2001, Chavez introduced a radical land reform law under which farm land would be taken from the huge landholdings of the wealthy and redistributed to poor farmers and former farm employees. Chavez also created new threats to property rights in the manufacturing sector, as he encouraged takeovers by the government and employees of privately owned factories that were not fully productive. In 2007 to 2008, Chavez nationalized the Venezuelan operations of a lengthy list of foreign-owned firms, including CANTV, CMS Energy, BP, Chevron-Texaco, Conoco Phillips, ENI, Exxon-Mobil, Statoil, Total, Lafarge, Holcim, Cemex, and SIDOR.

Chavez has often pointed to Simon Bolivar as the model for his political philosophy, centered on Bolivar's vision of a unified and independent Latin

America. In ongoing trade with Fidel Castro, Venezuela sold oil to Cuba at reduced prices in return for the assistance of professionals who would work in Venezuela. Chavez used Cuban doctors to create health missions in many low-income areas. A variety of other missions offered special assistance to street children, drug addicts, and the homeless. Chavez used Venezuela's oil revenue to assist other Latin American countries in ways that would enhance his Bolivarian vision. For many investors in Venezuela, the Chavez revolution suddenly brought a systemwide shift in political risks. For investors everywhere, Venezuela's experiences emphasize the need to evaluate the risks of major changes in political forces.

In contrast with the paradigm shift in Venezuela, this text refers frequently to many nations' liberalization reforms in recent decades. Some governments, such as China's, have shifted their political/economic paradigm gradually. Others, such as those in Russia and Eastern Europe, broke abruptly from communist central planning and government ownership. These widespread and extensive rejections of government economic intervention have created a host of new business opportunities for private sector firms. Yet liberalization reforms have left many barriers and challenges. The World Bank has created Investment Climate Indicators for most nations, and these can offer guidance to managers as they consider alternative investment locations. Numerous surveys have also pointed to the issues indicated by firms as a problem in doing business in each nation. The case excerpts at the end of this chapter enable students to assess and compare the remaining political risks in each of the Russian Federation, the Czech Republic, Hungary, Poland, and Romania. Students can prioritize these risks from the perspectives of various business activities and sectors. First, we turn to general indexes of systemic political risks and then to the complex challenges created by antitrust or competition policies.

Indexes of Systemic Political Risks

Prior to the 1990s, the political risks associated with interventionist governments were considerable and included government expropriation, regulations, and foreign investment restrictions. Many countries pursued the goal of economic self-sufficiency through extensive tariff and nontariff barriers to both trade and investment. Bribery often influenced government decisions. Today, such political risks have been reduced in many countries as a result of a new acceptance of free markets and a belief that international trade and investment are necessary for economic growth. Nevertheless, political risks still remain. The Index of Economic Freedom provides a country ranking of the degree to which political intervention impacts business decisions and offers summary statistics concerning the role of government in many countries (see www.fraserinstitute.ca and www.heritage.org/index). This index points to the various ways a government may take away potential profits, and this index can be analyzed to shed light on political risks. The Corruption Perceptions Index (www.transparency .org) indicates the extent of corruption in many countries. To the degree that a government has the power to regulate and intervene in matters that affect businesses, bureaucrats may be tempted to provide the desired approvals in return for bribes; so these indexes of economic freedom and corruption can be closely related.

The analyses of Chapters 2 and 3 enter this perspective on political risks. The widespread practice of corruption means that doing business in certain countries will require clear corporate practices in regard to bribery—ranging from the decision to enforce a zero bribery policy to the decision to permit specific types of "gifts" to the decision to authorize a local partner to undertake certain "assistance" activities in regard to government officials. As indicated in Chapter 2, U.S. legislation, for example, has made foreign corrupt practices a criminal offense for senior management in the firm. Furthermore, new control and audit practices may be necessary to operate in a culture where corruption is common and where employees may therefore not automatically adhere to the standards of honesty expected within the corporation. The following quotations indicate the nature and content of several indexes of political risks.

THE ECONOMIST INTELLIGENCE UNIT'S INDEX OF DEMOCRACY

The index provides a snapshot of the current state of democracy worldwide for 165 independent states and 2 territories (this covers almost the entire population of the world and the vast majority of the world's independent states). The EIU Democracy Index (see www.eiu.com) is based on five categories: electoral process and pluralism, civil liberties, the functioning of the government, political participation, and political culture. Countries are placed within one of four types of regimes: full democracies, flawed democracies, hybrid regimes, and authoritarian regimes.

INDEX OF ECONOMIC FREEDOM

The index comprises 23 components designed to identify how consistent institutional arrangements and policies in seven major areas are with economic freedom. The seven areas covered by the index are: 1) size of government, 2) economic structure and use of markets, 3) monetary policy and price stability, 4) freedom to use alternative currencies, 5) legal structure and security of private ownership, 6) freedom to trade with foreigners, and 7) freedom of exchange in capital markets.

Areas 1 and 2 are indicators of reliance on markets rather than the political process (large government expenditures, state-operated enterprises, price controls, and discriminatory practices) to allocate resources and determine the distribution of income. Areas 3 and 4 reflect the availability of sound money. Area 5 focuses on the legal security of property rights and the enforcement of contracts. Area 6 indicates the consistency of policies with free trade. Area 7 is a measure of the degree to which markets are used to allocate capital. Reliance on markets, sound money, legal protection of property rights, free trade, and market allocation of capital are important elements of economic freedom captured by the index. (See www.fraserinstitute .org and www.heritage.org/index)

CORRUPTION PERCEPTIONS INDEX (CPI)

The Transparency International CPI (2008) measures the perceived levels of public-sector corruption in a given country and is a composite index, drawing on different expert and business surveys. The 2008 CPI scores 180 countries (the same number as the 2007 CPI) on a scale from zero (highly corrupt) to 10 (highly clean). The CPI, which Transparency International first launched in 1995, is a poll of polls, this year drawing on 14 surveys from 7 independent institutions. The surveys reflect the perceptions of business people, academics, and country analysts.

Other indexes of political risk include:

- World Economic Forum Competitiveness Report (www.weforum.org)

- United Nations Trade and Development Index Country Ranking (http://unctad.org)

- Human Development Index (http://hdr.undp.org)

For natural resource sectors in particular, political risk may still be a "show stopper" for potential investors—where the risks of nationalization, special taxes, or new regulations are particularly severe. Many political leaders regard their nation's natural resources as an important element of the "patrimony" that is passed from one generation to the next. Managers in these sectors must consider whether the risks may be too high to justify investment. It remains helpful to seek the views of local political experts. One technique involves circulating a questionnaire to these experts, compiling the results, and returning the results to the respondents for further commentary. This "Delphi" technique facilitates the development of a consensus view on the political risks that a potential investor faces.

The analysis and management of political risks has become an important subject even when doing business in one's home country. It is not automatically true that country risks are greater abroad than they are at home. In Canada, Inco's experience with delays in its Voisey Bay project—as a result of environmental objections, the advocacy of aboriginal rights, and the issue of government taxes and subsidies—involved considerable difficulties compared with the relatively easy approval for mining projects in many less developed countries. When the question of Quebec's secession is added to these political risks, many Canadian corporations may conclude that political risks in Canada exceed those in many other countries, and, in this respect, certain less developed countries may offer a competitive advantage.

International investment agreements attempt to limit political risks. Both Canada and the United States have signed investment agreements with many other countries that promise financial compensation for firms based in Canada or the United States if their assets are expropriated, and these agreements promise that the amount of compensation will be determined in a fair and just manner. Under NAFTA's Chapter 11, firms can sue a NAFTA government on the grounds that they have been denied "fair and equitable treatment" in a way that is tantamount to expropriation. However, it is not clear how far Chapter 11 or other investment agreements go in protecting firms from new government regulations that increase costs or restrict prices. Political risk insurance may be purchased as protection against specific outcomes such as capital repatriation difficulties, expropriation, or war and insurrection. Canada's EDC offers credit insurance for many such risks (www.edc-see.ca), as does the U.S. government agency OPIC (www.opic.gov).

The World Bank, Organisation for Economic Co-operation and Development (OECD), and other organizations have developed indicators of public policies that impact investment, and these indicators serve as helpful references. World Bank investment climate indicators can be found in the World Bank's "Doing Business" database (see http://www.doingbusiness.org/). The World Competitiveness Yearbook (WCY) provides a general measure of the extent to which countries provide an environment that sustains companies' competitiveness (see www.imd.ch/wcy). The Economist Intelligence Unit (EIU) provides statistics reflecting the EIU evaluation of potential political risks (see www.eiu.com). The International Monetary Fund International Financial Statistics database provides statistics that include country tables, world tables, commodity prices, and other information (http://imfstatistics.org). Source OECD is the OECD's online library of statistical databases, books, and periodicals (http://new.sourceoecd.org).

Evaluating Each Nation's Political Risks

For firms that are searching for foreign suppliers and customers, as well as for firms that are evaluating investment opportunities, the analysis and evaluation of political risks has attained a new importance and a new complexity, requiring more careful differentiation among countries and business sectors. For example, instead of viewing Southeast Asia as a group of "tigers" that experienced an economic miracle in the 1980s and 1990s and a subsequent crisis in 1997, it is now necessary to carefully analyze the political situation in each individual country. It is important to examine alternative potential scenarios and projections and assign probabilities to each scenario in order to determine the risks and rewards connected with particular business opportunities. The events of September 11, 2001, and the rise of international terrorism have added another component to political risks. How to preserve the personal security of employees has gained a new prominence in business strategies. Here, significant differences exist among countries, as some appear to be experiencing a heightened antipathy toward foreigners. Specific plans for protection and exit must be based on an analysis of each country.

The relative significance of various political risks differs from one firm to another, dependent on many features such as type of business activity, experience in managing a certain risk, and financial strength. Hence, each firm has to develop its unique political risk strategies. The analysis and management of political risks is now of paramount importance in the context of globalization, the new economy, and the changing role of governments.

Competition and Antitrust: The Rise of New Political Risks

Governments everywhere are increasing their interventions to prevent monopolies and support competition. Mergers and acquisitions (M&As) have become commonplace and now involve huge MNEs whose pricing decisions impact residents of many countries. Consequently, many proposed M&As are now being analyzed by more than one government, sometimes leading to different decisions concerning the terms and conditions for approval. In particular, the European Union (EU) and the U.S. authorities each have the power to block any M&A, leading to increased uncertainties for the managers involved. A proposed merger of GE and Honeywell, for example, was approved by the U.S. authorities but was then rejected by the EU Competition Commission even though both firms were based in the United States. Cross-border M&As add to these uncertainties for managers as many nations have concerns about foreign takeovers of their domestic firms.

Meanwhile, antitrust authorities have taken a new interest in a range of potentially anticompetitive behaviors by large firms. Here again, more than one government may be examining the same firm behavior. With Microsoft, for example, U.S. authorities seriously considered the possibility of demanding that Microsoft be split into separate legal units. Otherwise, Microsoft's bundling of various software solutions would prevent potential entrance of new firms offering any of these software solutions. After several years of legal proceedings, the U.S. authorities reached a compromise with Microsoft in this regard. However, the EU Competition Commission continued its prosecution, imposing huge fines for Microsoft's apparent refusal to implement the Commission's decreed terms and conditions aimed at facilitating new entrants and enhancing competition.

With both M&As and anticompetitive behavior, the 21st century will see increasing attention to the possibility of international collaboration among antitrust authorities. At the same time, a series of new forces are also impacting this area of public policy, creating additional complexities. For all these reasons, competition and antitrust policies illustrate the challenges of new political risks and the ongoing changes in these political risks as a result of changes in other environmental forces.

Forces Driving Increases in Cross-Border Mergers and Acquisitions

The resource-based theory of the firm suggests that an organization's assets, expertise, and financial capability are built around and support certain strategies. Environmental transformation may require new strategies and resources, and cross-border mergers and acquisitions may facilitate these adjustments. In particular, trade and investment agreements are creating gaps between domestic strategies that provided success in the past and international strategies that are necessary in the context of the global business environment. Furthermore, technological advances, adopted more rapidly in some countries than in others, have also created a requirement for new strategies. A firm needs both time and finances to achieve the requisite transformation in its strategies and resources. However, a foreign firm may already have implemented successful international strategies. Hence, a cross-border takeover, divestiture, or merger may significantly reduce the time required and may provide the finances necessary for restructuring. These benefits may justify a share price substantially higher than current market share values. A foreign firm may have much to gain in enhancing value in a cross-border takeover target. For the foreign firm, this potential to enhance value may give an advantage to the merger and acquisition process compared with expansion through organic growth and greenfield operations.

With rapid and significant environmental changes, an organization must continually compare the costs, payoffs, and risks of achieving the requisite adjustments on its own with the terms and conditions of exit. Shareholders evaluate the prospects for the organization to achieve the necessary strategies on its own, and the market price of the shares prior to the merger or acquisition may reflect this relatively pessimistic evaluation. The acquiring firm evaluates the prospects for providing the necessary resources and strategies directly, and the acquisition offer reflects this more favorable evaluation. Domestic businesses in less developed nations increasingly face this pressure to exit as restrictions on imports and foreign ownership are reduced. It is also likely that businesses in Eastern and Central Europe will confront this paradigm as they have joined the EU and now compete more directly with firms in Western Europe. A divestiture to a foreign firm may provide the requisite resources and strategies to enhance international competitiveness.

With the growing number of cross-border M&As, antitrust has increasingly become an international issue. As an example, the European Commission dealing with antitrust rejected a three-way merger proposal valued at $10.6 (U.S.) billion between Canada's Alcan, France's Pechiney, and Switzerland's Algroup. The commission felt that the proposed merger would unduly limit competition in certain segments of Western Europe's aluminum industry. The commission counter proposed that if the trio were to divest certain strategic assets, the merged corporation's ability to control the market would be limited and the chance of the deal being accepted would be greatly enhanced. The parties believed that the price of acceptance was too high and decided not to pursue the three-way deal.

Changes in Forces Motivating Competition Policy and Antitrust

In previous decades, the concept of a product and its market was clear cut and precise; a Hirschman-Herfindahl Index (HHI) could be easily calculated, or some other market dominance test could be applied, and excessive market power could be readily noted. In an attempt to restrict large corporations from limiting competition, John Sherman wrote his now-famous antitrust law in 1890 on the basis of a philosophy that was relatively easy to understand and apply. "If we will not endure a king as a political power, we should not endure a king over the production, transportation, and sale of any of the necessities of life" (Boston, 1912, p. 348).

Today, however, many forces are obliterating traditional product boundaries and national markets. At the same time, changes in technologies are reducing entry barriers. As discussed in this text, low entry barriers may make a market "contestable" or subject to competition even if few competitors actually exist. If a firm were to raise prices above a competitive level, it would attract new entrants and existing firms would behave as if these new entrants were present. From many points of view, "market dominance" is quickly fading and few corporations can long sustain the "kingship" position that Sherman feared. Yet for the moment, antitrust agencies may see a dominant position that they believe warrants their involvement. For managers, this uncertainty adds to political risks.

In the context of rapid changes in industry structures, many countries have recently rewritten their antitrust legislation and regulations with the result that precedents are few and the implications of new government positions are not yet clear. The practice of collaboration among governments—most notably, the creation of a competition commission with authority over the entire EU—is also at an early stage, adding to uncertainties facing management. Meanwhile, firms operating in more than one country may face different types of investigations and required undertakings by each set of antitrust authorities. Due diligence in expansion planning will now require that managers devote more attention to the antitrust question. With possible merger or acquisition candidates, management will increase its chances of getting a positive response from antitrust regulators by understanding the forces that are impacting antitrust decisions.

THE GREATER THE AVAILABILITY OF SUBSTITUTE PRODUCTS, THE LESS THE LIKELIHOOD OF ANTITRUST PROSECUTION

The main reason the Standard Oil Company attracted antitrust intervention in the latter part of the 19th and early 20th centuries had to do with a lack of available substitute products. Individuals and firms had no choice but to pay the high prices established by Standard through its ability to limit supply. Today, product boundaries are disappearing due to technological change that creates multiuse goods and services, where a wider set of goods and services competes for the same demand. Preparedness to alter production and consumption patterns also seems to be increasing, creating an even wider range of substitutes within the marketplace.

Industries in which a variety of substitute products exist will be less able to practice anticompetitive behavior. A company that attempts to dominate a specific product category through anticompetitive activities may find itself unable to raise prices in spite of its mergers or acquisitions. The Canadian banks involved in proposed mergers in the late 1990s argued that the emergence of Internet banking would provide a viable substitute for the traditional brick-and-mortar branch system currently in place. This viable substitute, the banks argued, would ensure a reasonable level of competition in those markets that many feared would be adversely affected by the mergers. The Canadian Competition Bureau's report on the proposed bank mergers used a relatively short 2-year time frame to counter the bank's claim that Internet banking would eventually offer the consumer a viable substitute for the brick-and-mortar branch system. Had the bureau used a longer time frame, say 5 to 10 years, the report might have come to a much different conclusion. As the rate of consumer acceptance for Internet banking increases and e-banking proves to be a viable substitute for traditional branch banking, the Canadian government might well change its position and approve the proposed Canadian big-bank mergers.

AS INTERNATIONAL TRADE AND INVESTMENT BARRIERS ARE REDUCED, THE LIKELIHOOD OF ANTITRUST PROSECUTION MAY DIMINISH

Firms are facing an ongoing decline of trade and investment barriers, and this has the effect of increasing the number of competitors by adding foreign corporations to each product or service market. Geographic regions with open trade policies will, for this reason, be less likely to require aggressive antitrust policies. An exception to this trend remains with certain industries that are still viewed as essential for the nation and national sovereignty and are protected through a variety of barriers. Canada's banking sector illustrates this exception. The government's use of investment barriers, imposed to "protect" the nation's banks, has artificially limited the level of competition in the industry, which was the primary reason given by the finance minister for rejecting the proposed mergers. The Canadian government could remedy the bank merger situation by eliminating foreign ownership restrictions.

The proposed Pechiney-Alcan-Algroup merger noted above also confronted issues in regard to trade barriers. Aluminum producers in Eastern and Central European countries that were not members of the EU at the time were not factored into the Competition Commission's decision in turning down the three-way merger. Had the output from these countries been factored into the effect that the proposed merger would have had on the level of aluminum sheeting competition in the EU countries, the results of the Competition Commission's findings could have been quite different. Had management at Pechiney-Alcan-Algroup waited for Eastern and Central European countries to be admitted into the EU, their merger efforts would have had a greater chance of being accepted.

RECENT CHANGES IN INDUSTRY COST STRUCTURE HAVE REDUCED THE LIKELIHOOD OF ANTITRUST PROSECUTION

For many decades, economies of scale gave large corporations a competitive advantage and prevented the entry of competitors. Within this kind of industry structure, the threat of antitrust was important in preventing monopoly pricing. Today, however, in many sectors, recent technological changes have created the possibility of low-cost, small-scale production. For example, the market dominance of integrated steel mills has been shattered by the proliferation of mini-mills. As we look to the future, huge hydro complexes will face competition from small-scale gas or wind turbines, and telecom corporations based on traditional copper-wire networks will face competition from various types of wireless and cable ventures.

The "new economy's" emphasis on product differentiation through innovation has created industries that rest, to a greater degree, on human capital. The fixed asset investment needed for many high-tech startups is generally low compared with that required by many old-economy manufacturing facilities. The growth of venture capital in many forms has combined with this trend to reduce entry barriers for many new-economy industries. Furthermore, within many economies, the proportion of production that consists of physical goods has diminished, and the proportion that consists of services has increased. For the modern service economy, large-scale economies are less significant and the probability of market dominance is less likely than in the old economy of mass-produced goods.

The "new economy's" focus on innovation and human capital combined with the recent abundance of venture capital funding has lowered the financial barriers to entry in many emerging high-tech industries and resulted in a proliferation of new startups. The increase in competition from new market entrants can reduce the likelihood of antitrust prosecution.

INCREASING INTERNATIONAL PROTECTION OF INTELLECTUAL PROPERTY RAISES UNCERTAINTY SURROUNDING ANTITRUST ISSUES

Governments throughout the world are enforcing the protection of intellectual property by giving ownership to patents, trademarks, and copyrights in order to reward innovators and thereby encourage more research and development that will ultimately benefit society as a whole. An irony is that this process is purposefully creating and strengthening monopolies. The World Trade Organization (WTO) is becoming an increasingly important institution for enforcing intellectual property rights. China's entry into WTO membership focused attention on the issue of global intellectual property rights. Proponents of China's acceptance into the WTO feel that

> the inclusion of China within the framework of multilateral rules and obligations embodied by the WTO is the single best instrument we have to ensure continuing improvement in China's protection of intellectual property, because we know, first hand, that multilateral enforcement through the WTO offers a far more promising method of ensuring continued progress in China's intellectual property environment than does the threat of unilateral retaliation against China. (Holleyman et al., 2000, p. 1)

New-economy corporations rely on constant innovation to maintain an advantage over their competitors. Companies will continue to invest heavily in research and development only if they are guaranteed a period of "no competition," where they can earn the required return on their development costs. Patent and copyright laws must be maintained and expanded internationally in an effort to provide the necessary incentive for companies to continue their investments in developing innovative new products. The protection of intellectual property rights provides the owner(s) of these rights with the opportunity for the maintenance of a legitimate monopoly for a set period of time. The trend toward increased global protection for intellectual property rights can conflict with antitrust objectives, creating additional uncertainties for managers.

THE FASTER THE PACE OF AN INDUSTRY'S CHANGE, THE LESS THE LIKELIHOOD OF ANTITRUST PROSECUTION

The increasing rate of technological innovation has led to a rapid increase in new-product launches and has led to ongoing changes in industry structures, adding a time dimension to antitrust. Many of these new products can be substituted for older products that in past years had no such competition. Traditional product lines are disappearing, expanding the scope and definition of a product's "market." PalmPilots, with their unique operating systems, now compete directly with personal computers and the Windows operating system. Technological change has also had the effect of blurring product categories. Television sets equipped with "black boxes" can now surf the Internet, adding another product alternative to the standard PC.

It is becoming more difficult to dominate extremely dynamic industries. Early in its corporate history, Microsoft was able to predict the relative importance of operating systems and software applications over that of the soon-to-be commoditized hardware systems. Microsoft's insight allowed it to license its operating system confidently to a variety of hardware manufacturers, which eventually enabled its operating system to become the standard, forming a natural monopoly. When Microsoft initially used its monopoly power to launch its Internet browser, the Department of Justice may have had just cause to prosecute at that point in time. However, the current environment in the high-tech industry is one of rapid change, and it is becoming much harder for the industry players to predict the future. Microsoft initially underestimated the rate of growth and the emerging importance of the Internet to the high-tech industry. By the time the final word on the Microsoft case is given, the issue of Windows' dominance is likely to be much less relevant.

The harsh irony—one that Gates and other Microsoft officials are at pains to point out—is that this effort to defenestrate the company comes at a time when the world is moving away from personal computers to large-scale computer networks. (Quittner, 2000, p. 34)

Even if Microsoft had lost in the U.S. appeals process and had been broken up into smaller companies, the increasing level of competition in the industry would make it likely that these splintered divisions would be allowed to rejoin as one company at some point in the future.

Managerial Due Diligence

Certain specific sectors have often been owned and operated by governments or have been regulated by agencies dedicated to a particular sector. Throughout the world, privatization and deregulation are rapidly changing the structure of these industries. Telecoms, airlines, and various public utilities are undergoing radical transformations—and in many countries, it is now the responsibility of the antitrust agency to ensure that the new market is competitive. In the past, many countries had restricted the delivery of health care to organizations owned and operated by the government and/or had imposed clear price regulations on both hospitals and doctors. It is likely that the shift toward greater private-sector activity in health care will bring with it similar antitrust concerns. For participants in these sectors, M&As are particularly problematic.

M&As attract media attention and public interest. Inevitably, democratically elected governments are compelled to pay attention to public opinion in regard to certain expansion proposals. Huge international mergers raise the specter of global domination by giant organizations that could collude in ways that might ultimately result in higher consumer prices. Public opinion is becoming more important and more complex as antitrust agencies look toward factors other than economics that involve subjective judgment. For many corporations, the role of public opinion serves as a "wild card" that may suddenly intrude on expansion plans. Management is well-advised to devote attention to public opinion concerning potential M&As. Being proactive with explanations to the public in regard to future benefits concerning economies, innovation, and product diversification may be crucial in a successful expansion process.

The Internet has become the focus for a wide range of merged activities among corporations that are maintaining distinct corporate structures. Most dramatic, perhaps, was the decision of Daimler-Chrysler, Ford, and General Motors to build a unified electronic marketplace for trading auto parts, raw materials, and components. Whether such collaboration is acceptable from an antitrust perspective remains an important question for many firms. It is likely that many such collaborations will be examined individually by antitrust authorities.

> Now, instead of using a few broad rules of thumb to test for antitrust, they're digging down into the details of proposed mergers to look for anti-competitive problems. . . . And they're trying to forecast whether a merged company could raise prices excessively in the long run, even if it has no current pricing power. (Carney, 2000, p. 35)

For both firms and antitrust agencies, due diligence has become more time-consuming and expensive. The downside of announcing a merger or acquisition and being compelled later to walk away from the proposal argues in favor of placing antitrust issues near the top of the list in planning for a corporation's expansion. Abbott Lipsky, Jr. (2009) wrote an article in the *Antitrust Law Journal* in which he provides advice to business managers in their efforts to comply with what he refers to as "the continuing surge in global enforcement." He has emphasized that countries throughout the world are now creating new laws and enforcement procedures.

> This continuing proliferation of increasingly potent antitrust enforcement weapons is showing signs of acceleration, if anything, following an uninterrupted two-decade global surge. This trend will create ever-increasing compliance challenges for the rising proportion of businesses that operate across national boundaries within the increasingly integrated global economy.
>
> Continuing and dramatic antitrust expansionism requires corresponding increases in management vigilance and deployment of legal resources. (p. 965)

Lipsky (2009) describes the emergence of a new "global support network for competition enforcement." In 2001, some 13 competition agencies created a "virtual" organization that has since grown to include more than 100 agencies. This organization operates by consensus without any official sanction, but it has adopted common practices in regard to certain issues such as its "Recommended Practices on Merger Notification and Procedures." Nevertheless, managers still face a vast proliferation of criminal penalties, amnesty programs, private damages, and class-action procedures that differ from one nation to another.

The financial sector faces special concerns in regard to the maintenance of competitiveness. Stijn Claessens (2009) has emphasized that governments pursue several objectives at the same time and so reach different trade-offs among these objectives. Some governments may be most concerned about achieving efficiency in the financial sector, while others may seek universal access across geographic areas and types of businesses, and others may strive for stability within the financial sector.

Consequently, managers encounter different combinations of public policies in different countries. Overall, governments do view the enhancement of competition as a key overall objective. "Making in this way financial systems more open and contestable, that is having low barriers to entry and exit, has generally led to greater product differentiation, lower cost of financial intermediation, more access to financial services, and enhanced stability" (p. 84).

Prosecution in the Diamond Industry

With the expansion and strengthening of the EU, the European Competition Commission has gained significant power in its ability to institute legal action in response to what it determines to be anticompetitive action. This new role for a European-wide institution has been a major force in changing the global diamond industry. Although Europe was only one component of the global demand for diamonds, nevertheless, its threat of prosecution was powerful. A central concern of the EU's Competition Commission was that De Beers had signed a long-term contract with the Russian diamond producer Alrosa for all of its supply. The contract provided for purchases by De Beers of diamonds worth $800 million a year, and this agreement prevented potential competitors of De Beers from gaining any access to what was a major component of the global supply. The 5-year Alrosa agreement would significantly restrict the open trade in diamonds. Although neither De Beers nor Alrosa was an EU company, nevertheless, the European Competition Commission was empowered to intervene on behalf of Europeans who would have to pay higher prices than they would if the global market were more competitive. The Commission felt that even if Alrosa were to limit its sales to De Beers to half of its annual production, De Beers' position in the world market for rough diamonds would be unacceptably dominant. After considerable negotiation between the Competition Commission and De Beers, an informal settlement involved a phased reduction in the amount of diamonds that De Beers would purchase each year from Alrosa. Under the agreement, De Beers would be able to purchase $700 million of Alrosa diamonds in 2005, but this amount had to decline by $75 million each year thereafter until an annual volume limit of $275 million was reached. This agreement would ensure that competitors of De Beers would have access to a large supply of rough diamonds.

The shift from communist central planning to free enterprise management left many obstacles for private sector investors (see In Practice 10.1). Even in 2005, investors had to evaluate significant political risks. The following case excerpt presents a number of the World Bank Investment Climate Indicators and survey results.

In Practice 10.1 | Assessing and Comparing Political Risks

By 2006, Hungary had experienced more than 15 years of transition from central planning to free markets. The reform process had involved several distinct phases. The initial "leap to the market," with its widespread privatizations, included a dramatic deregulation with a "guillotine" procedure. A more refined process of "regulatory impact assessments" (RIAs) followed this period. A newly empowered competition office sought to strengthen the extent of competition within markets dominated by a single firm or a small group of firms. The goal of EU membership was a consistent driver of the reforms as early as 1991, since the EU model was compulsory for EU members. These years had been turbulent, and the transition was not yet complete.

Several exhibits compare aspects of political risk in Hungary with those of other Eastern European countries and Russia. Exhibit 10.1 provides three indicators of the regulatory burden that businesses had to endure in 2005.

Exhibit 10.2 presents seven issues that firms regarded as problems in doing business in 2005.

Exhibit 10.3 presents 12 World Bank Investment Climate Indicators for 2005 for each of several countries, as well as the OECD average.

Exhibit 10.1   Investment Climate Indicators 2005

Indicator	Czech Republic	Hungary	Poland	Romania	Russian Federation
Senior management time spent dealing with requirements of regulations (%)	2.1	4.0	3.0	1.1	6.3
Consistency of officials' interpretations of regulations (% of firms)	29.4	51.1	27.0	44.0	37.3
Unofficial payments for firms to get things done (% of sales)	0.4	0.5	0.4	0.6	1.0

Senior management time spent in dealing with requirements of government regulation (%): Average percentage of senior management's time that is spent in a typical week dealing with requirements imposed by government regulations (e.g. taxes, customs, labor regulations, licensing, and registration), including dealings with officials, completing forms, et cetera.

Consistency/predictability of officials' interpretations of regulations affecting the firm: Percentage of firms who agree with the statement "In general, government officials' interpretations of regulations affecting my establishment are consistent and predictable."

Unofficial payments for typical firm to get things done (% of sales): Average value of gifts or informal payments to public officials to "get things done" with regard to customs, taxes, licenses, regulations, services, et cetera. The values shown indicate a percentage of annual sales.

SOURCE: World Bank (2005b).

| Exhibit 10.2 | Issues Indicated by Firms as a Problem Doing Business (% of firms) 2005 |

Issue	Czech Republic	Hungary	Poland	Romania	Russian Federation
Anticompetitive practices of others	51	53	51	48	37
Corruption	49	26	45	49	40
Functioning of the judiciary	49	20	47	48	28
Uncertainty about regulatory policies	61	49	69	64	58
Labor regulations	51	36	46	41	20
Business licensing and permits	40	23	28	43	30
Customs and trade regulations	47	24	32	32	26

SOURCE: World Bank (2005b).

| Exhibit 10.3 | Doing Business Indicators 2005 |

Indicator	Czech Republic	Hungary	Poland	Romania	Russian Federation	OECD Average
Days required to start a business	40	38	31	11	33	19.5
Cost to start a business (% of income per capita)	9.5	22.4	22.2	5.3	5	6.8
Rigidity of employment (100 is most rigid)	24	37	37	59	30	35.8

(Continued)

Exhibit 10.3   (Continued)

Indicator	Czech Republic	Hungary	Poland	Romania	Russian Federation	OECD Average
Cost of firing (weekly wages)	22	34	25	98	17	35.1
Time to register property (days)	123	78	197	170	52	32.2
Cost to register property (% of property value)	3	11	1.6	2	0.4	4.8
Legal rights (10 is most protection)	6	6	3	4	3	6.3
Disclosure index (10 is most disclosure)	2	1	7	8	7	6.1
Time to enforce a contract (days)	290	365	980	335	330	225.7
Cost to enforce a contract (% of debt value)	9.1	8.1	8.7	12.4	20.3	10.6
Time to go through insolvency (years)	9	2	1	5	4	1.5
Recovery rate (cents on the dollar)	17.8	35.7	64	17.5	27.6	73.8

SOURCE: World Bank (2005a)

SOURCE: Conklin and Cadieux (2006).

Critical Thinking Questions

1. Evaluate the political risks in investing in Hungary. Which are most serious for an investor? Prioritize these political risks.

2. Compare Hungary's investment climate indicators with those of other countries. Do the World Bank's indicators provide an accurate and complete view of the political risks facing investors? What additional information would you want as a potential investor?

3. Will Hungary's membership in the EU eliminate these political risks?

References and Suggested Readings

Boston, C. A. (1912). The spirit behind the Sherman antitrust law. *Yale Law Journal, 21*(5), 341–371.

Carney, D. (2000, February 28). The new math of antitrust. *Business Week* (New York), p. 35.

Claessens, S. (2009). Competition in the financial sector: Overview of competition policies. *World Bank Research Observer, 24*(1), 83–119.

Conklin, D. W., & Cadieux, D. (2006). *Hungary's reform process*. London: Ivey. (Ivey Case No. 9B06M081)

Economist Intelligence Unit. (2008). *Economist Intelligence Unit's index of democracy*. Retrieved December 5, 2009, from http://graphics.eiu.com/PDF/Democracy%20Index%202008.pdf

Galbraith, J. K. (1958). *The affluent society*. New York: Houghton Mifflin.

Galbraith, J. K. (1967). *The new industrial state*. Princeton, NJ: Princeton University Press.

Heritage Foundation. (2009). *Index of economic freedom*. Retrieved December 5, 2009, from http://www.heritage.org/Index/

Holleyman, R., II, Lowenstein, D., Morgan, K., Murphy, E., Rosen, H., Smith, E., et al. (2000, February 23). *An open letter in support of China PNTR from America's creative industries*. Retrieved January 6, 2010, from http://www.iipa.com/rbi/2000_CHINA_PNTR.PDF

Hughes Hallett, A., & Piscitelli, L. (2002). Does one size fit all? A currency union with asymmetric transmissions and a stability pact. *International Review of Applied Economics, 16*(1), 71–96.

Lipsky, A. B., Jr. (2009). Managing antitrust compliance through the continuing surge in global enforcement. *Antitrust Law Journal, 75*(3), 965–996.

Quittner, J. (2000). Carving up Gates. *Time, 155*(19), 34–37.

Rugman, A. (2001). The impact of globalization on Canadian competition policy. In D. Conklin (Ed.), *Canadian competition policy: Preparing for the future* (pp. 30–44). Ontario: Pearson Education Canada.

Transparency International. (2008, September 22). *Corruption perceptions index*. Retrieved December 3, 2009, from http://www.transparency.org/news_room/in_focus/2008/cpi2008

World Bank. (2005a). *Doing business in 2005: Removing obstacles to growth*. Washington, DC: Author. Retrieved July 25, 2006, from http://siteresources.worldbank.org/EXTEDEVELOPMENT/Resources/DoingBusiness2005.pdf

World Bank. (2005b). *World Bank enterprise surveys: Bureaucracy and corruption*. Washington, DC: Author. Retrieved July 25, 2006, from http://rru.worldbank.org/ Enterprise Surveys/

Seizing Opportunities in Privatization and Regulatory Changes

11

CHAPTER LEARNING OBJECTIVES

On completion of this chapter, students should be able to

- recognize the motivations that underlie government decisions to nationalize, as well as decisions to privatize,

- recognize the motivations that underlie government decisions to regulate, as well as decisions to deregulate,

- recommend new investment opportunities that are arising as a result of privatization and deregulation,

- assess the risks and advantages of investing in public-private partnerships,

- evaluate a nation's changes in foreign ownership regulations and the implications for the firm,

- assess the shift of regulations from the national level to the regional level and global level.

In recent years, many societies have concluded that the benefits and costs of certain public enterprises do not justify continued government ownership and operation. Vigorous political debate has developed as to whether these enterprises should be sold to private owners, what the terms and conditions of a sale should be, and what form the arrangements for the organizational structure should take. The decision to privatize, or to sell shares to the public, is rarely a simple one. A government may decide to privatize part of the marketplace while maintaining ownership of its particular firm. This may be done by allowing private firms to compete against the government enterprise. Over time, the government enterprise may fill a continually decreasing share of the market, while new private firms become dominant. Nevertheless, the continuing role of state-owned enterprises (SOEs) remains a subject of contention, as firms may regard the pricing decisions of SOEs as unfair competition, with SOEs avoiding the constraints of profitability and interest payments. The sale of a certain portion of the ownership to a private entity involves a complex negotiation of many details. The specific share of ownership has to be agreed, and the private investors may require that they own more than 50% in order to be able to exercise management control over daily decisions. Some governments have retained a "golden share" that consists of a separate share class with veto power over specific types of management decisions. The "golden share" leaves the private investor in control of operational decisions but provides the government with a permanent right to make certain strategic decisions.

Rather than selling ownership, the government may offer a long-term lease of government-owned assets. Such a lease promises that eventually, perhaps not until 100 years have passed, the public will once again own the assets. This is particularly advantageous in view of the uncertainty of future events. For example, a jurisdiction may experience dramatic demographic changes. Population growth may result in increases in the demand for the services provided, resulting in economies of scale that add to profitability. Escalating land prices may increase the value of the assets. New technologies may create substantial added value for the investment. For example, telephony might be possible over electrical wires, so a hydro corporation might become a telephone company and a provider of television entertainment and Internet access. To sell the government ownership outright would deprive the public of any such future gains.

To the degree that a central focus has to do with operational efficiency, the government may sign a management contract with a private sector entity. Such contracts can take a wide variety of forms. At the extreme, the management contract may be to design, build, and operate the entire activity in return for remuneration that could be geared to the demand for services or could be a specific dollar amount. In recent years, concerns about privatization have led to advocacy of ongoing public-private partnerships. It is hoped that this new form of ownership will be able to combine the advantages of private sector involvement with the long-term interests of the public. However, such partnerships face a number of challenges. It is now generally believed that each public-private enterprise should have its own unique organizational structure with its own unique procedures for ongoing government involvement in management and investment decisions.

Regulations that differ among countries can form significant barriers to trade and investment, as the firm may have to modify its products or services to conform to each nation's regulations. Consequently, various agreements seek to harmonize regulations. The worldwide shift to deregulation may facilitate this process of harmonization. For financial institutions, regulations have differed among countries and attempts are being made to establish structures and practices for international regulations. Regulatory changes create new opportunities that managers can seize, as well as new challenges that they must manage.

What Governments Seek to Achieve Through Nationalization

Prior to the 1970s and 1980s, a vast literature emphasized the value to a nation of government nationalization of specific types of activities. Economists developed a literature in regard to "market failures" that would result from private ownership of certain activities. Rationales for government infrastructure ownership are illustrated by transportation systems. For the transportation infrastructure, the marginal cost of an additional user may be negligible. Yet to set price equal to the negligible marginal costs, as efficiency would require, would not yield enough revenue to make the project financially viable. This pricing issue is made even more difficult because many such projects are in a monopoly position. An industry as a whole may have declining marginal costs over the entire range of industry demand, so it is possible that the entire industry output can be produced at the lowest possible cost by a single firm. Consequently, declining marginal costs can be the basis for a monopoly. Any prospective entrant facing high initial costs might decide not to enter. If it did enter, the existing firm with its larger production would experience lower average and marginal costs than the new entrant and could underprice its new rival, presumably driving it out of the industry. One road, one canal, or one railway may provide adequately for all the needs of the population within the geographical area being served. Being a monopolist, the owner could set a price above the marginal cost. Other members of society would perceive such monopoly pricing as unfair and inefficient. Many believed that only government ownership and operation could provide for appropriate pricing.

Transportation infrastructures also demonstrate the problems associated with externalities and private contracts. With a new transportation system, the costs of many products might fall and the ultimate consumer would experience lower market prices for many purchases. In theory, a private owner might be able to capture all such indirect benefits. However, this would require price discrimination, charging each user in accordance with his or her gains from the system, and also significant borrowing to finance the system until future users could pay. Contracts with customers, both present and future, as well as contracts with the lenders of capital, may not be able to capture enough externalities and provide adequate financing to undertake such projects.

Some nations have accepted the above arguments for businesses such as iron, steel, and automobiles that are hoped to have a stimulating impact throughout the nation or throughout a particular region within it. Reluctance to accept foreign ownership of key sectors may also argue for government ownership. Furthermore, a government is able to redistribute income and wealth through pricing policies if it owns the activity. However, economically advanced nations may possess such a well-developed capital market that the contracting problems are not severe, so the extent of public enterprises may be reduced over time as the economy develops. Some countries have been more optimistic than others concerning the size of an activity's externalities or have stood in greater need of a solution to particularly high unemployment and slow growth. This perspective explains much of the difference among countries in government ownership and operation. New circumstances may lead a country to expand or reduce its ownership and operation of certain activities, creating new opportunities or challenges for investors.

In his book *Public Enterprise Economics,* Ray Rees (1984) discusses the rationale for public enterprise under four broad themes:

1. To correct market failure

2. To alter the structure of payoffs in an economy

3. To facilitate centralized long-term economic planning

4. To implement socialist ideology (p. 2)

With regard to market failure, Rees (1984) points to monopolies, externalities, and common-property resources. He also considers "dynamic" market failure, where new enterprises cannot be initiated because the capital market is not adequately developed or because private investors are too risk averse. With regard to the structure of payoffs, Rees refers to the distribution of income and consumption and the ability of society to alter distribution through the operation of public enterprises, particularly through pricing policies. With regard to centralized planning, Rees discusses the political perception that certain sectors are essential for growth, especially the infrastructure of transport, communications, energy, and steel. With regard to the socialization of production, ideology can play a role, and the motivation can be to eliminate what some people perceive as capitalist exploitation.

In their book *State-Owned Enterprise in the Western Economies,* Vernon and Aharoni (1981) emphasize that, for any one public enterprise, there may be several motivations, and this complexity confuses the simple evaluation of the enterprise in terms of fulfillment of its objectives.

Where the confusion begins is in the fact that state-owned enterprises are usually created with many different purposes in mind, with some parts of the body politic harbouring one main purpose while other parts harbour another. . . . It is in this multiplicity of goals that confusion lies. (p. 11)

In addition to the complexity of multiple objectives is the complexity of varying degrees of public ownership and control. In considering the future of public enterprise, Parris (1987) has emphasized "the continuing tendency for the distinction between public and private enterprise to become blurred" (p. 173). In recent years, the belief has grown that the administration of public enterprise can be improved through the infusion of private market forces and through a distancing from civil servants and politicians. Although still owned by the state, some public enterprises are now acting more like private firms, borrowing capital on private markets, being required to become profitable, and being exposed to private competition.

New Privatization Opportunities

The above section presents a summary of the arguments that have been used to support government ownership and operation of certain economic activities. Beginning in the 1970s, however, the view became increasingly widespread that weaknesses exist with government ownership and operation. A new body of literature has developed in which economists refer to "government failures." One might argue that these government failures could become apparent only through the practical experience of government ownership and operation.

Civil servants or bureaucrats may not be as keen to assist customers as is the situation in privately owned enterprises. Some observers conclude that government employees expect to have permanent employment. Without the risk of being dismissed, they do not go to extra lengths to respond to particular needs of their customers. They can ignore customer complaints. They can refuse to offer special help to customers who need it. From this perspective, privatization promises a more intense and ongoing responsiveness to customers. Privatization also promises improvements in the quality of service. Employees have to be more conscientious in their daily work.

Related to this attitude on the part of government employees is the argument that they lack concern for efficiency and productivity improvements. Some observers point to the compensation scheme within governments as a principal cause of this phenomenon. In general, governments offer a rigid pay scale without the opportunity for bonuses based on performance and with promotion based on seniority rather than achievements. With the second half of the 20th century, economists have increasingly emphasized productivity improvements as an essential element of the economic growth process. For any society, future economic well-being and the nation's economic growth rate are seen as depending on the ability to introduce continual improvements within the functioning of each enterprise. Privatization promises to raise general living standards by offering greater value at lower cost.

The previous section presents arguments in favor of government ownership and operation in order to implement prices and investment strategies that would be in the interest of the general public. However, in practice many observers feel that political responses to public pressure groups inevitably result in prices and investments that are inappropriate in the context of efficiency and productivity. Politicians are not in a position to make decisions that will be optimal for society as a whole or that will be optimal from the perspective of the long-term interests of society. Furthermore, politicians are not able to negotiate market-level wage agreements because they cannot withstand the political pressures that a strike would create. Economists have developed an extensive literature in regard to "public choice" in which they analyze the process of government decision making in the context of pressure groups and elections. Privatization can avoid these pressures and can bring prices and investment in line with market realities.

Many authors have argued that in regard to creativity and spontaneity, the individual initiative and personal risk taking of the entrepreneur contrast sharply with the obedience to bureaucratic rules, concern for proper process, and reference to chains of authority that mark the government employee. Bureaucracies are endemically resistant to change. Thompson (1969) emphasizes that "in the case of the bureaucratic organization, there is special need for caution with regard to change" (p. 19). Specialization is part of the bureaucratic structure, and those who have become proficient at one particular activity have a strong vested interest in opposing change. Furthermore, the employees become "specialized in working with one another. . . . Consequently, any suggestion for change must be measured against its effect on the co-operative system as a whole. Bureaucratic organizations must plan and control change" (p. 19). Perception and creativity are not encouraged—and may even be discouraged. Thompson carries this view further.

> Many studies attest to the fact that groups, over a period of time, exert powerful conformist pressures on their members. Consequently, there is nothing about groups as such that can be guaranteed to increase individual creativity; they could, in fact, have just the opposite effect. (p. 14)

All these forces argue in favor of privatization.

Participating in Public-Private Partnerships

Public-private partnerships are playing a bigger role in capital projects across all areas of government, such as transportation, communications, power generation, energy, delivery, water and wastewater, waste disposal, courthouses, hospitals, jails and even legislative assemblies. (Murphy, 2008, p. 99)

In recent years, a new literature has advocated the creation of public-private partnerships (P3s) for activities that were once seen as appropriate for government ownership and operation. Proponents in favor of these new structures believe that such arrangements can achieve all the advantages of the private sector that are discussed above. The involvement of private sector ownership will automatically lead to improvements in efficiency and quality. The enterprise will achieve a new responsiveness to the needs of consumers. The enterprise will be capable of more active entrepreneurship and will achieve ongoing innovation. At the same time, these new structures will provide government involvement that is necessary to protect the long-term interests of the public in regard to the enterprise's strategy and future investments. The public will continually gain benefits from the innovation and technological improvements that will result from private sector involvement. The partial government ownership will create a vehicle for continual involvement on behalf of the public. This perspective suggests that regulatory structures may be simplified and there may be less need for public involvement in a regulatory structure. Government involvement in ownership will provide ongoing transparency and accountability.

Private sector entities have become actively involved in investing in P3s throughout the world. In 2008, Morgan-Stanley created a $4 billion fund to invest in such partnerships, while Credit Suisse and General Electric created a fund of more than $5 billion. The manager of the Credit Suisse–GE fund has emphasized that his organization will bring operational expertise to investments anywhere in the world.

"What really differentiates us from other infrastructure funds is our ability to apply our operational expertise," he said. "Many infrastructure companies and assets have not really been exposed to the management techniques that most well-run industrial companies adopt, either because they were government-owned or (they) operated in monopoly or quasi-monopoly environments." (Guerrere, 2008, p. 1)

Some analysts suggest that P3s may be the only way to access the large amounts of capital needed for 21st century infrastructure investments. Some now suggest that each city must create a strategy that will link a list of necessary public investments with specific opportunities for private sector involvement. As reported in Canada's *Globe and Mail* May 21, 2008, an international analyst argued that the city of Toronto must

> Make a dramatic move to attract private-sector money for public projects like its massive light-rail expansion plans.
>
> But to attract that money, cities should develop and promote a "prospectus"—just like a private firm looking for investors—with a list of "investment-ready" projects, structured to bring in private-sector money and promoted with expected rates of return. (Grey, 2008, p. A11)

Timothy Murphy (2008) has emphasized the advantages of P3s. Private sector involvement can build infrastructure faster because of the greater ease in accessing capital. Cost overruns are absorbed by the private sector. The private sector will bear the significant risks in design and construction, as well as the risks in operating and management. P3s will improve efficiency and cost effectiveness. Reliance on direct charges for usage provides a strong incentive for maintaining high-quality customer service. The P3 structure allows government to focus on the overall outcomes, as well as key problems, leaving daily issues to the private partner.

However, Murphy points to five arguments that have been levied against P3s:

1.   Opponents argue that P3s will be more expensive because the private sector inevitably faces higher costs in borrowing from the public. Furthermore, P3s have to earn a profit. They may also face higher procurement costs. Murphy argues that in practice, the evidence indicates that P3s do offer cost effectiveness. Furthermore, this structure eliminates significant risks that could create major costs for the government.

2.   Opponents argue that the private sector will seek to create lower quality design and service. Murphy emphasizes that this argument points to the need for carefully crafted service and quality standards, as well as effective ongoing oversight. Murphy also recommends the importance of penalty clauses and cancellation clauses as mechanisms for ensuring ongoing service quality.

3.   Opponents argue that P3s involve less accountability and more secrecy. In response, Murphy argues for the institution of value-for-money assessments at various stages in the construction and operation of the enterprise. The agreement must include provisions for ongoing monitoring of the project with benchmarks for performance achievement.

4.   Opponents argue that P3s are a threat to workers' rights and will inevitably reduce the number of employees. Murphy recommends provisions in the agreement that will obligate the private sector to hire public sector employees, and he argues that there is no compelling evidence of large job losses. Nevertheless, it should be expected that private sector

involvement will introduce new compensation programs such as incentive pay, bonuses, and profit sharing.

5. Opponents argue that P3s will result in a loss of public policy flexibility. In particular, commitments will be made for decades to come. A long-term commitment is a requirement of the P3 concept, so it must be recognized that some policy flexibility will be lost. This emphasizes the importance of the detailed negotiations for any particular P3. In addition, some opponents argue that future trade agreements could entrench the rights of foreign investors in ways that could limit future government interference in strategic decisions.

Murphy emphasizes that to be successful in P3s, governments must develop effective project and contract management skills. This contracting expertise may not be present and may have to be created.

> To do this effectively, the government needs the requisite independent expertise to make sensible value-for-money comparisons, to run a fair and effective procurement process, to ensure effective allocation of risk, and, finally, to effectively monitor and enforce contractual compliance. (Murphy, 2008, p. 99)

A recent literature expands on the challenges that governments face in designing and implementing P3s. The World Bank now sees P3s as an increasingly significant investment vehicle throughout the world, and it has created a Public-Private Infrastructure Facility to provide funding of P3s. Ongoing challenges include the creation of an organizational structure that will facilitate joint decision making between the private and public representatives. To some degree, this challenge is similar to that found in strategic alliances between corporations, such as outsourcing arrangements, so these bodies of literature provide guidance. For example, it may be appropriate to create a committee with representatives from both the private and public investors, which has the power to bind both sets of investors. How to resolve disputes that will inevitably arise forms a related challenge. It may not be possible to project with much certainty what the optimal future investment strategies may be. At some point, the private and public partners may recognize that they have differences in strategic preferences and financial capabilities concerning future investments. Governments may have a political need to offer concessionary rates for specific groups, such as those with low incomes, or to specific firms in order to attract them to the jurisdiction. How to combine the public interests in such situations with the private sector's desire to maximize profits may present an ongoing challenge. Governments may have an obligation to provide transparency and public accountability that may not be shared by the private sector investor.

It is clear that each P3 has to be designed to deal best with the unique interests of the various parties in the context of the specific type of business activity. The history of P3s has been brief, so the disadvantages may not be seen for many years or decades. In particular, many of the attributes of the private sector rest on the central reality of market competition. The creation of a P3 by itself may do little to enhance the market competition on which efficiency, productivity improvements, and innovation depend. Different governments are reaching different decisions in regard to ownership, privatization, and P3s, and for many governments these decisions are changing over time. Managers must continually evaluate the new opportunities being created by privatizations and P3s.

Adjusting to Regulatory Changes

Regulations may be directed at a myriad of features and attributes of a product and its production process. Governments can choose any of these elements as the focus for regulation, including, for example, the working conditions of employees; the impact of production facilities and waste materials on the purity of air and water or on the aesthetic appearance of the community; the appropriateness and accuracy of advertising and marketing programs; the health and safety of customers who use the product; and the financial obligations of the producer to its suppliers, employees, customers, and government. For any aspect of any economic activity, a government may conclude that private decision making could be contrary to the best interests of the society as a whole. Through regulations, a government is able to withdraw any particular economic decision from the direct participants and make that decision collectively. Furthermore, for decisions that it leaves to individuals and firms, a government is able to restrict the freedom of choice. From these perspectives, a government may be able to achieve its objectives through regulation without the difficulties involved in government ownership and operation.

George Stigler (1971) has analyzed regulations as a means by which firms can increase their profits as they "capture" the regulatory process. Stigler claims that "as a rule, regulation is acquired by the industry and is designed and operated primarily for its benefit" (p. 3). Firms in a particular industry and professionals in a particular occupation inevitably pressure governments to impose various regulations that will restrict entry, thereby enabling them to charge higher prices than they otherwise could. In many societies, a general perception has developed that the benefits of regulations have not, in practice, been as great as had been hoped when they were first imposed and, furthermore, that the costs of administration and compliance have exceeded original expectations. Out of this perception, a trend toward deregulation has developed in many societies. Support for deregulation is based on the disappointing results in practice of particular types of regulation. The theme of deregulation was a major plank in many political platforms as early as the 1980s, including those of Margaret Thatcher in Britain and Ronald Reagan in the United States.

In designing regulations, a government can institute many kinds and degrees of legal standards and can enforce its regulations in a variety of ways. Interpretation and enforcement are often delegated to public servants, and this raises issues of the appropriate role of legislators and of the judicial system. The processes for evaluation of costs and benefits of a regulation are not clear-cut or straightforward, and they often involve difficulties in quantifying certain attributes such as cultural sovereignty, clean air, and public safety. In recent years, many countries have adopted deregulation programs on the grounds that efficiency and growth are reduced by the compliance costs and distortions caused by regulations. Another central theme is the tendency for changing circumstances to render some regulations obsolete. A regulation that appears to be appropriate at a certain time may later be seen to encounter practical difficulties that limit its usefulness. Long-term impacts may turn out to be less desirable than short-term impacts. Many regulations interfere with international trade and investment, so international agreements are increasingly focusing on these regulations and are seeking to restrict or harmonize them in order to create a level playing field for businesses. In view of these issues, regulations can be subject to considerable uncertainty and frequent change, requiring that managers continually adjust their strategies in response.

In recent decades, legislatures have frequently delegated the making of particular kinds of regulations to specialized agencies. For most countries, this proliferation of agencies has resulted in the development of extensive bodies of administrative laws. The agencies have often been granted the power to enforce their regulations, so administrative bodies have adopted judicial powers and processes. Often, such bodies can examine evidence and impose penalties for violations. Relationships between regulatory agencies and the court system have sometimes been unclear, with uncertainty as to the rights of the firm to appeal the decisions of the agencies. Nations differ in regard to the relationships and reporting practices between regulatory agencies and their legislatures. They differ in the relationships between the administrative law of regulatory agencies and that central body of law that has been approved explicitly by the legislature. They differ in procedures for appealing the decisions of regulatory agencies. Within each nation, significant differences exist among the various types of agencies with regard to each of these issues. Meanwhile, the European Union (EU) has worked toward the international harmonization of its member countries' regulations. Two broad areas of regulation of particular concern to international investment illustrate these issues: foreign ownership regulation and banking regulation.

Foreign Ownership Regulations

For the multinational enterprise, a particularly important set of regulations relate to government policies that restrict foreign ownership. In the 1970s and 1980s, many developing countries imposed economy-wide restrictions on the percentage of foreign ownership that was permitted within each business entity. In some countries, restrictions have been aimed at a large number of specific sectors. In other countries, only a few sectors have been subject to foreign ownership restrictions—often telecoms, airlines, and banks. In recent years, a major portion of foreign direct investment (FDI) restrictions have been reduced or eliminated, generally as a requirement of new trade and investment agreements. In the North American Free Trade Agreement, for example, Mexico pledged to open a lengthy list of previously restricted sectors. China's entry into the World Trade Organization included China's pledge to permit FDI, subject to specific remaining limitations in a set of previously restricted sectors. These agreements have created a host of new international investment opportunities, yet some restrictions still impact international business strategies.

Government restrictions on the percentage of equity ownership held by foreigners often compel foreign investors to accept domestic partners. Given this situation, host country partners are in a strong bargaining position in regard to the amount of financial and other resources they bring to a joint venture in exchange for their equity share. To the extent that the resources provided by host country partners are below the value represented by the ownership share they acquire, equity ownership restrictions can act as a tax on foreign investors, a tax that accrues not to the host country government but to host country nationals. Furthermore, the providers of resources other than capital are at risk in terms of the success or failure of an enterprise, and some believe that all those at risk should be able to influence business decisions with governments serving as their agents. Equity ownership by a domestic government and membership on the board of directors can act as a government window on the inner workings of a firm and can assist in developing effective regulations.

Many countries have had some type of case-by-case screening and approval process for FDI proposals. The nature of this process has varied considerably, and for most countries, it has changed over time. Countries have often allowed exceptions to their general ownership restrictions for investments that are thought to bring exceptional benefits. Governments have been willing to trade off the perceived costs of foreign equity ownership for benefits such as increased exports, transfer of advanced technologies, upgrading of domestic raw materials, location in remote regions, and job creation.

Many countries have liberalized their FDI frameworks by gradually introducing exceptions to their basic restrictions, such as raising the size threshold above which approval is required. Governments have also stipulated shorter time limits on the approval process. Some countries have moved to a "notification" and "approval" system, under which the foreign investor could simply notify the relevant screening organization and provide it with certain information. This government agency can then accept the notification as received, request additional information, or inform the investor that the application will have to go through a more formal approval process. If the investor does not receive a reply within a specified period, the application is deemed to have been approved. The problems engendered by foreign ownership restrictions have induced foreign investors to engage in a wide variety of activities to circumvent them. Governments are often fully aware of these actions and sometimes have even cooperated in them. Consequently, it is important to be cautious in accepting a nation's legislative intent as reality. Corporate records may have indicated a transfer of shares to domestic investors, but at the same time, the domestic "investors" may have signed undated share transfer agreements, and they may not be involved in any corporate decision making. Back-to-back transfers of shares have also been used to evade these provisions.

Most governments worry that their country's unique cultural identity could be undermined if FDI were allowed in media and cultural industries. Many countries, for example, have been particularly fearful of being absorbed into the United States' cultural milieu, given the huge relative size of the United States and the ease with which U.S. radio and television broadcasting can cross the border. Similarly, many countries have sought to maintain domestically owned media networks to support a distinctive national analysis of political developments. In some countries, the media have been an organ of the state, used to carry out the mission of the government in power. Foreign investment in the media has been seen as diminishing this government regulatory power. The rationales for liberalization in recent years have involved a growing recognition that technological advances, such as satellite broadcasting and the Internet, have reduced the effectiveness of trade and ownership barriers at national boundaries. There has also been increased recognition that information has become a key competitive advantage and that there is now a need to improve information access and speed up its flow internationally. However, the relative slowness of change in foreign ownership restrictions in mass media and culture reflects the predominance of political rationales for these restrictions.

The Basel Accords: A Model for Future Regulatory Frameworks?

In the early years of the 21st century, international negotiations were undertaken in regard to the capital requirement of financial institutions.

The Basel Accord of 1988 had specified a target of 8% as a level of capital that all banks operating internationally must set aside against their loans in order to ensure a minimum level of safety for depositors. It was hoped that this agreement would prevent financial catastrophes. By 1999, many felt that this target should be raised and it should be differentiated in accordance with the nature of each bank's assets. International differences of opinion developed in this regard. In particular, German banks felt that the 8% capital-adequacy ratio was unduly high for their property loans, which had traditionally been a very safe portfolio. Banks in other nations were reluctant to accept the German position in view of the traditional volatility of real-estate prices and in view of the competitive advantage this would give the German banks.

The basic concepts involved in calculating risk were also being challenged as the Basel Accord modification was debated. A key question was how many categories should be established for risk and the degree to which these different categories should have different capital ratios. Related to this was the question of whose corporate risk rating should be used for corporate loans. For example, U.S. banks might have an advantage since a higher percentage of companies in the United States had credit ratings than was true in Europe.

Chart 11.1 shows how the 8% capital ratio could be modified in accordance with the various risk categories. The chart presents percentages of the standard 8% ratio. For example, a 20% rating means a 1.6% capital requirement. Basel II sought to create minimum capital requirements that would be geared to the risks inherent in each type of loan. It was expected that banks would determine the risks that they faced and classify their loans into categories, where each category would have a particular weighting in regard to calculating necessary reserves. Loans would be classified into five weighting categories of 0%, 20%, 50%, 100%, and 150%, with this percentage being applied to the standard 8% capital requirement. For example, bank holdings of government treasury bills and bonds would have a weight of 0% in calculating the bank's required capital. At the other extreme, loans to the nonbank private sector would generally require a 100% weighting or the full standard 8% capital requirement. Apart from these minimum capital requirements, Basel II sought to impose standard supervisory reviews of financial institutions, as well as transparency with full disclosure of loan risks.

Ironically, Basel II was to be implemented beginning in 2008, just as the global financial crisis was becoming increasingly severe. The crisis itself raised the question whether future attempts to create more extensive global regulations could minimize the risks of insolvency of financial institutions.

Chart 11.1   Basel Balance Proposed Weightings (%)

Claim	AAA TO AA−	A+ to A−	BBB+ to BBB−	BB+ to B−	Below B−	Unrated
Sovereigns	0	20	50	100	150	100
Banks: Option 1[a]	20	50	100	100	150	100
Banks: Option 2[b]	20	50[c]	50[c]	100[c]	150	50[c]
Corporates	20	100	100	100	150	100

SOURCE: Basel Committee on Banking Supervision (1999).

a. Based on risk weighting of sovereign in which the bank is incorporated

b. Based on the assessment of the individual bank

c. Claims on banks of a short original maturity, for example, less than 6 months, would receive a weighting that is one category more favorable

The EU Harmonization of Regulations

In its determination to create a single market, the EU has promulgated a set of regulations that each member has to adopt. This Acquis Communautaire consists of several documents:

- The founding Treaty of Rome as revised by the Maastricht, Amsterdam, and Nice Treaties

- The regulations and directives passed by the Council of Ministers, which concern the creation of single market

- The judgments of the European Court of Justice in regard to conflicts of interpretation

The Acquis has expanded considerably in recent years and now includes the Common Foreign and Security Policy and Justice and Home Affairs, as well as objectives relating to the single currency European Monetary Union. Countries wishing to join the EU have to adopt and implement the entire Acquis on accession, though there has been some flexibility as to timing. The European Council has ruled out any partial adoption of the Acquis, as it feels that this would raise more problems than it would solve and would result in a watering down of the Acquis itself.

In addition to transposing the body of EU legislation into their own national law, candidate countries have to ensure that EU law is properly implemented and enforced. This could mean that administrative structures have to be set up or modernized, legal systems need to be reformed, and civil servants and members of the judiciary have to be trained. The European Commission has been in charge of an annual assessment of each new member's progress. Meanwhile, many other international agreements have also sought to achieve a harmonization of regulations and, in many cases, to reduce the degree of government regulatory intervention.

The following case excerpt illustrates many of the issues that arise with changes in political forces and the role of government (see In Practice 11.1). For many years, India had relied on government ownership and regulation to operate its telecom sector. Attempts to privatize and deregulate created a series of opportunities and challenges for private sector firms.

In Practice 11.1	Assessing Risks and Opportunities in Privatization and Deregulation in India's Telecom Sector

India appeared to be a nation of enormous investment opportunity, with its population of 1 billion people and its relatively high growth rate. India's telecom sector, in particular, appeared to offer first mover advantages, as the government of India promised to institute economic reforms that would privatize government-owned telecom systems and that would give telecom corporations much greater freedom from traditional government regulations.

In 1994, the government announced the National Telecom Policy (NTP), which defined the objectives for growth of the telecom infrastructure in India. NTP 1994 also recognized that the required resources for achieving these targets would not be available out of government sources and concluded that private investment and involvement was required to bridge the resource gap. The NTP paved the way for the entry of the private sector into telecom services and the introduction of cellular and value-added services.

The 1994 telecom policy reforms had certain shortfalls, and the liberalization process failed to get off the ground. First, allocations of licenses for basic and cellular services were based on the highest bid, which led to companies quoting unrealistic amounts in their attempt to be awarded the circle (the telecom policy defines a circle as a region for which licenses are granted). Also, the government had set a minimum reserve price for the licensee fee. Bids for basic services were therefore not received for eight circles because prospective bidders found the license fee too high. It also resulted in the entry of operators who had not been evaluated rigorously in terms of their cost-revenue projections, their ability to manage the capacity build-up and operations, or their motive in participating in the bidding process (for instance, to sell the license later if permitted). Finally, only six licenses were awarded for basic services for the 21 existing circles for cellular services.

By 1999 the targets as envisaged in the objectives of the NTP 1994 had remained unfulfilled. The private sector entry was slower than was envisaged in the

NTP 1994. The cabinet approved its "New Telecom Policy" in March 1999, and the policy was implemented in April 1999. It included:

- A significant shift from the fixed license fee regime to a license fee based on a revenue-sharing mechanism occurred. The share of revenue to be paid as the license fee was set at a maximum 15%.

- Licenses for access services (basic, cellular, radio paging, radio trunking) were issued for an initial period of 20 years, extendable by 10 years.

- Sharing of telecom infrastructure by all service providers was permitted. Interconnectivity among various service providers within the same area of operations was also permitted.

- Lastly, the national long-distance services sector was opened to competition from January 1, 2000.

While there had been a rapid rollout of cellular mobile networks in the metros and states with more than 2 million subscribers, most of the projects were facing problems. The main reason, according to the cellular and basic operators, was that the actual revenues realized by these projects were far short of the projections, and the operators were unable to arrange financing for their projects and therefore complete their projects on time. Basic telecom services by private operators had commenced only in a limited way in two of the six circles where licenses were awarded.

The licensing, policy making, and service provision functions were under a single authority. The government decided to separate the policy and licensing functions from the service provision functions. The Department of Telecom (DoT) and Department of Telecom Services (DTS) became Government of India Departments under the Ministry of Communications. DoT had its role in policy making; licensing; and coordination matters relating to telegraphs, telephones, wireless, data, facsimile, and telematic services, and other like forms of communications. In addition, DoT was responsible for frequency management in the field of radio communication in close coordination with international bodies. It also enforced wireless regulatory measures for wireless transmission by users in the country. DTS was the premier telecom service provider in India. The main functions of DTS included planning, engineering, installation, maintenance, management, and operation of voice and nonvoice telecommunications services all over the country.

A central concern had to do with the extent and pace of economic reforms. Liberalization had begun in 1991, at the urging of the World Bank and IMF, and in reaction to a foreign exchange crisis. However, this "New Industrial Policy" had retained foreign ownership limits of 51% in many sectors, including telecoms, with the need to obtain specific government approval if a foreign owner wished to exceed these 51% limits. State governments still exerted considerable regulatory

(Continued)

(Continued)

power, quite apart from the national government, and the pervasive bureaucracy carried with it the possibility of corruption in attaining regulatory approvals. Furthermore, labor legislation and strong unions could also present challenges, and contracts were often subject to further negotiations.

SOURCE: Minhas and Conklin (2001).

Critical Thinking Questions

1. Analyze India's telecom privatization process. Why was the privatization process so slow?

2. Analyze India's telecom regulations. Why was the process of deregulation so slow?

3. Evaluate the challenges and opportunities in India's telecom sector from the perspective of a foreign investor. Would you attempt to enter this market? Why or why not?

References and Suggested Readings

Basel Committee on Banking Supervision. (1999, June 5). Banking regulation: Growing basel. *The Economist,* p. 70.

Grey, J. (2008, May 21). City urged to tap private sector. *Globe and Mail,* p. A11.

Guerrere, F. (2008, May 12). Funds get $10bn to tap global expansion. *Financial Times,* p. 1.

Minhas, H., & Conklin, D. W. (2001). *Lucent in India.* London: Ivey. (Ivey Case No. 9B01M047)

Murphy, T. (2008). The case for public-private partnerships in infrastructure. *Canadian Public Administration, 51*(1), 99–126.

Parris, H. (1987). *Public enterprise in Western Europe.* London: Croom Helm.

Rees, R. (1984). *Public enterprise economics* (2nd ed.). London: Weidenfield & Nicolson.

Stigler, G. (1971). The theory of economic regulation. *Bell Journal of Economics and Management Science, 2*(1), 3–21.

Thompson, V. (1969). *Bureaucracy and innovation.* Tuscaloosa: University of Alabama Press.

Vernon, R., & Aharoni, Y. (Eds.). (1981). *State-owned enterprise in the Western economies.* New York: St. Martin's.

Ongoing Impacts of Trade and Investment Agreements

12

Each trade and investment agreement can change the terms and conditions under which managers make their trade and investment decisions, so it is important for managers to provide input into the negotiations preceding new agreements. Trade and investment agreements expand the scope of the market and may facilitate the achievement of enhanced efficiency through economies of scale. Furthermore, they may facilitate the transfers of technologies and managerial skills that accompany international investment. Managers may suddenly face new opportunities, as well as new competition, so analyses of these agreements are essential. Many trade and investment agreements seek to reduce the wide array of political risks and uncertainties discussed in the previous chapters of this text. Negotiations seek to create a more level playing field for international flows of trade and investment by limiting each government's freedom to distort relative costs and prices, restricting each signatory's decisions in regard to its public policies.

In this process of international discussions and negotiations, the decisions about certain types of public policies are shifting from the individual nation to multinational forums. In previous chapters, we discuss various agreements that seek to achieve harmonization in regard to specific public policies and reductions in barriers to trade and investment. Membership in many trade and investment agreements has required a reduction in foreign ownership restrictions, as has been the case in Canada and Mexico (under the North American Free Trade Agreement [NAFTA]) and Spain (with the European Union [EU]). Indonesia's membership in the General Agreement on Tariffs and Trade (GATT) put some pressure on the government to liberalize its foreign equity ownership restrictions. The desire of the Republic of Korea to join the Organisation for Economic Co-operation and Development (OECD) had the same effect. Most significant, China's membership in the World Trade Organization (WTO) entailed a commitment by China to reduce its investment restrictions substantially. The large number of such agreements, with many countries having signed many agreements, adds a challenging complexity for managers.

There are now dozens of international agreements. Some are bilateral, such as trade agreements the United States has negotiated with Chile and Israel. Some are regional, such as the Canada-U.S. Free Trade Agreement and its successor, NAFTA. Some cover several regions, such as the Asia Pacific Economic Cooperation Agreement (APEC). GATT and its successor, the WTO, have provided a forum for global agreements. For managers, this complex set of rules with significant differences among agreements requires ongoing attention, with analyses of the implications for each business sector of changes in these rules and in their interpretation. The protection of intellectual property has become a vital issue for many business sectors, and a series of international agreements has focused on this subject. Environmental issues have also become the focus of international agreements. Both intellectual property and environmental agreements receive special attention in this chapter.

In recent years, many of China's policies have given rise to a plethora of trade and investment disputes, and these illustrate the wide array of ongoing potential conflicts. The WTO agreements provide formal structures for the adjudication of trade disputes. These procedures can grant rights of trade retaliation to the country whose businesses have been hurt. Retaliation includes countervail duties and import quotas directed at specific products. However, prior to taking a trade dispute to this WTO process, the parties can meet for the purpose of reaching a compromise solution. China has become involved in a number of disputes where a memorandum of understanding has been agreed to in hopes of rectifying the situation. As a result of these various factors, trade disputes have created a cluttered economic landscape that can be confusing for managers.

The Changing Interests of Businesses

A major factor causing changes in business interests has been the globalization of assets. Many firms have been losing their identification with a single nation. Many shareholders do not live in and are not citizens of the country where their corporate facilities are located. Linked with this is the globalization of production. For many years, all multinational enterprise (MNE) decisions were made in the head office and subsidiaries produced as instructed. Usually, the product mix was identical to the parent's product mix. The subsidiary had short production runs that were high cost. Today, for many MNEs the head office is a marketplace for evaluating competitive bids for world mandates. Each subsidiary produces for the world market and enjoys economies of scale. In the past, the local enterprise sought tariffs to protect its sales domestically. However, many MNEs were able to negotiate special duty remission agreements as part of their rationalized production and global mandates. For many countries, a major portion of imports and exports are now intra-MNE transactions, many of these being intermediate rather than final products. In this way, free trade was established within MNEs prior to international political agreements, and trade agreements can be seen as a political response to the changing interests of businesses.

Today, firms often seek alternative government assistance instead of tariffs. The growing significance of technology leads more firms to seek research and development assistance. Through innovation, a firm may alter the global industry structure for its products. In the extreme, a firm might achieve a world monopoly, as in the case of new pharmaceutical products. A substantial body of trade literature deals with competitive behavior when few producers exist such that decisions of one firm directly affect the profitability of the others. Game theoretic analysis suggests a variety of strategic reactions. Much of this discussion is relevant in considering the use of subsidies by governments in order to maximize their producers' interests vis-à-vis those of other nations. For example, governments in Europe have subsidized Airbus in hopes of gaining market share from Boeing, which has been subsidized by the U.S. government.

The relatively greater role of services in the production and employment of most modern economies has also changed the interests of businesses. Protection, if it is to be achieved, must be implemented through alternative instruments such as immigration restrictions, professional regulations, or limitations on foreign investment. At the same time, the growth of services has meant that tariffs, since they affect goods prices only, are an increasingly arbitrary form of taxation. From this perspective, tariff reductions can also be seen as a type of tax reform that may establish a more uniform tax system. Furthermore, the expansion of trade itself can alter a nation's industrial structure in ways that change the protective interests of businesses located there. High-income countries may no longer have the labor-intensive industries that seek protection from cheap Chinese imports, for example. Together, these changing interests of businesses have diminished the relative strength of political support for protective tariffs.

The Expanding Scope of Trade and Investment Agreements

Trade agreements deal with much more than trade and tariffs. Most agreements provide for a reduction in restrictions on foreign investments, facilitating international flows of capital. In many agreements, the signatories promise that they will provide "national treatment" to foreign-based firms, pledging that governments will make any decisions that impact them as if they were domestic firms. Any domestic programs of financial assistance or any taxation provisions will be at least as generous to foreign firms as to domestic firms. Some agreements go beyond the promise of "national treatment" to include guarantees concerning the risks of government expropriation. In recent years, some argue that expropriation should include any government action that could substantially reduce the future flow of a firm's profits. NAFTA promises investment protection in Chapter 11 of the agreement, but its meaning has involved considerable uncertainty. A U.S. firm selling a fuel additive in Canada suddenly found that new environmental provisions would prohibit the use of its fuel additive. In response, the U.S. firm sued under Chapter 11 and was given financial compensation. Ironically, a trade agreement may provide investment guarantees to foreign firms that domestic firms may not enjoy.

International investments generally require the temporary posting of expatriates to the new business and the regular travel of executives to manage, or at least to supervise, the activities there. In view of these realities, trade agreements generally provide for the reduction or elimination of restrictions on travel or immigration for business purposes. As Chapter 11 of this text discusses, each country has implemented a host of regulations for various purposes. Many regulations are unique in their wording and enforcement and may form barriers to trade. A firm may simply find it uneconomical to provide different products or services for each nation in order to comply with each nation's regulations. A firm may require a detailed level of knowledge and a degree of relationships with enforcement agencies that make the compliance process too complex and time-consuming. In response to these realities, many trade agreements seek to achieve the "harmonization" of regulations with common sets of standards for each sector. Consequently, trade agreements often contain chapters devoted to specific sectors, with each chapter focusing on sector-specific regulations.

Agriculture and food processing are often the focus of considerable debate since most governments try to protect their farmers and food safety is of great concern to the public. Some issues may involve different national attitudes toward the health risks created by certain products. In recent years, North American farmers have adopted genetically modified crops and feed additives for livestock. Many Europeans regard these modifications as possibly carrying risks for cancer or birth defects and wish to prohibit food imports that involve genetically modified crops or certain feed additives. The risk of mad cow disease or other communicable diseases can also be of concern and may underlie trade agreement provisions for the continuation of import barriers under certain conditions.

Textiles and clothing have traditionally been labor-intensive, offering relatively low-skilled employment opportunities. A flood of imports could throw large numbers of employees into permanent unemployment, particularly in towns that have depended heavily on these jobs. Hence, many trade agreements have maintained ongoing import restrictions or have provided for only a slow reduction of these restrictions over time.

Government procurement has been seen as a means to achieve many political objectives, including preferential assistance to minority groups, stimulus to innovations, and the economic development of disadvantaged regions. Consequently, many trade agreements leave scope for the continuation of certain types of domestic preference. Government procurement is an area where informal preferences cannot be detected easily by foreign firms, making it difficult to mount legal challenges even if the trade agreement promises equal access.

It is not obvious how much domestic value-added content should be required in order for a product to cross a border free of tariffs. Trade agreements often state specific rules for specific sectors, and these rules require that each firm keep records that trace all of its imports, its value-added costs, and its selling prices in order to prove, if challenged, that its products should cross the border free of tariffs. The NAFTA value-added test, for example, was 62.5% for automobiles, light trucks, engines, and transmissions and 60% for other vehicles and parts. In textiles and apparel, NAFTA established a triple transformation test, requiring that apparel be made in a member country from textiles made in a member country from yarn made in a member country.

Many nontariff barriers are exercised by subnational governments, so the rights and responsibilities of subnational governments form an essential component of this subject. In many federal states, the subnational governments have been guaranteed certain powers in a constitution, but these powers differ considerably among nations. Included in this more politically complex sphere could be various kinds of subsidies, sector-specific or region-specific tax concessions, government-owned enterprises, sector-specific regulations, and government procurement policies. With these policies, subnational governments may have rights and powers that a national government cannot bind in international agreements.

The establishment of freer trade requires a harmonization of government practices and policies in the signatory nations in order for similar price ratios and investment incentives to exist. From this perspective, the extent and nature of free-trade agreements will be determined by the degree to which potential signatories share common producer and consumer interests. It appears that such commonalities of interests are most extensive among countries that are geographically close. Hence, we see a reason for more thorough agreements on a regional level rather than on a global level, as in the agreements of the EU and NAFTA. This perspective includes similar attitudes toward government ownership, toward the regulation of particular sectors such as financial institutions and telecommunications, toward subsidies for economically disadvantaged regions, and toward subsidies for new technology and for education and retraining. It is only with a similar pattern of producer and consumer interests that societies can agree to a similar pattern of price distortions and consequently a meaningful free-trade agreement covering these government interventions in the market. Recent global shifts toward restraining the role of government and relying on free markets make free-trade agreements more feasible.

Whereas much trade literature has been based on static analyses and the calculation of individual interests as currently perceived, the writings of Olson and his followers have emphasized the dynamics of economic growth and the importance of continual change in the growth process. The future interests of the society as a whole may not be attained if vested interests determine political decisions. Hence, the creation of free trade can result in substantial benefits for future generations. One of the most significant economic relationships demonstrated with a high degree of consistency over the period since 1945 is the greater rate of economic growth enjoyed by outward-looking countries pursuing liberal, market-oriented policies than by countries whose governments interfered extensively in the economy. This optimistic perspective has supported the global shift toward freer trade and investment. It remains to be seen whether this faith in free markets will be diminished by the post-2007 global financial and economic crisis.

The GATT and the WTO: The Need to Adjust to Continual Changes

GATT came into effect in 1948 and formed a framework for multinational trade negotiations until 1994. Under GATT, there were eight rounds of negotiations to reduce trade barriers:

1947 Geneva, Switzerland

1949 Annecy, France

1951 Torquay, England

1956 Geneva II

1960 to 1961 The "Dillon Round"

1964 to 1967 The "Kennedy Round"

1973 to 1979 The "Tokyo Round"

1986 to 1994 The "Uruguay Round"

In the early rounds, most of the negotiation agenda concerned the reduction of tariff rates. Recent negotiations have increasingly focused on the other barriers to both trade and investment and on the public policies that distort relative prices and create an unfair competitive advantage. Consequently, international agreements have greatly increased in complexity. For many firms in the developed nations, the protection of intellectual property is necessary to prevent a flood of counterfeit products. The recent growth of services has resulted in demands for freer access by personnel to foreign markets. The export of services requires a local presence to foreign markets, so investment provisions have acquired a new significance. The final GATT Uruguay Round included many of these new subjects, so member countries concluded that a new organizational structure, the WTO, should be developed to extend the scope and authority of GATT.

The WTO has imposed tighter exemptions for developing countries with balance of payments difficulties, requiring a heightened degree of transparency. The WTO has established clearer disciplines and reporting obligations for state-owned enterprises. It has clarified the relationships between preferential regional agreements and the WTO provisions. The WTO deals explicitly with government procurement policies. It attempts to reduce agricultural subsidies. Signatories agree to translate nontariff import barriers into tariffs, thereby making them more transparent and subject to systematic reduction. For many years, a Multinational Multifiber Arrangement (MFA) had allowed economically advanced nations to retain import quotas on textiles and clothing. The WTO created a schedule for the 10-year elimination of the MFA with the expectation that this sector would be subject to the same type of treatment as other sectors. Countries considering the imposition of antidumping duties would have to engage in a public and transparent adjudication process.

Trade Related Investment Measures prohibit government policies that require stipulated local content as a condition for investment approval. Trade Related Intellectual Property Rights have become a major component of the WTO's activities. The WTO has established new procedures for dispute settlement, seeking to clarify and expedite the decision-making process. A nation lodging a complaint is guaranteed the right to a dispute settlement panel. Strict time limits are placed on each step in the process. Signatories agree to adopt panel reports and to bring their laws into conformity with panel decisions within specified time limits.

However, signatories have not granted the WTO any real enforcement powers. Generally, all that the WTO can do is give a country the right to impose retaliatory trade measures against another country whose actions are judged to have violated the WTO rules. In practice, nations have sometimes ignored WTO decisions. If the nation judged guilty does not export much to the country its policies have harmed, then the threat of retaliatory trade measures may have no practical meaning. A small nation cannot impose retaliatory trade measures with much impact on large countries. On the other hand, retaliatory measures threatened by the United States or the EU generally carry substantial power. Hence, the WTO serves as a set of guidelines for public policies, but its success depends largely on the voluntary compliance of its members.

The WTO initiated the Doha Round in 2001. Many developing countries felt that the earlier rounds had provided substantial benefits to the rich nations but relatively few benefits to them. Earlier rounds reduced developing countries' tariffs on imported manufactured products and opened their markets to foreign businesses and investors. However, their principal exports were agricultural goods, for which the rich nations have retained high import barriers. Also, the rich nations have consistently given substantial subsidies to their farmers, thereby reducing their costs and prices. For the developing countries, these rich-country subsidies prevented them from competing on a level playing field. Their exports to the rich nations faced a cost disadvantage, and their exports to other markets confronted subsidized products from rich nations. Hence, the trade in agricultural products became a central subject in the Doha Round. In particular, a major goal was to reduce agricultural subsidies. An agreement in agriculture seemed necessary in order to achieve freer trade in services, more reductions in tariffs on industrial goods, and a clarification of rules on antidumping actions. Meanwhile, within the EU, an agreement between Germany and France promised to maintain the Common Agricultural Policy (CAP) and its subsidies until 2013.

In the United States, Congress traditionally gives the president "fast-track negotiating authority" in which Congress promises not to vote on each provision of a tentative agreement but only on the agreement as a whole. In the final stages of the Doha negotiations, a fear was that the U.S. president's fast-track authority might expire, making it impossible in practice to get any tentative agreement passed by Congress; so for a number of reasons, the Doha Round was at risk of failure.

Participating in Trade Disputes

A trade agreement is a living document with continual changes in the interpretation of various clauses. In many cases, trade disputes arise from conflicting interpretations and procedures for dispute resolution that lead to decisions about the meaning of the relevant clauses. In the Canada–U.S. Free Trade Agreement, for example, each country retained the right to place barriers on imports of agricultural goods, while free trade was established for nonagricultural products. A dispute arose over whether ice cream was an agricultural product, in which case Canada could retain its import barriers, or a manufactured good, in which case Canada's import barriers had to be removed. It was decided that ice cream was an agricultural product, so Canada's import barriers would remain. Under the Canada–U.S. Free Trade Agreement, country-of-origin provisions were established to ensure that adequate value was added domestically (at least 50%) to classify the product as Canadian or American for duty-free border crossing. U.S. trade officials challenged the exports from a Canadian-located automobile plant on the basis that it failed to achieve 50% Canadian content. In its defense, the Canadian plant claimed to have reached the required level by including interest payments to Canadian banks as part of its value added in Canada. This issue was clarified in the subsequent NAFTA, where interest payments were disqualified as contributors to domestic value added. Each trade agreement results in a host of disputes that lead to new interpretations.

Managers must now be aware of potential trade disputes in their business sector anywhere in the world and must develop scenarios as the basis for creating contingency plans. Ongoing collaboration with government officials has become essential since the firm must turn to its government to defend its interests within bilateral and regional agreements, as well as within the WTO—both in terms of negotiating agreements and also in terms of dispute resolution. For many years, an ongoing trade dispute between Canada and Brazil focused on a wide variety of government programs that provided assistance to Bombardier in Canada and Embraer in Brazil. It was not clear which if any of these programs constituted unfair competition.

In Practice 12.1   Subsidies and Unfair Competition: The Example of Aircraft

The Canadian government lodged a formal complaint with the WTO in regard to Brazil's *Programma de Financiamento as Exportações* (PROEX), which was implemented in 1986 to foster Brazil's export market. As a developing economy, under WTO regulations, Brazil was allowed to compensate for its "country risk." This risk raised the cost of financing in Brazil since interest rates had to be higher to attract investors. PROEX was designed to "pay back" a portion of this risk premium.

The PROEX program was not applied only to the commercial aircraft industry. It covered thousands of products. However, Bombardier claimed that PROEX had created subsidies to that industry of over $1 billion U.S. a year. Bombardier claimed that the PROEX interest equalization was being applied to firms that were obtaining financing *outside* of Brazil and, thus, amounted to a subsidy of roughly US$4.3 million over the standard 15-year financing period (Morton, 1998), or US$2 million off the purchase price (Shifrin, 1998). Considering that the Embraer jets were priced at nearly US$4 million lower than Bombardier's CRJ-100 series, this was a major advantage.

Meanwhile, Embraer (1998) described a lengthy set of "operations and mechanisms," which they felt were direct and indirect subsidies to Bombardier.

- Use of the so-called Canada Account, a fund not subject to public debate, used to support export transactions where the Canadian government, acting on behalf of its national interest, operates where the Export Development Corporation cannot do it because of the size or risk of the operation.

- Unrefundable financing and zero-cost loan guarantees provided by the Export Development Corporation.

- Current and previous programs of TPC (Technology Partnerships Canada), which is the major source of subsidies to the Canadian aerospace industry, through the creation of funds for aircraft design and manufacture.

- Benefits provided by the Quebec government.

- Financing to research and development through the Defense Productivity Program, which has been replaced by interest-free loans and not refundable TPC for unspecific times. (Embraer, 1998)

- When Bombardier entered the aerospace industry, it did so by taking over Canadair for around $100 million after the federal government absorbed over US$1 billion in debt.

- In 1992, Bombardier paid less than US$40 million for de Havilland, saving thousands of jobs. The Ontario and federal governments agreed to provide over $400 million in subsidies.

- In 1994, Bombardier received an $18-million interest-free loan to expand its Canadair plant through the Canada-Quebec Agreement on Industrial Development.

- In October 1997, Ottawa agreed to lend Bombardier $87 million under the Technology Partnerships to help improve the fuel efficiency of the CRJ-700 and $57 million for the de Havilland DHC-8-400 in 1996 (Dwyer, 1998). The funds are repayable once a program becomes financially viable.

- Bombardier used the Export Development Corporation (EDC) to finance its sales with alleged low-interest loans, guarantees, and equity infusions, which were sometimes significantly lower than market expectations. In 1995, then president of the EDC, Paul Labbe, said that the "EDC is happy if it earned inflation-level return on its assets and admitted that 'in the real world' it should be seeking a return between 13 and 20 per cent" (quoted in Dwyer, 1998, p. 42). He later stated that "The Canada Account is for someone who is looking for financing below market prices" (quoted in Dwyer, 1998, p. 42).

SOURCE: Conklin and Hunter (1999).

Critical Thinking Questions

1. In the Bombardier versus Embraer dispute, which government provisions were unfair subsidies?

2. Should developing countries such as Brazil have the right to give special subsidies in order to create high-tech jobs?

3. Can you compare the degree of "unfair competition" between Bombardier and Embraer, or are the various government provisions too extensive and complex for you to make a comparison?

Protecting the Firm's Intellectual Property

Earlier chapters discuss the dependence of a firm's profitability on its ability to create products or business practices that are unique or at least differentiated from those of competitors. Many firms devote substantial time and expense to the research, development, and marketing that underlie the search for differentiation. For them, the sustainability of profitability rests on the prevention of other firms from simply copying their success without approval or authorization. Today, governments regard the innovative process as a means to increase their nation's productivity and, hence, their growth rates. Without the guarantee of global protection of intellectual property, firms might not invest in the innovative process to the degree that would be optimal for society as a whole. The risk of copying or piracy from firms in other nations has shifted this subject into trade and investment agreements.

There is a long history of international agreements in which each signatory nation pledges to respect the patents, trademarks, industrial designs, geographical indications, and copyright that are given protection by any other of the signatories. However, developing countries may be tempted to increase their growth potential by not enforcing the intellectual property rights of firms located in the rich countries. For firms in developing countries, a simple route to success may lie in copying internationally successful products and business practices. Low wage rates may create a competitive advantage in the manufacture of products originally created in the rich nations. International laws to protect intellectual property involve more than a matter of guaranteeing a fair business reward for research and innovation. They also involve the creation of jobs in one's own country as opposed to jobs in other countries. Furthermore, to the degree that public funds have paid for the relevant research, this is directly of financial concern to the donor government.

Lower wage rates have led to a shift in the manufacture of many products from the United States and Europe to Asia. MNEs have taken an active lead in technology transfer, creating subsidiaries "offshore" to take advantage of lower wage costs. However, newly industrialized countries—such as China, Hong Kong, Singapore, South Korea, Brazil, Mexico, and many others—have the capacity to copy the latest in technology and then sell the products into the North American and European markets. Recognition of this new offshore capability is a central element when considering legislation that protects intellectual property. Increasingly, domestic legislation in North American and European countries can offer little protection. Domestic legislation to protect intellectual property may even be undesirable in that it may simply shove employment opportunities offshore to countries where the protection is not honored. Unfortunately, the economic interest of many countries lies in the rejection of protection for intellectual property. Why should these countries honor the property ownership of others when their own manufacturers can create jobs and prosperity through piracy and counterfeiting?

Developing countries may lack the legal systems and social norms that underlie effective enforcement of these rights. Some analysts point to the impact of traditional values as a basic cause of failures in Chinese compliance with intellectual property rights. "Successive Chinese governments have adopted model intellectual property laws from the United States and Europe and their citizens (and often courts) have continued to ignore them" (Lehman, 2006, p. 1). John Lehman has argued that intellectual property was not considered in traditional Chinese thought or in traditional Chinese legal codes; so there exists no ethical foundation for intellectual property rights. "The basic problem with enforcing intellectual property rights in China is not legal or based on stages in economic development, but arises from intellectual and cultural dissonance" (p. 8). Consequently, adherence to international agreements that China has signed may not occur soon.

Of particular concern are the advances in pharmaceutical products. Developing countries may place a high priority on offering inexpensive drugs to their low-income populace and may be tempted to encourage low-cost generic production in defiance of international agreements. The proliferation of unauthorized copies carries with it the risk that trade may bring inferior products to consumers who do not recognize the inferiority and who may be harmed. Faulty automobile parts or inappropriate drugs could result in personal injury or even death to the consumer. Yet both the owner of the intellectual property and its government may face great difficulties in proving that the copies are not "real." For managers today, the protection of intellectual property has become a major public policy issue whose scope is now international, as well as domestic.

Many governments have signed the Paris Convention for the Protection of Intellectual Property, which was initiated in 1883, as well as the Berne Convention for the Protection of Literacy and Artistic Works, which was initiated in 1886. Signatories of the Patent Cooperation Treaty pledge to recognize the patents filed in other signatory countries just as if these patents had been filed in their own country. Similarly, the Madrid Agreement Concerning International Registration of Marks and the Madrid Protocol provide for the international registration of trademarks. The Hague Agreement Concerning the International Deposit of Industrial Designs offers a procedure for international registration of industrial designs. The Lisbon Agreement for the Protection of Appellations of Origin and their International Registration registers brands related to country or region of origin.

In 1970, the United Nations created the World Intellectual Property Organization (WIPO) to coordinate these international agreements and to modify them as circumstances change. WIPO seeks to harmonize rules and practices in regard to the granting of intellectual property rights and their enforcement. In recent years, WIPO coordinated the development of new treaties to prevent unauthorized access to and use of works on the Internet. These "Internet Treaties" consist of the WIPO Copyright Treaty and the WIPO Performance and Phonogram Treaty. Copyright does not require the kind of formal registration that relates to other types of intellectual property. Copyright occurs automatically as relevant material such as software is created, although many counties do offer an optional system of registration. WIPO generates more than 90% of its annual budget through its various international registration services, supplemented by contributions from its member governments.

While WIPO works on an ongoing basis to provide for registration of intellectual property and to encourage the enforcement of its ownership, the WTO serves as a forum for the negotiation of international rules on key issues. An additional complication arises from the process of international dispute resolution. Violation of agreements concerning intellectual property cannot be stopped quickly or easily. Today, a technological advance may offer a competitive advantage for only a few years; it may quickly be overtaken by other advances or rendered obsolete by changing tastes. By the time an international dispute is resolved through a judicial process, the innovating firm may have missed the opportunity to profit from its intellectual property and might even be bankrupt.

Some critics argue that the current patent system is failing, in that government agencies and court systems lack the ability to analyze the complexities of modern technologies. Government agencies must evaluate patent applications, but civil servants may not understand the intricacies of the proposed products or production processes, so they may approve questionable patents. Perhaps too many patents are being issued. Disagreements exist as to whether certain biological procedures should be patentable, particularly in the realm of genetic modification. When challenges concerning patent infringement are brought before a court, the judges may lack the capability to make wise decisions. Some patents may overlap with other patents, complicating the question of ownership. Furthermore, some small startup firms and universities may not have adequate funds to file or enforce patents.

For managers, the issues involved in the protection of intellectual property pose many questions for business strategies. Should a manager seek a patent? Might the patent registration process reveal technological advances that could stimulate unauthorized copying, and might it be better to rely on secrecy within the firm? In considering investments in China, is there too great a risk of unauthorized copying as a result of geographical proximity to potential "pirates"? Can technological advances be protected better from business locations in North America and Western Europe, or even in countries such as India where the legal system may be more inclined than China's to enforce relevant laws? If a firm's intellectual property is violated, is the legal enforcement process worth the costs that would be incurred? How can a firm be sure that its technological advances will be considered different enough from existing patents to avoid the charge of patent infringement? What terms and conditions of patent ownership are reasonable in research arrangements with universities? Managers must give serious ongoing consideration to these questions.

Adjusting to New Environmental Agreements

Whether trade and investment negotiations are the optimal forum for environmental issues or whether separate agreements focused on specific environmental issues should be pursued has become an increasingly complex subject. At the core of this analysis are the differences among nations in regard to regulations and their enforcement and the shift of responsibility for setting standards from the nation to the international community. Many leaders of developing nations have taken the position that their political priority is rapid economic growth in order to reduce widespread poverty with its diseases and generally poor health. Only when per capita incomes and lifestyles reach a certain level can developing nations afford the luxury of imposing the costs associated with environmental protection and sustainable development. This burden must be delayed until they can afford it. Meanwhile, some political leaders view the costly regulations of rich nations as creating an unfair competitive advantage for developing nations, enabling them to attract foreign investment that will bring more jobs, managerial skills, higher tax revenues, and a stimulus for economic growth. Yet the achievement of environmental protection and sustainable development will require global public policies. How to deal most effectively and equitably with this conundrum poses an ongoing challenge. For managers, the relevant public policies and their enforcement do differ among nations, creating a set of issues to be considered in their list of investment location determinants. Yet the rules are changing, and the potential negotiation of new international agreements creates an ongoing shift that managers must anticipate as they decide on the production machinery and equipment they will acquire and the product variants they will develop.

A series of international agreements have been negotiated. Some have aimed at the reduction of acid rain. Others have sought the elimination of the CFCs (chlorofluorocarbons) used in refrigerant equipment, which threaten the ozone layer. Recently, the threat of global warming has generated international agreements on public policies to reduce "greenhouse gases," particularly carbon dioxide. The NAFTA agreement was signed in 1992 under the authority of the first President Bush. Bill Clinton felt strongly that NAFTA should deal explicitly with environmental and labor standards, so when he became president in 1993, Clinton negotiated side accords to NAFTA. The side accords created new permanent international institutions to monitor these issues within the NAFTA countries, to promote compliance within each country of its own regulations, and to administer new dispute settlement procedures. An objective was to investigate situations where regulations were not being enforced and in this process to encourage transparency and voluntary compliance. Joint pollution monitoring and voluntary control programs were established. However, the NAFTA members were reluctant to surrender significant national sovereignty to the new institutions. In disputes, an arbitration panel could levy a fine. Trade sanctions could be imposed only in exceptional circumstances where a country refused to pay the fine and continued to inadequately enforce its own environmental laws. In recent years, many members of the U.S. Congress have expressed their view that future trade and investment agreements must contain provisions to establish and enforce environmental standards and also labor standards. For some proponents, this position is simply a means for preventing the loss of U.S. jobs as firms shift their activities to countries with lower standards and, hence, lower production costs.

Although the Kyoto Protocol is an important example of an international agreement on environmental issues, it is not groundbreaking in the sense of being the first such agreement. The Montreal Protocol on Substances that Deplete the Ozone Layer signed in 1992 is an important alternative model. The impetus for the Montreal Protocol was the thinning of the ozone layer over the earth that was allowing increased levels of cancer-causing ultraviolet light to penetrate the earth's atmosphere. This protocol is of interest because it addressed several of the weak points currently existing in the Kyoto Protocol. First, the Montreal Protocol provided for specific sanctions for nations not meeting their objectives. Second, it built in major incentives for developing nations to join the pact. Last, it ensured that there were no economic incentives available for nations violating the pact.

On the surface, the Montreal Protocol appears to have been extremely successful. Between 1986 and 1993, world CFC production fell 60% (Lerner, 2001). It would appear as though CFC levels are easier to regulate than greenhouse gases because CFCs can be eliminated completely, while it is unlikely the same could be done with greenhouse gas emissions. Despite the apparent success of the protocol, during the same time period (1986–1993), production of CFCs by developing nations increased 87% (Powell, 2001). An underground market developed with estimates that 20% of sales were illegal, many originating in developing countries (Wickham, 2001). It has been speculated that one of the reasons behind this is that the incentives allocated to encouraging developing nations to adhere to the pact were not fully provided. Another concern that arises over the Montreal Protocol is its perceived inconsistency with the export/import provisions set out in GATT and the WTO. Many nations participating in the underground trade in CFCs argue that trade restrictions make the protocol invalid since they violate these trade agreements.

The reduction of acid rain provides an additional example of government intervention to protect the environment. Many analysts have been very positive in evaluating the success of acid rain programs.

> The greatest environmental success story of the past decade is probably America's sulphur dioxide scheme, aimed at reducing acid rain. . . .
>
> The key was the introduction of tradable rights, combined with a credible threat of punishment for non-compliance. This spurred the development of a vibrant market and lowered emissions beyond expectations. ("Economic Man," 2001, p. 74)

It appears that each environmental concern may have to be addressed individually based on the particular environmental problem and existing treaty obligations and with an understanding of the incentives and disincentives for adherence for each stakeholder group. This individualized approach to agreements on environmental issues will create a myriad of challenges and opportunities for many firms.

Deciding Whether to Comply With Sanctions

Generally, one nation imposes trade and investment sanctions against another nation in an attempt to make that nation change certain public policies. A firm generally must adhere to sanctions imposed by the country in which it is incorporated. Otherwise, the firm and its executives would be subject to prosecution. Furthermore, a foreign subsidiary of a firm incorporated in a nation issuing sanctions will generally need to adhere to those sanctions because the parent company may otherwise be subject to prosecution. Even for firms with no ownership links to the nation imposing sanctions, another nation's sanctions pose a variety of dilemmas. There may be the reality of "extraterritorial" enforcement, as in the U.S. Helms-Burton Act, where a firm's directors may face personal prosecution and shareholders may face the risk that assets in Cuba or in the United States may be expropriated.

A firm may fear that its transactions with the nation issuing sanctions might be impeded either by the government of that country or by interest groups within that country. The Internet today facilitates the coordinated efforts of potential customers and other interested individuals in various attempts to damage a firm that appears to be violating ethical positions as they interpret them. The political situation in Myanmar (formerly Burma), for example, attracted widespread public reaction quite apart from the U.S. government's somewhat limited sanctions. The National League for Democracy, under the leadership of Aung San Suu Kyi, won Burma's general election in May 1989. However, the military leadership of the State Law and Order Restoration Council (SLORC) refused to accept the election, placed Suu Kyi under house arrest, and violated human rights in its attempts to prevent insurrections. Over the years since that time, Suu Kyi has repeatedly called on nations everywhere to impose sanctions against Burma in hopes of causing the overthrow of SLORC. A multitude of individuals have responded to this plea, boycotting products from Myanmar. Many governments at the municipal and state level—as well as the national level—have joined public boycotts of Myanmar's products.

There may be an ethical dimension for business executives, as they may respect the position underlying the sanctions of another nation. In recent years, shareholders have come to take positions in regard to these ethical dimensions. For example, the Canadian oil company Talisman Energy undertook joint venture oil operations with the government of Sudan. In view of the Sudanese government's violation of human rights in its persecution of religious minorities, shareholders of Talisman joined by religious leaders protested Talisman's business involvement, both publicly and at shareholder meetings. Confronted with this public outcry, Talisman sold its interests in the Sudan.

It is generally agreed that the sanctions imposed by many nations against South Africa's apartheid policy were a key factor in leading to the overthrow of the white political supremacy government and the adoption of equal rights for black South Africans. In 1962, the United Nations General Assembly passed the first of many resolutions calling on UN members to sever trade and investment links with South Africa, and many nations throughout the world imposed economic sanctions against the government of South Africa as an economic opposition to its apartheid policies. The South African economy was heavily dependent on trade and foreign investment and was vulnerable to this international pressure. South Africa's economic prosperity and growth potential were generally acknowledged as being placed at risk by sanctions. Consequently, sanctions strengthened the political position of those in South Africa who opposed apartheid. Most observers have felt that sanctions played a key role in the release of Mandela, the domestic political opposition to apartheid, and the domestic negotiation with black liberation movements to repeal apartheid legislation. At issue is whether other targets of sanctions are as vulnerable as South Africa was and whether success requires the near universal application of sanctions by most nations. Can a single nation, even with the economic power of the United States, achieve results using sanctions, or will the target simply shift its trade and investment to other nations?

The president of the United States has the right to issue executive orders that impose sanctions in situations that "constitute an unusual and extraordinary threat to the foreign policy of the United States" and where the president "declares a national emergency to deal with that threat." Some of these executive orders have covered an entire nation and its residents; some have named specific persons and have given the secretary of the treasury, in consultation with the secretary of state, the right to designate additional persons (where persons may include corporations). Each executive order has prescribed penalties for violation of the order; those are generally financial penalties, as well as imprisonment.

Sovereign Wealth Funds and State-Owned Enterprises as Investors and Competitors

In recent years, a new phenomenon has arisen in this subject area: the growth of sovereign wealth funds as accumulations of current account surpluses. China's foreign exchange rate policies have resulted in huge and rapidly growing international reserves, generally in the form of U.S. dollars. Oil exporting nations have gained windfall profits from escalating oil prices. Not surprisingly, these nations are now tempted to invest in equities rather than fixed-income instruments. However, the nations that face the prospect of government-owned foreign direct investment are expressing fears that essential elements of their economy may be directed in the interests of the foreign government and these interests may diverge from their own national interests.

> Bain Capital and its minority Chinese partner, Huawei Technologies, have shelved their $2.2 billion deal to acquire 3Com, a U.S. computer networking company, saying a key Washington committee charged with vetting foreign investments in sensitive sectors has told Bain it would not approve the purchase. ("Concern Over Foreign Investments," 2008, p. 1)

The *Financial Times* has referred to the "China Fear" and "rising protectionist sentiment in the U.S." as political forces that intervened to prevent Huawei from purchasing a mere 16.5% of 3Com. While 3Com developed security software for the government, Bain announced that it would sell the security software division to other investors as part of the proposed deal. Huawei had claimed to be a private company separate from the government of China, but this theoretical independence could not keep it from being seen as a potential instrument of China's government. National security concerns now extend to a wide range of potential investors and investments, making sovereign wealth funds and state-owned enterprises an important subject within the international investment literature. China's investments in the natural resource sector have raised fears that China may achieve an undesirable degree of political, as well as economic, power. China's investments in African nations and other developing countries have raised fears that China may use these investments to exert pressure on governments to support China's political positions, thereby tipping the geopolitical balance of power.

Estimates in 2007 placed the value of sovereign wealth funds at $2,000 billion to $3,000 billion, and it was expected that these could rise fivefold in the next decade. Apart from China's many state-owned enterprises, the China Investment Corporation was established in 2007 and now stands as the potential purchaser of enormous foreign equity positions. In the period of several years, China's international reserves climbed quickly to reach approximately $1.5 trillion U.S. by 2007. China's political leaders increasingly questioned their policy of using these funds to purchase bonds, particularly as U.S. interest rates fell in early 2008. China's inflation concerns led to a policy of "sterilizing" the money supply expansion caused by massive purchases of foreign bonds. However, the process of issuing bonds to domestic purchasers became more expensive as China raised its interest rates above U.S. levels. Equity purchases offered the promise of higher returns than foreign interest payments and also offered the promise of avoiding the paper losses resulting from the international interest rate gap. At the same time, the rising oil prices created windfall profits for oil-exporting governments, adding to the possibility of takeovers by foreign funds.

Many dramatic situations attracted public attention. In 2005, CNOOC, China's third-ranked oil firm, attempted to purchase the American oil corporation Unocal but withdrew in the face of U.S. political objections. In 2006, the Dubai Ports' Authority purchased P&O, a British port management firm. P&O owned and operated facilities at several U.S. ports. In the face of media reports and political criticisms, the Dubai government withdrew its proposal. In the 2007 to 2009 financial crises, many U.S. banks suddenly experienced enormous losses that threatened their capital adequacy ratios, and major financial institutions turned to sovereign wealth funds to acquire new equity. In January 2008, the government of Singapore Investment Corporation led a group who invested some $12.5 billion in Citigroup. Merrill Lynch raised $6.6 billion from investors who included the Kuwait Investment Authority, the Korean Investment Corporation, and a Japanese bank. "Morgan Stanley analysts pointed out that 93 per cent of the $79 billion that has been invested in western financial companies so far has come from just five states: Singapore, China, Dubai, Abu Dhabi and Kuwait" (Larsen, 2008, p. 16).

In February 2008, the government of Australia announced a new set of six principles to guide its decisions concerning whether to permit sovereign wealth fund investments. Among these principles, Australia will evaluate the degree to which prospective investors operate at arm's length from their government. Australia will consider the financing arrangements and corporate governance procedures. A central concern is the lack of transparency in regard to the sovereign wealth funds. Ad hoc reactions by the United States and Australia, as well as underlying concerns shared by France, Germany, and others, have led to the proposal for a global code of conduct. The subject of government ownership has once again claimed international attention and threatens to alter many industry structures within which managers make business decisions.

Ever-Closer Integration

The chapters on political forces demonstrate an increasing shift of public policy determination from the national level to international forums and agreements. As a result of this process, firms will continue to encounter frequent and substantial changes in the business environment within which they make decisions. The harmonization of public policies should ultimately ease some of the challenges firms currently face as they try to adapt to significantly different policies in the various nations where they trade and invest. Yet for some policies such as taxation and subsidies, national differences may persist over the foreseeable future. The business world will remain a complex and ever-changing mosaic.

New opportunities and challenges will continually arise, requiring ongoing analyses and a capacity to adjust and adapt.

China's transition from communism with its central planning and state-owned enterprises has involved the transformation of many business and government practices. Not surprisingly, progress in this transformation has been slow, and many business and government practices have continued to distort trade and investment patterns, resulting in an ongoing series of trade disputes. Prospects for resolving these disputes remain unclear.

In Practice 12.2 **Coping With "Unfair Competition" From China**

When China applied to join the GATT in 1986, it was essentially a centrally planned economy with an opaque trading regime with high tariffs and a plethora of nontariff barriers. Its main trading partners were socialist countries such as the USSR and Yugoslavia. It was not until 1992 when China declared its intention to establish a "socialist market economy" that it began to lower tariffs. The simple average Chinese tariff rate was reduced from 42.9% in 1992 to 16.6% in 2001. After accession, the average tariff dropped to 9.8% (Greene, Dihel, Kowalski, & Lippoldt, 2006, p. 12).

China's trade disputes illustrate the wide variety of issues that still confront the negotiation and enforcement of international trade and investment agreements. By 2009, China's exports had increased dramatically from $250 billion in 2000 to a projected $1,500 billion in 2009. This enormous growth of exports has severely damaged competing businesses in the advanced nations, particularly the United States and Europe. China's entry into the World Trade Organization (WTO) in 2001 guaranteed China's right to export to these nations, but at the same time the WTO required China to adhere to certain rules that sought to support fair trade and create a level playing field. Several sets of issues have given rise to a series of trade disputes: the protection of intellectual property, health and safety concerns about China's products, China's manipulation of its currency, and costs and prices determined by the government rather than free markets.

Many of China's manufacturers are accused of replicating the designs and product characteristics of western manufacturers and then of using low-wage labor to destroy profit margins and sales volumes of the established Western firms. Domestic legislation in North American and European countries can offer little protection. The government of China seems not to enforce criminal procedures and penalties for such violations. The economic interest of many newly industrialized countries lies in the rejection of protection for intellectual property. Why should these countries honor the property ownership of others when their own manufacturers could create jobs and prosperity through piracy and counterfeiting? From this perspective, China's trade disputes over the protection of intellectual property involve principles that are increasingly important globally.

(Continued)

(Continued)

China has not yet created the same health and safety standards that are enforced in Europe and North America. Hence, the consumers of China's exports face the risk of contracting illnesses and diseases related to these products and the risk of being hurt when these products malfunction. A series of upsetting complaints by consumers have led to calls for import barriers against certain products and for more thorough inspections of imports from China. The industrial chemical melamine can be used to raise protein readings in food inspections. Questions have arisen about this practice in some of China's food industry, including pet food and even baby food. Melamine can form crystals that can block the kidneys, leading to death as a result of kidney failure. A vast array of toys is now seen as having design and manufacturing flaws that have led to consumer concerns and large-scale recalls. Some toothpaste made in China contains diethylene glycol, which has been responsible for at least 200 deaths. For China to adopt and enforce Western standards of health and safety may take many years or even decades. Yet import restrictions by Western governments can severely limit the concept of free trade.

Western nations have established extensive regulations in regard to labor and environmental standards. For business establishments located in these nations, compliance with these regulations can add substantially to their costs. China has not yet imposed similar regulations, so business establishments located in China enjoy an unfair competitive advantage. China's refusal to sign the Kyoto Protocol is a particularly striking example. In response, some legislators advocate that a special "carbon tax" be imposed on imports from China. How to incorporate labor and environmental standards in the international trade system remains an unresolved issue.

China has supported its exports by keeping the value of its currency below the level that would be determined in a free market for international exchange. Consequently, foreigners can purchase Chinese-made products for less foreign currency than they would otherwise have to pay. This conscious manipulation of China's foreign exchange rate has helped to create jobs for the annual migration of millions of rural inhabitants to the cities, but foreign competitors see this practice as unfair competition.

Apart from these broad subject areas, a host of trade disputes focuses on various fiscal incentives that China extends to specific businesses, tariff exceptions for certain imports into China, and preferential lending arrangements to Chinese firms. Many traditional Chinese government interventions can be interpreted as providing cost advantages to certain Chinese firms. Perhaps inevitably, China's transition from a centrally planned economy to free markets means that many Chinese businesses do not yet operate on the basis of free market prices and profit maximization. From this perspective, the government of China is involved in an ongoing transition to free and fair competition and is learning how to best adjust to the WTO rules.

A difficult legal issue concerns the ability to prove that non-Chinese firms have actually been hurt by these actions and that they have been discriminated against in regard to receiving financial benefits from the government of China. In many cases, certain Western firms gain from the ability to purchase low-price Chinese products. Often, retailers align themselves with China's positions, while firms that add value to Chinese exports such as steel also support a welcoming position for imports from China. A difficult practical issue concerns how to enforce WTO decisions within China. Enforcement involves the "principal-agent" dilemma that has been analyzed extensively in political science literature. Even when China's central government wishes to enforce intellectual property protection, how can the central government find and prosecute the violating firms? Furthermore, local governments may allow or even encourage violations in their attempts to support local jobs. Corruption can also enter these situations, as local firms may offer bribes to prevent enforcement.

SOURCE: Conklin and Cadieux (2009).

Critical Thinking Questions

1. What is your advice to the government of China in regard to the protection of intellectual property?

2. What procedures and policies could enhance the health and safety features of China's exports?

3. Do China's lower labor and environmental standards create a permanent unfair competitive advantage for firms located in China?

4. Does China's foreign exchange rate policy give firms located in China an unfair competitive position?

References and Suggested Readings

Concern over foreign investments scuppers $2bn deal for 3Com. (2008, February 21). *Financial Times*, p. 1.

Conklin, D. W., & Cadieux, D. (2009). *China's trade disputes*. London: Ivey. (Ivey Case No. 9B09M018)

Conklin, D. W., & Hunter, T. (1999). *Bombardier versus Embraer: Charges of unfair competition*. London: Ivey. (Ivey Case No. 9A99M004)

Dwyer, R. (1998, October). Bombardier goes into battle. *Airfinance Journal*, 42.

Economic man, cleaner planet. (2001, September 29). *The Economist*, p. 74.

Embraer. (1998, July 23). *Embraer press release*. Sao Paulo, Brazil.

Greene, M., Dihel, N., Kowalski, P., & Lippoldt, D. (2006). *China's trade and growth: Impact on selected OECD countries* (Working Paper No. 44). Paris: Organisation for Economic Co-operation and Development.

Larsen, P. T. (2008, January 16). Sovereign wealth goes to Western reserves. *Financial Times*, p. 16.

Lehman, J. A. (2006). Intellectual property rights and Chinese tradition section: Philosophical foundations. *Journal of Business Ethics, 69,* 1–9.

Lerner, I. (2001). Fluorocarbon industry adapting to regulations. *Chemical Market Reporter, 260*(10), 10.

Morton, P. (1998, November 4). Canada, Brazil make their cases to Geneva panel: First WTO round. Both seek to end "illegal" subsidies in aircraft sales. *National Post,* p. C15.

Powell, P. (2001). The refrigerant issue: Is the debate cooling off? *Air Conditioning, Heating & Refrigeration News, 212*(10), 13.

Shifrin, C. A. (1998, July 20). Canada-Brazil dispute returns to WTO. *Aviation Week & Space Technology, 149*(3), p. 40.

Wickham, J. (2001). International trade and climate change policies. *Journal of Environment & Development, 10*(3), 298.

Zahniser, S., & Crago, Z. (2009, March). *NAFTA at 15: Building on free trade.* Washington, DC: U.S. Department of Agriculture, Economic Research Service.

Summary and Conclusions 13

Having analyzed a wide array of environmental forces, a manager can compile a list of issues that are relevant for his or her firm. With this list, it is necessary to prioritize the issues using two criteria: importance and urgency. It is helpful to map the relevant issues against these two criteria, as in Figure 13.1. The relative importance is ranked on the vertical axis, and the relative urgency is ranked on the horizontal axis. Managers should then focus on the issues in Quadrant 4, which are of both high importance and high urgency.

The literature in regard to issue management emphasizes that some issues can be managed most effectively if they are dealt with early in their development. With this in mind, managers should study issues in Quadrant 2 to

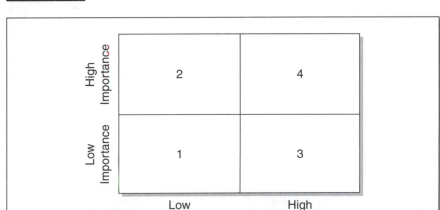

Figure 13.1   Prioritizing Environmental Forces

determine for which issues they should take preemptive action before these issues become highly urgent. While some issues may remain in Quadrant 2 for many years, there are likely some issues that may soon shift into Quadrant 4. These should be a focus for management at a time when they have not yet created problems for the firm and have not yet attracted extensive public and media attention. For each issue, it is necessary to decide where the decision and appropriate action should occur within the firm. It may be appropriate to delegate responsibility to the organizational structure at the country level. However, there will be many issues of relevance for the firm's operations in more than one country. For firms with a regional organizational structure, it may be appropriate to delegate responsibility to the regional organization. Of course, some issues such as elevating ethics or corporate social responsibility (CSR) within the corporate culture are relevant for the entire firm and will become the responsibility of the firm's head office.

This mapping of issues results in a continually changing diagram. Managers should put in place a process for modifying the prioritization over time. Some issues will shift away from Quadrant 4 as the firm manages them successfully. Some may shift to Quadrant 2, remaining highly important but losing the urgency. Such changes may enable the firm to focus on other issues in or near Quadrant 4. The firm can put in place a process for delegating issues in Quadrants 1 and 3 to employees whose jobs may be impacted even though the issues are of low importance for the firm as a whole.

From time to time, unexpected crises will arise due to significant changes in one or more environmental forces. Apart from the process of regular ongoing prioritization, it can be helpful to create a crisis committee of the board of directors. Such a committee can be called into action with temporary responsibility for managing the crisis. This process enables the firm's managers to continue with their regular responsibilities without the distraction of shifting their energies and time to the unexpected crisis.

In this chapter, students can be encouraged to apply Figure 13.1 to a particular firm at a particular point in time. Students might choose a bank prior to the 2007 to 2009 financial crisis, for example, or a manufacturer prior to the ensuing recession. Alternatively, students may focus on any one set of environmental forces, mapping each issue created by those forces. Reference to current financial statements and Internet reports can enable students to compile a relevant list of issues for many firms. Chapter 13 summarizes the issues discussed in the text, so a review of Chapter 13 can assist in this process. Students can then consider how each of these issues could be managed. Development of alternative scenarios in regard to this issue management can assist students in applying theoretical concepts to real situations.

Social Forces

Social forces pose many important challenges for managers, and often there are no clear or universal solutions. For each firm, relevant social forces differ among nations and they change over time. Furthermore, business/society interactions often include many stakeholder groups, as well as government agencies and nongovernmental organizations (NGOs). Each firm has to create its own set of strategies to deal with the particular social forces that it faces, and some of these strategies may have to be designed differently for each nation in which it operates. These responses have to be integrated into the firm's other strategies in ways that impact the entire range of the firm's activities, as well as its internal organization. Proactive positions are generally necessary, rather than just reactions to issues as they arise. The pervasiveness and complexity of social forces mean that management must ensure it is continually aware of issues as they develop. Management must put in place global governance and reporting structures that facilitate appropriate decision making, as well as a set of metrics that measure the firm's performance and a communications program that minimizes misunderstandings and conveys the firm's intentions with honesty and transparency.

The subject of ethical codes and CSR crystallizes many social challenges. At the one extreme are those who, like Milton Friedman (1970/2001), advocate the guiding principle of shareholder value maximization as the sole determinant of managerial decisions. At the other extreme are those who expound an altruistic philanthropy based on philosophical beliefs concerning universal ethics, such as those related to human rights. Within this range of perspectives, many authors offer distinct typologies for analyzing social forces and for developing appropriate firm responses to each set of social forces. Meanwhile, the rise of activist groups who threaten public criticism and boycotts means that even Friedman's dictum of maximizing shareholder value now requires a wide range of CSR strategies.

Some analysts, such as Porter and Kramer (2006), believe that each firm should create a competitive advantage through appropriate CSR strategies. From this perspective, CSR morphs into political strategies through which a firm's reactions can be designed in order to achieve desirable government decisions. For multinational enterprises (MNEs), it is clear that CSR has become a subject of major importance, but the complexity of dealing with social forces that differ among nations has created uncertainties about the optimal strategies. The pursuit of least-cost alternatives in each country conflicts with the objective of creating globally consistent strategies. Meanwhile, international NGOs and national governments are negotiating CSR agreements to create global standards. For the MNE, corporate governance with division of responsibilities between the parent and its subsidiaries adds confusion to the implementation of global strategies and adds difficulties to the creation of appropriate procedures for global reporting and enforcement. CSR has become a central management issue in a world where public expectations, legal requirements, and social needs all differ significantly among nations and where the MNE must continually reconcile its universal ethical positions with nation-specific realities.

A major force underlying the CSR challenges in international business is the difference in culture among countries. The impacts of cultural differences extend beyond CSR to include the business behavior of local management and employees, as well as the preferences of consumers. For the MNE, there are advantages in creating a globally consistent set of organizational structures and incentives and a unified marketing program. Yet there may be many instances where exceptions geared to the local culture may be most effective. Countless articles have utilized the typology created by Hofstede and Bond (1988) in order to analyze the implications of cross-country cultural differences for management decisions. On the basis of extensive surveys, Hofstede and Bond conclude that each country's culture can be best examined in accordance with five dimensions: individualism/collectivism, uncertainty avoidance, power distance, masculinity/femininity, and long-term versus short-term orientation. Not only do cultural differences impact CSR, they also impact consumer preferences and marketing, as well as structures within firms and industries.

Academics have also examined the motivations of consumers from different cultures and have concluded that marketing strategies have to take these differences into account to be most effective. For example, cultures differ in regard to the weight they place on attributes such as quality, privacy, service reliability, the introduction of breakthrough services, and the means of consumer communication with the firm. The retail MNE in particular must create an international expansion strategy on a country-by-country basis, focusing on differences in consumer preferences and the need for market segmentation.

For many cultures, personal relationships are built on an ongoing exchange of favors. Personal relationships and trust form a central determinant of success, both within the firm and in its external interactions. In China, the pervasive importance of *guanxi* demonstrates the benefits that MNEs derive from developing ongoing and long-term exchanges of favors that link individuals, as well as the organizations in which they work. Government approvals can be expedited, and informal preferences can place an MNE ahead of its competitors. Furthermore, without a tradition of business jurisprudence, rapid contract enforcement may become impossible with the result that one must rely on personal relationships to cope with misinterpretations and misunderstandings. Continual changes in the environment of business may require ongoing renegotiation of contracts—a process that may be most effective in the context of longstanding personal relationships and trust. The literature on joint ventures and strategic alliances repeatedly emphasizes the need to create procedures for decision making that are conducive to the building of trust among firms. These behavioral characteristics may be more significant in predicting the degree of success than any structural or organizational features among firms. Yet the exchange of personal favors may raise questions related to ethics.

Personal relationships that involve an ongoing exchange of favors may be criticized as petty corruption that can pervade all types of business transactions, both between firms and also with government employees. While some of this bribery can simply expedite decisions and actions, other situations may involve a distortion of business outcomes. Meanwhile, government officials in positions to alter the firm's overall profitability may receive substantial payments. Funds that rightfully belong to the public may be diverted into private hands. Firms that would have paid fees to the government may be able to reduce their financial obligations. Corruption distorts free market outcomes, resulting in business and government decisions that reduce efficiency and so reduce a nation's aggregate production. Some investors may reject potential business dealings in certain cultures because of the presence of corruption. Recent years have witnessed global attempts to reduce corruption, and many nations now treat corruption as a crime. In this context, management encounters issues that challenge ethical positions and that involve risks of legal prosecution, as well as impacting potential profits.

Managers today must be continually concerned about preventing fraud. New governmental reporting requirements seek to enhance transparency and accountability. New legal provisions increasingly add to the responsibility of boards of directors in providing accurate information to investors. At the core of these concerns is the need to develop a corporate culture that provides ethical guidelines to all the firm's employees so that decisions throughout the firm are socially acceptable.

For the MNE, these issues are linked in a host of multidimensional decisions that require ongoing responses, hopefully within a consistent set of strategies that create a competitive advantage while maintaining an ethical code of conduct. Social forces are changing as the MNE confronts these issues. People throughout the world are now watching the same television and movies, reading the same books, purchasing globally branded products, and communicating via the Internet. For many, there is now an ongoing adaptation to global norms and values. Migration is creating new international relationships that may alter cultures in both the old home country and the new. Much of the academic literature has ignored youth's rapid degree of adaptation to the realities of cultural differences, as opposed to the intransigence of older groups in this regard. As the years go by and the youth age, each national culture will likely be modified. Changes in each nation's demographic profile over time can also impact certain cultural characteristics. Meanwhile, there is an ongoing interplay between social forces and other forces—with an ongoing modification of many other elements in the environment of business.

Technological Forces

Among cultural differences, the role of personal relationships and trust is a key determinant of the nature and extent of social capital, linking these cultural differences to their implications for entrepreneurship. While physical capital obviously differs among countries, the more ephemeral social capital also differs among cultures. Social capital has important implications for managerial decision making, particularly in relation to innovation and entrepreneurship. Networks based on personal relationships and ethnic trust can facilitate business transactions and risk taking. Social capital impacts the degree of cooperative behavior that the firm can expect from its employees, as well as its customers, government agencies, and other stakeholders. Hence, it influences the firm's ability to develop new forms of value creation. Social capital can play a key role in market entry decisions and in the creation of new products, services, or procedures. Firms differ in their ability to utilize social capital within each culture, so the enhancement of a firm's ability in this regard may lead to a competitive advantage for the firm.

Many authors use the social capital perspective to analyze differences among countries in regard to economic growth and the productivity improvements that drive growth. For the World Bank, this subject has been the focus of considerable research—much of it linking social capital with human capital. Cultures differ in regard to the degree to which they encourage and reward risk taking and innovation. These differences impact a country's legal, financial, fiscal, and education systems. For the MNE, an understanding of these cultural differences is essential in reaching optimal investment decisions and business practices.

Until recent decades, innovations were generally created as responses to specific challenges within particular circumstances. The printing press, for example, resulted from a desire to improve on the time-consuming process of writing by hand. The steam engine resulted from a desire to increase efficiency in the removal of water from mines and to achieve a more rapid pace than that of horses. Often, the innovation process then involved the diffusion of such technological breakthroughs to additional uses. Many business opportunities grew out of the array of potential applications related to a single basic concept.

While this process is still prevalent in today's business environment, what is new is the creation of innovation procedures that aim to achieve continual cost reductions and improvements in products and services. What is new is the conscious pursuit of knowledge that can lead to ongoing competitive advantages for the firm. What is new is the development of a learning organization whose culture and practices are designed to stimulate and facilitate the innovation process on a continual basis. This vision of the firm often includes the involvement of all of the firm's employees, as well as the involvement of customers and suppliers throughout the value chain. For many firms, this vision also includes new partnerships, particularly with universities and government research institutes. This pervasive impact of technological forces has created new paradigms for strategies and management. New success indicators relate to the firm's capability in acquiring and managing knowledge. A "balanced scorecard" includes more than just financial results, and intellectual capital focuses on the firm's strategy for building and managing its knowledge activities.

Each nation, and each region within each nation, has its own unique innovation system that forms a key component of the environment of business. These innovation systems differ significantly, with some offering distinct advantages for the firms located there. This reality rests to a large degree on culture, social capital, education, and entrepreneurship. For each nation or region, a set of crucial characteristics includes the nature and strength of attitudes toward risks and rewards, the entrepreneurial quality of university relations with businesses, the willingness of all members of a value chain to become partners in the pursuit of knowledge, and the extent to which innovations within the financial system support this process. Current success creates conditions that support future success in repeated cycles of new technological advances, each of which may move from the research phase to widespread diffusion throughout the economy.

The United States has attained a position of global leadership in the new knowledge economy. Some Western European countries have also attained outstanding success. For much of the rest of the world, a central question relates to their capacity to adopt the technological advances of the United States and Western Europe. The motivations and procedures for technology transfer have become an essential element in the growth prospects of less developed nations. The linkages between international investments and the advanced technologies that are embodied in these investments place the MNEs at the center of this subject. MNEs may regularly transfer the manufacture of new products from the developed nations to the less developed nations in order to reduce costs through payment of lower wage rates. Many governments of developing nations wish to break out of this product cycle by creating their own innovation systems through investments in universities and research institutes. However, much must first be transformed within a nation's social, economic, and political forces in order to create an innovation system.

Advances in information technology have combined with innovations in microelectronics to create a host of new opportunities for e-business activities in every business sector. The Internet has become the new infrastructure that can reduce costs, improve communication, and enhance management practices. Porter (2001) has emphasized that

> the greatest threat to an established company lies in either failing to deploy the Internet or failing to deploy it strategically. Every company needs an aggressive program to deploy the Internet throughout the value chain, using technology to reinforce traditional competitive advantages and complement existing ways of competing. (p. 77)

Managers can collect, analyze, and distribute a myriad of information that enables them to develop new insights and create new business relationships. Managers can make decisions with greater flexibility, adjusting in real time to changes in production and consumption realities. Traditional boundaries in regard to products and services have become blurred, requiring firms to reexamine their vision and mission. Logistics and supply chain management have experienced dramatic changes, with more sophisticated inventory control and interfirm integration being offered through third-party logistics. Innovation in microelectronics is being facilitated by outsourcing of components to electronics manufacturing services. Managers are developing new skills and practices in electronic partnering. Meanwhile, a digital divide exists between developed and less developed nations. A series of obstacles has retarded the expansion of e-business activities in some countries. The nature of the telecom system and the cost of accessing it can play a determining role. More durable obstacles may involve managers' attitudes toward risk taking, the difficulties in calculating return on investment, the legacy of brick-and-mortar facilities, access to capital, and achievement of a critical mass in numbers of suppliers and customers online. For e-business leaders in the United States and Western Europe, new strategies and management practices can offer a competitive advantage when investing in lagging nations, creating a new set of incentives for the international expansion of MNEs.

For many nations, a digital divide may exist between regions, age groups, and income and educational levels. Advanced local loop technologies and broadband service may not be available at a reasonable cost everywhere. The nature of the digital divide underlies the need for e-market segmentation with distinct strategies and practices for different market segments. For many firms, e-business is changing the relative bargaining power in the employer/employee relationship and is changing the nature of human resource activities. In the knowledge economy, ongoing employee education and retraining programs have a greater importance and a central role in supporting the firm's competitive advantage. E-business is changing the competitive positions of incumbents and new entrants, making startups easier and challenging monopolies. E-business has created a new set of ethical and social issues. The ease of accumulating and distributing an array of information about each individual challenges the concept of privacy rights. "Spamming" and online marketing to children can enter a gray area in terms of ethics, while certain criminal activities such as identity theft and fraud are facilitated by the Internet.

The traditional pharmaceutical business model is being threatened by a new biotech model and by generic manufacturers. In the past, each pharmaceutical firm commanded a value chain that it integrated from clinical trials through production and marketing. Each firm would generally test an array of compounds in a trial-and-error method in the search for an optimal drug to treat a widespread illness. Today, an alternative discovery procedure rests on the scientific analysis of how a specific disease develops and the design of a drug that can interfere with the disease process. "Rational drug design" can lead to medicines that are customized for specific subgroups of people who may have somewhat different versions of a disease. This emphasis on scientific research has led to a host of partnerships between universities, research institutes, and biotech firms. Meanwhile, the traditional value chain is being separated into distinct segments with individual firms specializing in each segment, including specialized clinical research organizations, drug manufacturers, and providers of sophisticated drug delivery systems. As a result, the industry structure has changed, redefining the role of Big Pharma firms with a new focus on the coordination of these separate firms and the marketing of the final products.

Governments have come to play a decisive role in the pharmaceutical industry. Clinical trials remain a key element of the drug development process, and governments in many nations have assumed responsibility for analyzing the data from clinical trials in order to reach decisions concerning drug approvals. The United States, Europe, and Japan have instituted somewhat different practices in regard to drug approvals. In recent years, the discovery of serious side effects has led many governments to recall certain drugs that they had earlier approved. Governments have also been actively involved in the regulation of advertising, the provision of financial assistance for research and development (R&D), and the setting of retail prices. Faced with significant differences among countries in regard to government policies and the innovation system, all firms within the pharmaceutical sector confront difficult decisions in strategies and management, including where to locate various activities.

A "drug divide" exists between the developed nations and the less developed nations. The United States, Western Europe, and Japan consume nearly 85% of the world's production of pharmaceuticals. Big Pharma firms have focused their research on health issues of the high-income populations, often searching for lifestyle drugs. They have tended to ignore diseases that are prevalent in the low-income, less developed world. Furthermore, while firms in the developed nations have built their R&D programs on the expectation of patent protection, the less developed nations have often ignored these patents. Generic production with much lower prices has led to a growth in parallel trade. In response, international trade negotiations have sought to create global standards for patent protection, largely unsuccessfully.

New social and political forces are compelling firms, particularly those in the developed countries, to create technologies that can reduce their usage of materials and energy, improve the efficiency of production processes, expand recycling practices, and improve end-of-life product management. These challenges have led many firms to institute Environmental Management Systems in order to integrate new environmental technologies more completely into their traditional business goals and activities. Some authors argue that the pursuit of these innovations can enhance a firm's profits and its international competitiveness. Consequently, more stringent government standards may benefit the firm, as well as society as a whole.

Global warming has been receiving widespread and increasing attention. Managers confront a variety of alternative strategies as possible responses to the impacts of greenhouse gas emissions. The creation of emission trading schemes means that managers must compare the costs of purchasing certified emission reduction credits with the costs of implementing new emission reduction technologies. Some countries are not bound by the Kyoto Protocol's commitment to emission reductions and have not imposed emission caps. Consequently, managers must decide whether interjurisdictional differences in standards should be considered in their investment location decisions.

Global warming has focused attention in particular on alternative electricity generation technologies. Among the potential renewable resources that could generate electricity, wind has gained prominence because of its relatively low cost and because of various drawbacks of other technologies. New technologies have greatly reduced wind generation costs. Wind generation facilities can be built on a relatively small scale, so individual firms and consumers can now consider investments to satisfy their own needs. Governments have instituted subsidy programs, as well as standards that mandate certain targets for generation by renewable resources. In many jurisdictions, electricity distributors must ensure that specific percentages of their electricity are derived from "green" energy. These pressures are creating many opportunities for entrepreneurial responses. For a number of reasons, the United States may not be the most attractive market for these investments. Hence, even U.S. firms may be tempted to invest in wind electricity generation in other nations. Meanwhile, government programs and policies are expanding quickly and consumer preferences are changing quickly. Managers must remain flexible in their strategies and practices in order to respond to these changes.

Economic Forces

Economic forces differ among nations and continually change over time. Analyses of their likely impacts and the creation of appropriate economic strategies can be the central determinant of a firm's success. The attractiveness of a particular market depends on its industry structure, including the competitiveness of existing firms, the threat of substitutes and new entrants, and the bargaining power of suppliers and customers. New communication technologies have facilitated international outsourcing, enabling each firm to locate each activity in whatever country offers the optimal combination of cost, quality, and other attributes. New organizational structures may be required to coordinate international networks and to stimulate international innovation.

An industry's profit potential depends on the structure of that industry, and industry structures differ in significant respects among nations. For managers, this perspective is crucial in international business decisions. Where a single firm dominates the marketplace, the interrelationships between that firm and its customers can have a unique configuration, where the firm has power to maintain prices and profits above competitive levels. The degree of the monopolist's strength in price negotiations will be impacted by the threat of new entrants and the threat of substitutes. If these threats are weak, then a monopolist may gain exceptionally high profits. However, even if no substitutes currently exist, the threat of new entrants may make the market "contestable," such that a monopolist has to act as if potential entrants were already in the marketplace. Recognizing these realities, firms may devote considerable effort and expense to the maintenance of existing barriers to entry, and to the erection of new barriers. Barriers may rest on R&D that can create unique product or service modifications or marketing that can control the distribution system and mold buyers' preferences. Governments may regard monopoly behavior as achieving inappropriate levels of prices and profits and may intervene to reshape the industry by creating competition or to regulate prices and profits directly, or may even take over the ownership of the firm.

When only a small number of firms exist in an industry, the investment, price, and output decisions of any one firm impact the decisions of the others. Game theory provides frameworks for analyzing these interfirm reactions. Each firm knows that if it raises prices, it may lose market share. However, if its competitors also raise prices to a similar extent, then the profits of all firms in the industry may increase. Hence, each firm makes its decisions based on its expectations about the responses of its competitors. This reality can result in an unstable market, with prices and market shares shifting dramatically. Alternatively, this mutual interdependence may result in price agreements that seek to stabilize prices at higher-than-competitive levels. In the extreme, firms may cooperate to raise prices with much the same result that the monopolist might achieve. From this perspective, the threat of government intervention is similar to that of the monopoly structure, and each firm must make its business decisions with this threat in mind.

With modern communications and transportation technologies, outsourcing can involve any nation; so the value chain has become an international web. Many firms participate in value chains where their profitability depends on cooperation. A group of firms may work together to expand the value that is added by their group as a whole. While the group as a whole faces competition from other groups, the organizational dynamic within each group may seek to improve the outcomes for all participants. This international web will strive continually to create unique goods and services so that potential substitutes are further removed from the final customer's purchasing decision. Coordinating this complex network so that it involves an ongoing innovation process has become a key determinant of each firm's success. To achieve innovation, a firm can no longer simply accept the components or products it is offered by export agents or distributors from other countries. Firms must now create organizational structures that facilitate an ongoing international collaboration focused on the innovation process. This may require an exchange of personnel among firms on a regular basis, as well as ongoing dialogue and exchange of research information.

The MNE must choose investment locations in the context of each nation's ever-changing macroeconomic variables. Growth rates, unemployment and inflation rates, and foreign exchange rates may all impact a firm's business plans. Technological progress can increase a nation's growth rate and income levels so that consumer demand offers new opportunities. Each nation's international competitiveness differs among industries, so each nation's relative attractiveness as an investment location is not the same for all firms or all business activities. Consequently, each MNE must develop its own combination of strategies and management in response to economic forces. Governments use macroeconomic policies to achieve several objectives. Generally, people expect that their government will ensure full employment, and the specter of social unrest caused by unemployment is a primary concern for many governments. Some governments, following the 1930s Depression and challenged by Keynesian economics, have officially pledged to maintain low unemployment, and this objective remains a central focus of macroeconomic policies. Inflation can destroy personal savings and disrupt business plans, so governments have also pledged to restrain inflation—often within specific targets, such as 0% to 2% annually. Growth in the form of annual increases in gross domestic product and per capita incomes has become another target of macroeconomic policies. In recent years, the objective of attaining high growth rates has increasingly come to depend on productivity improvements that involve increases in output per unit of labor or per unit of some combination of labor and capital. To facilitate international trade and investment, many governments include the stability of their exchange rate as a further objective. For some governments, such as China, this objective includes the decision to keep the pegged exchange rate below an equilibrium level in order to stimulate exports and employment. The adoption by many European Union members of a single currency eliminates exchange rate fluctuations among them in order to advance the objective of creating a single European market.

In recent years, the macroeconomic objective of maximizing economic growth has also led governments to implement certain industry-level policies. Governments have devoted greater attention to privatization and deregulation, education, skills training, and funding of R&D in the expectation that these programs will increase the nation's productivity and, hence, increase its growth rate. In the formerly communist nations, liberalization reforms have been extensive and have altered industry structures in significant ways. Particularly in the less developed nations, unemployment has generally not been perceived as a result of inadequate aggregate demand. Rather, analysts have emphasized inappropriate human skills, obsolete technologies, and inadequate capital stock. Here as well, certain sector-level policies and programs seek to ameliorate these shortcomings. Consequently, government policies may impact industry structures, competitiveness, and national economic prospects in ways that managers must understand and to which managers must adapt their strategies.

In *The Competitive Advantage of Nations*, Michael Porter (1990) analyzes the basis for a nation's competitiveness by drawing a diagram of a diamond, where each of the four corners represents an underlying feature: factor conditions, demand conditions, related and supporting industries, and firm strategy structure and rivalry. He emphasizes that for any particular industry in a specific country to be internationally competitive, it must have a strong domestic presence of each of these four features as they relate to that industry. From this perspective, the international competitiveness and the future income and growth of a nation's firms will be determined by strengths and weaknesses with regard to these four features.

A nation's competitive advantage will not be spread evenly across all industries. Each nation will have a unique combination of these factors. This unique combination will be best suited for only certain kinds of industry. Consequently, a nation will have a cluster of industries that depend on a similar combination of factors and that will form the competitive advantage for that particular nation. Within such a cluster, there will often be many different firms in the same industry. These competing firms or rivals may all be internationally competitive. Backward and forward linkages to suppliers and purchasers are necessary to create a vertical cluster that is internationally competitive. Successful strategies and management require an understanding of these economic forces.

Political and Governmental Forces

Political and governmental forces are related to each of social, technological, and economic forces. These forces play a key role in the building of social capital, the fostering of entrepreneurship, and the facilitation of immigration. There are many ways through which cultural values shape political forces and through which interest groups influence government decisions. The attempt to reduce corruption illustrates the reverse flow, in which laws and their enforcement seek to change common business practices. In the context of these interactions, the firm must adjust its strategies and management practices in response to social and political forces, but the firm may also seek to influence these forces through lobbying of government and by relating with interest groups.

Political forces are also related to technological forces through the development of "the knowledge economy" and ongoing partnerships within the "triple helix." Government ownership and regulations can influence the speed with which firms adopt information technologies, microelectronics, and e-business. Governments determine the nature of the pharmaceutical industry, subsidizing research, approving new drugs, and controlling drug prices. Increasingly, environmental concerns are leading governments to encourage the implementation of new technologies. In all of these respects, analyses of technological forces involve the discussion of political forces.

Governments continually attempt to alter the functioning of specific markets. Each firm's industry structure is subject to government intervention in response to externalities or third-party effects and monopolistic pricing. Yet many governments have recently engaged in liberalization programs with privatization and deregulation in the hope of stimulating economic growth and particularly the productivity improvements that underlie it. Meanwhile, a government's fiscal, monetary, and exchange rate policies determine the economic environment within which the firm operates.

Public policies differ among nations, and these differences can impact the firm's trade and investment decisions. Some public policies interfere with business strategies, while others can support and assist the firm. Many countries have been altering their public policies in order to attract more international investment. Some have created special economic zones or high-tech corridors within which investors are promised particularly attractive public policies. In view of these situations, a firm can create a competitive advantage through its ability to relate with and adapt to the political process in each country. Furthermore, a firm may be able to influence the process of making laws and regulations, both directly in its lobbying of politicians and civil servants and indirectly in its communications with NGOs and the public. Consequently, it is important for firms to develop nonmarket strategies that underlie and are integrated with their market strategies. Government policies that traditionally were regarded as "domestic" have now become of international importance, as they can distort price ratios and, hence, trade patterns or even act as trade barriers. However, trade and investment agreements contain provisions that place constraints on each signatory's public policies for the purpose of creating a level international playing field.

For MNEs, relevant public policies include ownership, regulation, taxation, and subsidies, all of which impact business strategies and management. Most nations have created impediments to certain types of investment. In some nations, the use of price regulations can alter projected rates of return. In others, businesses may confront sanctions, screening agencies, or continual government intervention in business decisions. Some, such as Venezuela under Chavez, are implementing new restrictions on foreign investment. Yet in recent years, many nations have implemented liberalization reforms that reduce the degree of government intervention in order to stimulate economic growth. China, India, and Eastern Europe illustrate the challenges and opportunities created by liberalization reforms.

Many nations have devised schemes to offer foreign investors special incentives. They seek to attract not only foreign capital but also advanced technologies and managerial skills. As early as 1979, China created special economic zones with modern infrastructure and tax concessions. Many nations have copied this model. Some, such as Malaysia, have focused their zone on the attraction of high-tech firms. Meanwhile, the relatively advanced nations have been striving to retain jobs in the context of corporate "offshoring" to low-wage countries, and some have created special subsidy programs for this purpose. However, such government policies may conflict with provisions of trade and investment agreements, such as the World Trade Organization.

For some issues, a new trend has developed in the creation of international, rather than national, public policies. The protection of intellectual property requires that all nations adhere to a consistent set of government rules. The physical environment is a global phenomenon as the pollution of each country becomes the pollution of all countries. In this context, some businesses may be tempted to reduce costs by shifting their investment locations to countries that have lower standards or poorer enforcement. Competition or antitrust policy now needs to be based on international market behavior rather than just national market behavior. The internationalization of financial institutions has led many to advocate global regulations. This new interconnectedness within the global economy is shifting certain public policies toward an international level, but how these international agreements should be formulated and enforced remains a subject for debate.

Trade and investment disputes are a continual threat for MNEs. In particular, China's rapid and substantial expansion throughout the global economy has created a host of concerns about unfair competition and distortions that prevent the creation of a level playing field. Sanctions can suddenly disrupt established trade and investment patterns. Some nations see the growth of sovereign wealth funds as a potential danger for their own national sovereignty, leading to pressures for new protectionism. In the context of these new developments, firms must manage many ongoing transformations in their environment of business.

References and Suggested Readings

Friedman, M. (2001). The social responsibility of business is to increase its profits. In T. Beauchamp & N. Bowie (Eds.), *Ethical theory and business* (6th ed.). Upper Saddle River, NJ: Prentice Hall. (Reprinted from *New York Times Magazine*, September 13, 1970).

Hofstede, G., & Bond, M. (1988). The Confucius connection: From cultural roots to economic growth. *Organizational Dynamics, 16*(4), 4–21.

Porter, M. (1990). *The competitive advantage of nations.* New York: Free Press.

Porter, M. (2001). Strategy and the Internet. *Harvard Business Review, 79*(3), 63–78.

Porter, M., & Kramer, M. (2006, December). Strategy and society: The link between competitive advantage and corporate social responsibility (Reprint R0612D). *Harvard Business Review,* 1–14.

Author Index

Subject Index

About the Author

David W. Conklin (PhD, Economics, MIT) is a professor at the Richard Ivey School of Business where he teaches courses in the Environment of Business and Business in a Political World. He has written ten books, including *Soviet Profit Reform, Comparative Economic Systems, Foreign Ownership Restrictions and Liberalization Reforms, Re-engineering to Compete: Canadian Business in the Global Economy,* and *Cases in the Environment of Business: International Perspectives.* He has also published 90 business cases and has edited 16 published conference proceedings. His publications focus on the interface between corporations and public policies.

Professor Conklin has taught at universities in many countries in Economics and Political Science Departments as well as in Business Schools. He has worked in the civil service and research institutes as well as in the private business sector. He has undertaken research, teaching, and consulting projects for MNE's, financial institutions, individual governments, and international governmental agencies.

Supporting researchers for more than 40 years

Research methods have always been at the core of SAGE's publishing program. Founder Sara Miller McCune published SAGE's first methods book, *Public Policy Evaluation*, in 1970. Soon after, she launched the *Quantitative Applications in the Social Sciences* series—affectionately known as the "little green books."

Always at the forefront of developing and supporting new approaches in methods, SAGE published early groundbreaking texts and journals in the fields of qualitative methods and evaluation.

Today, more than 40 years and two million little green books later, SAGE continues to push the boundaries with a growing list of more than 1,200 research methods books, journals, and reference works across the social, behavioral, and health sciences. Its imprints—Pine Forge Press, home of innovative textbooks in sociology, and Corwin, publisher of PreK–12 resources for teachers and administrators—broaden SAGE's range of offerings in methods. SAGE further extended its impact in 2008 when it acquired CQ Press and its best-selling and highly respected political science research methods list.

From qualitative, quantitative, and mixed methods to evaluation, SAGE is the essential resource for academics and practitioners looking for the latest methods by leading scholars.

For more information, visit **www.sagepub.com**.